WINTER IN LONDON

WINTER IN LONDON

By

IVOR BROWN

With drawings by
LYNTON LAMB

1952
DOUBLEDAY & COMPANY, INC.
Garden City, New York

TO MY WIFE
who really is a Londoner

Acknowledgments

THE AUTHOR is most grateful to the following authors, executors and publishers for permission to quote from the under-mentioned works :

RHYS DAVIES: *Boy With a Trumpet* (William Heinemann)

HILAIRE BELLOC: *Collected Poems* (Methuen)

ARNOLD BENNETT: *Riceyman Steps* (Cassell)

G. K. CHESTERTON: *The Secret People* (Methuen)

JAMES-POPE HENNESSY: *London Fabric* (Batsford)

A. E. HOUSMAN: *A Shropshire Lad* (The Society of Authors as literary representatives of the trustees of the estate of A. E. Housman and Messrs. Jonathan Cape Ltd.)

Contents

Illustrations

Excuse

WHEN I WROTE a book about Shakespeare I excused myself, justly I hope, for that intrusion with the plea that the subject was already overworked. To add one voice to a myriad is to commit only a very minor nuisance: it is not to be obstreperous; but to invade a theme on which there are only a few works of authority requires great courage and preparation. In the same spirit I do not apologise for another book concerning London, a city whose literature is gigantic according to its merits: one does not seriously trespass where so many have already trod.

But there should be some reason, beyond mere itch to write, for a new volume on such a subject. My defence, or rather my explanation, is this. I have been trying to compose a book of compensations as well as of affections. For the Greater London of to-day is a region, not a town, a mass too big to be lovable in its entirety. Winter, even though it arrive in the beauty of autumn's autumn, can, in a city, be very bleak and grey. Let us enjoy it as we may. Like so many of London's inhabitants I am not of it by blood or by birth. By accident of my father's profession and of my own I have lived there, off and on, most of my life. London is not in me, though I am in London. But, whether aboriginal or immigrant, a man is a fool who does not study and savour the place in which he lives.

The many parts of the monster that is London are still sufficiently small and separate to have their own personalities, which both the old inhabitants and the new arrivals can, if they have the sense to do so, appreciate and cherish. The London of my liking is a patchwork of bits and pieces of which I have tried in this book to render my sense of appreciation. Also, as a London Scot, I am saying ' Thank you ' to a hostess.

In my chequer-board of predilections certain elements are conspicuous. London, for me, is Hampstead and Highgate, Kew and Richmond, the Southwark shore, because of its history, and the centre because of its arts, society, and entertainments. The man who comprehends and relishes this London corner or that is under no obligation to feel passionately about Snorer's Park, if some new adjunct of that name be added to the sprawl of suburban dormitories.

If London were smaller, Londoners would be far more curious about its looks and its doings. But the gigantic size, the massive impersonality of it, deaden the appetite for exploration. Millions never deviate from the track that leads them to and from their work, never take a lunch-time stroll when the day invites, or employ a spare hour to peek and peer round the corners and up the alleys.

Our senses have been numbed by the sight of the vast open bomb-sites, with their architectural skeletons, their old boots and tin cans, their redeeming weeds and their coverlet of willow-herb. The acreage of ruin, even the square mileage, has become accepted, and we have been slower than most afflicted nations to grapple with the mess. We no longer stop to curse the devilry that did it or to wonder what a similar devilry may have next in mind. But, even with so much of interest and of beauty splintered into a dusty nothing, there is plenty left for the perambulation of the curious. The size of London, in many ways a disadvantage, has at least this merit, that the entire place could not be destroyed. The remains are plentiful, despite the loss of so much richness. From such strength could the Monster discard under pressure. Rose Macaulay in her fine novel *The World My Wilderness* has driven into the pathos of London's tumbled history, the romance of the rubble.

Wandering up the street and looking round the corner, that really is the matter of this book. The things described and made matter of comment are all easily reached: no great wealth, no special privilege, no knowledge of the right person to approach are needed to see any of the places and view any of the performances that are mentioned. Most of the subjects are obvious: yet the obvious is continually overlooked. Any street of your acquaintance has a secret history: it is not just the site of drab façades that meet the incurious eye. Strange events and strange people caused it to be built in what was once a meadow or a fowler's marsh to Tudor London. Great men have lifted their fictions from these pavements: the ghosts of any London lane are infinite.

There are some unhappy people with the capacity for being bored anywhere. Put them back into Periclean Athens, Cleopatra's Egypt, or Shakespeare's London and they would yawn their heads off. The owners of such watery spirits will regard London with lack-lustre eye: to them a Mean Street is just that and nothing more. They can visualise nothing but the visible. The faded elegance of a fan-light or a classical portico in a slum suggests nothing to them; but the drama of a city's ups-and-downs, the rise and fall of roads and districts, the romance that is hinted in an old street name or a tavern title, the scenes which the great novelists used, the scaffolding of actual history—all these are there for him who takes a bus ride or a stroll. All that is needed is an hour of leisure and an eye for the laughter and the fretting, the jests and grumbles, the assaults on the senses and the occasional caresses, of a city as it moves to and fro, through crumbling to renewal.

I am perpetually surprised that so few people amuse themselves in that way. Perhaps one reason is that such journeying is so inexpensive: its plebeian nature disappoints the snobs of the purse. Another, rather similar, cause may be the conviction of

so many Londoners that it is absurd or impossible to walk anywhere. In their opinion bus, tube or taxi must be taken to avoid
even a ten minutes' stroll. From the two last and from half of
the first of these vehicles nothing can be seen. They are useless
to questors, except for getting to the expeditionary base. I do
not write for avid, untiring pedestrians, but for the perambulator,
to use a term favoured by James Bone, author of *The London
Perambulator* and *London Echoing* and by the Islington Perambulator
before him; also for the economical who do not resent a thing
because it is cheap or free.

The selected pleasures are, I hope, of sufficiently diverse kinds.
I have not made the slightest attempt to 'do' London; that
would be impossible in a book of this size and scope. My response
to architecture is only emotional. I have no specialised knowledge
and lack the jargon. I have left out many of the notable sights,
except one or two that are visited in childhood and henceforward
forgotten. The excursions that I have made and recommend are
brief and easy and ask no more than the odd hours of a week-day
or week-end. Bernard Shaw, writing of his own youth, long
ago pointed out that the best education in the world was free,
or nearly so, to any Londoner who could use his wits and take
his chances in museum, gallery, and library. I would add 'in
the streets as well.' And not education only: but entertainment
at no cost and that in cordial abundance.

CHAPTER I

Salute to November

———————⟨≈⟩———————

WINTER IN LONDON begins, for me, in November, whether
that be officially autumn or not. It is the first of the Four
Dark Months, or rather of the Short-Day Months, as I would
prefer to call them. Nightfall is early, but the noons and afternoons are often sufficiently warm and radiant to defy the
slanderers of these thirty dwindling but likeable days. Every
kind of abuse has been thrown at the droop of the year: November's head does, indeed, bow before the encircling gloom as
December enters, but there is no need to pelt it with false
assertions, as Thomas Hood ingeniously, but inaccurately, did
in his familiar rhyme.

> *No sun—no moon!*
> *No morn—no noon!*
> *No dawn—no dusk—no proper time of day.*
>
> *No warmth, no cheerfulness, no healthful ease,*
> *No comfortable feel in any member—*
> *No shade, no shine, no butterflies, no bees,*
> *No fruits, no flowers, no leaves, no birds,—November!*

This is all more false than true. No sun, no noon? I am
writing this in a haze of sunshine on the morning of November
6th. No leaves? The trees on Hampstead Heath, where I have
just walked for an hour, are well-laden and the foliage of the
willows beside the pond where Keats took the air and Shelley

sailed boats for Leigh Hunt's children—or so it is nice to believe
—is neither wilting nor discoloured.

It has been a strangely untinted autumn, due, I gather, to the
summer's drought. Without sap in them and without a nip of
frost working on this foison, leaves will not play at oranges and
lemons or turn to russet for their farewell party. So this year
in the great beeches of Ken Wood, November invites me not
to watch a drift of falling gold but to observe the obstinate
survival of shades as green as any in high summer. Had there
been more rain, November would have been, as usual, a month
of yellow and scarlet in the many woodlands of London, woods
far more numerous than most Londoners suspect. I have often
walked in Highgate Woods, for example, a dark plantation in
the dip between the hills of Highgate and of Muswell, and met
nobody at all, though millions were adjacent. In the parks the
lingering chrysanthemum, the tardy and tenacious rose still defy
winter. ' No fruits, no flowers, no leaves, no birds '—nonsense
every way! My neighbour's pear-tree is still well charged with
fruit and tosses me a share of useful windfalls when the wind
rises. Some will be there for a week or two yet.

As for birds, they are always more visible as the leaves thin
out; thus December is as happy a month for the amateur
ornithologist as any. He misses the migrant warblers, but he
finds in plenty the invading water-fowl. No birds! Did Hood
ever survey in November the estuary of London river or such
reservoirs as his London possessed? Did he ever go to Richmond,
where even I can lift my head while golfing beside Kew Gardens
to observe swans and herons in flight, duck soaring, a kestrel
living up to his fine name of windhover, a pheasant or two, a
covey of partridges, as well as those monstrous Thames Valley
carrion-crows which seem to grow fatter and more raucous here
than anywhere else in my experience. No birds!

After a frosty night there will be a misty morning. Up in
Hampstead one often dodges the fog that may linger almost till

noon lower down: sometimes, naturally, we catch and hold a hill-mist which the levels are escaping. It is not unpleasant, it is indeed almost amusing, when going into town in the morning, to drop down the hill, along the heath's dew-bright edge, to the bus at Pond Street and there find the lingering murk. One walks out of clear radiance into a world of mixed gloom and glitter and into odd fantasms of departing fog. There is clear sky above all this and the sun, as I see it from my bus top, seems not to be itself, not to belong to the sky at all, but to be glued on to it like a small red disk; it resembles one of those labels which they put on pictures in galleries after the exhibit has been sold. It is as though someone had purchased this ochre blanket above me and registered the fact in red.

The disc will in half an hour be dissolving misty and the blanket will be folded up: the sun will suddenly uncrimson itself and return to normal gold, at least until tea-time: then it will change tint and turn scarlet in the fall of the day and become enormously large as well as lurid. I have never understood why the sun, seen through the morning mist, looks so remarkably small while, when it sets, in the evening haze, it appears to be double its early size.

That evening haze of November, arriving all too early as the month advances, often has a richness that is little observed. People are indoors or going about their business in a hurry; but could they look westward at four o'clock down the street or, better still, over the river or across some open space, they would often see a flaming sky and sometimes a rare delicacy of mingled tints. The flaming sky reminds me of those tar-dyes you occasionally notice in the middle of a road or asphalt surface, something so gay as to be almost out of English nature: the delicate tints of a winter sunset recall the necks of those London pigeons, who circle and swoop round the charitable donors of bread in Trafalgar Square: with wine-grey pink and tender blue these city-haunting mendicants present the many-tinted image of a winter sunset when the sky is clear enough. They are very brief, these November lighting-up times, but they have the subtlest fascination for an eye that has the chance to catch their brief existence.

Evening can put a diadem on towns, especially those winter evenings which close a day of keen and bracing quality. The lights come pricking out in the high buildings of the great offices and hotels. A patine of bright silver underlies the starry plateau overhead, where glitters Shakespeare's patine of bright gold. Now the streets are relieved of drabness; they call to pleasure, as central squares and boulevards should do. Later on, when the masses come pouring from desk and counter to the bus halts and the stations, one may easily feel engulfed and submerged. The London crowds appear always to grow in size and scarcely to improve in manners.

It is preferable, if one can arrange it, to wait instead of joining this hurly-burly of desperate fugitives. How frantic is their struggle to escape! They seem to fear, that, if they miss the 5.40, their villas, even their whole suburbs, will have vanished before they get there. Why not some dalliance? For now, even in times of austerity, there is a happiness, both of young excitement and of elder serenity, reflected upon human tempers from the sparkle of a town lit-up. It is the hour of release. We may have written that awkward letter and held that tiresome interview: or we may have dodged them both. In either case they are out of mind. It is a dry winter evening and the town is getting into its nocturnal trim. November? Well, yes, but are not those lamp-lit streets and blazing buildings of pleasure more gaily accosting, more warmly welcoming, than the dusty avenues of a sultry summer evening?

For the wealthier it is cocktail time. For the million others it is time for tea, for the pictures, for the pally-de-danse. Streets aglow, shop-windows with a beckoning gleam, and lofty mansions starred with a thousand casement-lights are part of the November picture in any great swarming-place of man. New

York, where November is usually an exquisite month of challenging air and of hard, clear radiance, is especially magical at this time. The monster buildings, which in daytime suggest the Stonehenge of the Steel Age, become like giant Christmas trees with all their lanterns kindled. London too, though on a lesser scale, has a lucent glory of its own. Watch our modest cliffs of brick and stucco round Hyde Park or by the river in the dwindling of a November day. Far less in size than the bastions of Manhattan, they yet have their twinkling majesty and proclaim the praise of electricity, cleanest, less cruel, least corrupting of man's nineteenth-century inventions. A city conceals, inevitably, or at least distorts, much of its architectural splendour at night. But it also brings out for show a notable part of its regalia.

A good way in which to see London thus bejewelled is to stand upon one of the river bridges at sundown. If I have been down to Richmond, I like to come back by way of Waterloo —only thirteen minutes in one of the half-hourly non-stop trains—and then to walk across Hungerford Bridge to Charing Cross, a trifling step. If I time it correctly, I am there as the pigeon's-neck sunset is just fading in the west while, upon the north bank, from Westminster to City, from Abbey to St. Paul's, the curving shores begin to glitter with the fine points of incandescence in the windows and finally with the complete illumination of the Embankment and of its tributary streets. For a November nocturne there is nothing to beat it in London, though many a foreign capital has even more electrical largesse for the eye. Not New York only, but Stockholm with its urban islands, seen at lighting-up time with the fiords as mirror to the kindled town, are superb in this kind of five-o'clockish iridescence.

London, however, has its own display and it is odd, as I walk south across the bridge to Charing Cross, to breast the storm of walkers making for Waterloo and the trains to their Surrey homes. Head down they hasten, looking not at all to the wonderment on their left or to that necklet of eye-jewellery away to the east, but pressing forward, apparently convinced, as I said before, that their villas will have vanished if they do not get there at the appointed, the expected moment. True, from Hungerford Bridge you do not see up-river well: the railway bridge intervenes. But the down-river spectacle is tremendous and a winter afternoon will best provide the emergence from twilight of a myriad flashing lamps and window-panes.

You can see London from the top of a bus, but not from a taxi or a car. For the best way in which really to appreciate a town is on foot, pausing as you please, free, deviating, vagabond. In summer that is hard work. I am frightened of summer in London. May has its glory of sun and breeze together, but later the heat is nearly always of a humid kind and one fine day leads on to head-oppressing cloud and the gathering, menacing murk of a thunder-storm. Pleasant occasions are unpleasantly crowded. The Centre Court at Wimbledon becomes a bowl of perspiration. As for cricket at Lord's, one can only get in with comfort when the game is of minor importance. The July pavements are intolerable to the feet and to tread the softening asphalt is like walking on warm glue. One may get on a river steamer, but only by queueing.

That is one thing in which the walker is uniquely happy. He does not have to line up for the train to start and the boat to be undocked. He can go and he can stop when he likes: and this is a very important matter when London becomes more heavily over-populated with an ever-growing rush of the centripetal millions in the morning and of the centrifugal millions at night. All sports and entertainments of any appeal soon become alto-gether too appealing: one can only get to them by risk of suffocation in a tube or of roadside frustration in a mile of blocked and fuming traffic. If I choose to wander off to some corner of London well-loved or unexplored, I have a liberty denied to all those arena-bound, even though they be of the privileged spectator class, members with special entrances and private enclosures or holders of guinea seats. Not that I am anti-athletic. Give me a big rugby football match at Twickenham and there shall I be, arriving somehow. But that happens in winter: it is the summer crushes from which I shrink.

I know what can be said for the other side. The first caress of genuine, consoling sun, not the thin, wintry sunshine that only deceives by its queer, crimson radiance, the glory of a cloudless sky over the sleeper-happy lawns in the parks—all these you can praise to the full. But I chiefly remember sweltering offices, unbearable scrimmages for transport, the hot pant and stink of over-heated motor-engines in the street—all this with a general infection of fatigue, general because that summer weariness is not only of the limbs but of the spirit. I do not want to see London in July: I do not want to be in this sizzling bowl a day longer. There are mountains. There are seas. There are rivers which make the right kind of noise, not surly, silent, muddy meanderers, so often and so properly called the Ouse, but jocund, frothing, clattering beauties, whose babble haunts me through a London heat-wave. Beyond far Inverness, by Affric's peaty fountains, there would I be. And here I am surveying the urchins bathing in, and even swallowing, the muck that is the water of the Thames.

It would be absurd to idealise a London November. It can be as black as night, and far more frightening, with the kind of fog that is piled up carpet-wise above the streets: it can be a dense and dirty yellow-brown with the kind of fog that seeps up from the river and the canals and the ponds in the parks and lies impenetrable in the streets. It can offer, too, the long assault of bludgeoning rains when the south-west wind hurls over the Home Counties all the buckets it has failed to empty over Dartmoor and Salisbury Plain, Cotswold stone and Surrey heather. All I insist is that we do not be intimidated by Hood's negations.

Take one of them alone—'No comfortable feel in any member.' Surely the drowsy numbness of a dog-day's scorching is much less comfortable to any normal person than the readiness to be up and about which the decline of the year engenders. Naturally those who are too old to be in any way active or are crippled by muscular and nervous afflictions will not agree with me. But for most of us there is surely a surge of spirit in the autumn, a challenge in the air, a summons to discover and to relish things. Mr. T. S. Eliot has observed that 'April is the cruellest month.' Not always: even an autumn-lover can respond to proud pied April and the flush of May. But it is significant that the most beautiful of all poems on the English climate was written on autumn by a Londoner, John Keats. Keats omitted, be it noticed, to write an Ode to Spring, a season which has evoked all the world's worst verses. At this point I cannot forbear to quote the preposterous lines of Emerson:

> The April winds are magical
> And thrill our tuneful frames,
> The garden-walks are passional
> To bachelors and dames.

I am sure that November never produced nonsense as overwhelming as that.

I am not discussing what time best suits the terrestrial oceans of the undulant Yorkshire moors, the peaks of Wales, or the fantastic jumble of glory at the top of Borrowdale. They have their seasons. What time does best suit the sweltering London pavements that attacked and consumed our feet in June? Plainly the time of cooling, the time before the snow has come and turned to urban slush, before the east winds nip the muscles and provoke lumbago's torturing paralysis, in short the leader of the winter months, the libelled, slandered, and accursed November.

CHAPTER II

Torracorranex

THIS NAME is neither Mexican nor Antipodean. It may suggest a snake-dance as described by D. H. Lawrence or one of the back-blocks where Boldrewood's bushrangers have now been peaceably transmuted into budding Bradmans. But in fact the pentesyllabic-monster belongs to London, West Central 1. It signifies the Tottenham Court Road. But that must be explained.

When I was a boy, living in a tranquil crescent called Hampstead Hill Gardens, I first travelled to and from Oxford Street by way of Camden Town and this shopping avenue called Tottenham Court Road; our vehicle was a horse-bus. Going down hill from the Northern Heights, as the house-agents love to call them—it will be the North London Highlands before long—was easy work. But coming up again was real coaching; we took on an extra horse and became a three-in-hand at Chalk Farm and then again at Rosslyn Hill in order to surmount these escarpments, to use the military writers' term. The descent took us about forty minutes and the reascent some fifty. There was a seat beside the driver for which a small boy darted, braving the weather of the uncovered top-deck in order to profit by the company, the general sense of equine acquaintance, and the commanding position. So with a not outrageous day and a good, genial, fruity conversational driver as your guide and commentator on the London scene—and such men there were —the journey could be total bliss.

I remember driving home in this style after the opening— the world-première we have to call it now—of Stoll's Coliseum. This globe-topped monster was to be the wonder of the town. The management started with the preposterous hope of filling it four times daily, at twelve, three, six, and nine o'clock. It was Christmas Eve when the high occasion came and my brother and I attended what was, in fact, the third celebration, i.e. the six o'clock house of the first day's operations. There was to be a horse race, all alive and kicking, with real nags galloping against a revolving stage.

This was the Coliseum's answer to the neighbouring Hippodrome, which was then actually hippodromic, that is to say a running-place for horses—and also a diving-place. There was a circular pool where the front stalls are now and into this a one-legged cyclist would drop from the roof, disengaging his machine *en route*; or a bevy of sleds and droshkys and galloping Cossacks would plunge into the water in the breath-taking episode called ' Siberia.' Aquatic shows are part of London history; the old, well-watered area of Sadler's Wells depended on the application of the natural springs to the man-made spectacles. Early in the century everybody expected a Hippo- drome to be as good as its name and not just another music-hall; in Central London it was both hippic and aquatic. To compete with this came the majestic Coliseum and its primal venture of a mimic Derby.

So we were to see the Race: were to see, but did not see. At the ill-omened six o'clock house, which we had unluckily chosen to attend, there came, after the wintry session on the open bus top, a real blast of misfortune. The curtain became irremediably stuck just before the Great Event. We had sat through a very respectable Variety Programme—for this was to be a Family House and none of your common or raffish

Tottenham Court Road in the days of the horse-bus

music-halls with people ordering bottled stout to be served in their stalls. We had sat in rather far-away seats and in the highest expectation. Outings of this kind undoubtedly meant far more to boys and girls in those days, in which films were a rare and unattractive flicker and wireless quite unknown. To-night was the night. There would be The Race.

But there was no race at all, at least not for us. Two earlier houses had revelled, no doubt, in the static gallop as the frustrated horses plodded on against the counter-revolution so cleverly organised to check them, until the audience was deemed to be sated with the spectacle and one steed was urged or permitted by his jockey to get a winning nose in front. But in our case the curtain of that stately Pleasuredome fell and would not rise. Its obstinacy ended the evening just as the horses should have been going to the post. We saw nothing of the masterpiece. We got plentiful managerial apologies, but we did not get our money back. Apparently, as we had only missed the last item, last and certainly most lavish, we did not qualify for compensation. I have borne a tacit, unforgettable feeling of distrust in the Coliseum ever since, despite many notable evenings there, with all manner of diversions from the inspired solitudes of Grock to the massed choruses of mammoth ' musicals.'

So, with the Christmas spirit considerably dashed, we returned to the bus and soon were jogging up Torracorra, which was, and to some extent still is, a Londonese slurring and abbreviation of the seigneurially entitled Tottenham Court Road. It was a cold, clear night with everybody hearty and not a few hiccuping. Call the old days good or bad, whisky and gin were twopence a nip. So there was a sound of the more squalid revelling in Torracorra and more riot still as we clattered up past the Camden Theatre, whose pantomime I always attended, and the Bedford, whose varieties I was supposed to avoid. With the drunkenness of those days there was also, even in sobriety, a kind of friendliness that has nearly vanished from our teeming, pushing, nervy, strident, surly London with its over-worked mechanised transport.

But that is a familiar complaint and it should not be heavily urged. That kindly London could be damnably sordid too. I have ugly memories of a Saturday night after-theatre journey back to Hampstead in a horse-tram. This rattled its way from the Euston Road end of Torracorra up the Malden Road to the Fleet Road; this is really the grandfather of Fleet Street since both take their names from the same river, the Road being near the source of the rivulet and the Street running where the notorious old Fleet Ditch once coursed with its murky flood of refuse under Holborn to Blackfriars. The slatternly car was full of drunken sluts who were repulsive and even terrifying to a small boy: they were creatures as obscene of talk as foul of aspect. You would not see their kind to-day. No, I am not going to romance over Phil May's London as seen, smelled, and heard on a wet night in the neighbourhood of Torracorra.

The horse-bus (and tram) were on their last, hard-worked legs. We were soon to dive into the bowels of Belsize Park and be taken for twopence—the horse-bus fare had been threepence, I think—on the Tube to Oxford Street in a quarter of the old time, speeding like magically accelerated moles under tunnelled Torracorra. It was the custom, on the earliest Tube trains, to have a guardian to every carriage. His job was to open and close the doors and also to warn the passengers of the station next ahead, so that they should be on tip-toe to alight. Such admonitions were delivered with a grinding vocal roar which telescoped all the details of the information as an accident may telescope the railway carriages. Those extraordinary, and surely to a foreigner quite incomprehensible, noises ended when the presence of guardians in each coach was deemed superfluous.

But the relentless yelling survives in the curious screams which are delivered by platform officials at the central stations of the London Tubes when crowds are largest at the rush-hour. They are commanded to hurry on, with orders raucously bellowed into the ears of people already being pushed and almost trampled down in the scramble to get somehow wedged into the train. When a person who is fighting desperately to insert himself into a packed carriage has his ear-drums assaulted with the kind of savage exhortation (possibly merited by sluggards half-asleep or immobile) he experiences the last, infuriating horror of such travel. I cannot think why the rulers of London Transport permit, or even encourage, this cacophonous discourtesy. The melancholy wail of 'Idor,' which presumably means 'Mind the Doors,' is harmless enough; it is the nagging stream of 'Hurry on there' when one is being hustled almost to extinction that drives one to frenzy.

As we left Goodge Street going south in the old days the voice of the guardian roared 'Torracorranex,' informing us that our next stop would be the Tottenham Court Road. So the street has remained Torracorra for me; also it has retained a certain fascination, despite all its drabness, because it was my first avenue to the pleasures of the West End. Torracorranex! We were in the heart of things.

The road was once a rural thoroughfare leading to the Adam and Eve Pleasaunce, hard by Tottenham or Tatnam Court which, the home of the Fitzroy family, stood near our Fitzroy Square; this square is now largely a hospital island with the Bohemian waters lapping grubbily about it. The Adam and Eve is still there at the corner of Warren Street and Hampstead Road, and is now a very urban public-house. Gone are the London gardens famous for their syllabubs, a dish which sounds a trifle sickly nowadays since it had a milk basis and was curdled with wine. It was popular with the Restoration ladies who carried their virtue, rather precariously, for an airing in the famous pleasure-grounds and tavern-gardens of the town. There was opportunity enough for sillybubbery—or should it be syllibibery? Two misses, deeming themselves repressed and frustrated, as we say nowadays, discuss their bondage in Wycherley's *The Gentleman Dancing Master* :

PRUE: 'Tis true, Miss, two poor young creatures as we are!
HIPPOLITA: Not suffer'd to see a play in a twelve month!
PRUE: Nor to go to Punchinello nor Paradise!
HIP: Nor to take a Ramble to the Park nor Mulberry-garden!
PRUE: Nor to Tatnam-Court nor Islington!
HIP: Nor to eat a sillybub in new Spring-garden with a Cousin!
PRUE: Nor to drink a Pint of Wine with a Friend at the Prince in the Sun!
HIP: Nor to hear a Fiddle in good Company!
PRUE: Nor to hear the Organs and Tongs at the Gun in Moorfields!

Plainly the town had copious opportunities.

Earlier, in the days of Shakespeare and Jonson, resort to Tatnam had been common for the purpose of eating cream and there was the sweet of the year when Torracorra smelled all April and May so that Gay could write of a street car (named Desire?) making for amorous thoughts in green shades, doubtless with syllabubs attending.

> *Love flies the dusty town for shady woods,*
> *Then Tottenham Fields with roving beauty swarm.*

There is still rusticity. Leaving Oxford Street you see the northern hills and woodlands on a summer evening surging gently up behind Camden Town: and on a clear day in winter you may have the same glimpse too. These slopes were long the cherished view of London's inhabitants; that is why what is left of the houses in Euston Road have their gardens, now yards, in front of them. This was the verge of the town before the railways came and naturally the railways established their three great termini where the town began. The house-owners liked to sit and look outwards to the north-westerly heights whose agreeable curves moved skyward behind the villages of Somers

Town, Kentish Town, and Camden Town; so they arranged their gardens for such sessions and, when you go from Warren Street to Euston, you can still see the houses on your right set back with what was once a gazebo or observation-post as well as a pleasaunce in front.

· Lovers now, if they fly from the town for shady woods, need not go very far. A journey of four miles will bring them to the great beeches of Ken. But they will discover small relief of that kind in Torracorra; the joys are urban and up to date, 'jive' in London's Harlem or the racket of the Fun Fair. Cakes gluey with cream-substitute—is this the product of the soya bean?—replace the syllabub. But still, with a clear sky, you may lift up your eyes unto the hills and feel some balm from that not far horizon.

It is an extraordinary place, this Torracorra, with its seigneurial past and its plebeian look. The imposing and historic shops on the East side are contrasted with some lamentable shabbiness on the West. It largely furnished Victorian London and a good deal of our own. Behind its plate-glass windows have gleamed a noble array of mahogany sideboards, of august four-posters, and of the shiniest bedroom suites in the modern style. Wandering down the street of a morning—I was a Bloomsburian once—I often thought what a pleasing surprise it would be for Maple's staff, if, when they clocked in, they discovered that a weary tramp, or even a couple, had somehow penetrated their vast mansion during the night and had gone happily to sleep in one of those great beds displayed in the vast windows. Some boozy Christopher Sly of St. Pancras, all fumes and rags, would well have become such an invasion. Indeed, the trick might have been played the Sly way, with a posse of rowdy students depositing a drunk and incapable member of their rout to sleep it off in such grandeur and then wake to find himself famous —or at least a 'front-page top' in the early editions of the evening papers.

The great days of Torracorra were when Shoolbred stood shoulder to shoulder with Maple. In an age of shine and shoddy Shoolbred's was doomed by nature; it was a store as solemn as a kirk elder and as reliable as oak. It retained the shop-walker, in solemn black, tail-coated I think, or even frock-coated, to the end. It retained leisure and a grave brand of courtesy. You could really shop in Shoolbred's instead of being caught in a wave of bargain-hunting, stunt-lured myriads. It sold everything and its catalogues were encyclopædias. I miss my store-catalogue English in these times; ' the same, japanned.' Do we still japan? The particular glory of the house was its home equipment, beds, blankets, ironmongery and so on. It did not vulgarly bellow its bargains or beckon the young couple about to set up house in the suburbs; sagacious parents led them down Torracorra as the right, indeed the only, thing to do; here was the Mecca of the mattress-minded.

Up the East Side, from Charles Baker's where I bought my schoolboy suits, to Wolfe and Hollander and Bartholomew and Fletcher, it used to be solid worth all the way. Heal came in with the New Look, reminding the Road that it was the verge of Bloomsbury as well as the bed-maker for Baron's Court. Heal brought in style and Shearn gave it nuts. I never felt that the Torracorra was the right place for vegetarians. It was the natural sideboard for a large roast, when such things were, not for a pot of herbs. This is not to impugn the admirable service of roots and fruits with which Shearn's met the uncarnal at the counter or the lunch-table. I merely feel, as I walk down Torracorra, that this is no street for ' an attachment à la Plato for a bashful young potato or a not too French French bean.' It is true that the Road has never been renowned for restaurants since the old ' Tatnam for syllabubs ' times. But before the coming of Shearn in the middle and of the Corner House at the end, its public-houses offered, I fancy, considerable comforts to the Victorian Londoner

Who's fond of his dinner
And doesn't get thinner
On bottled beer and chops.

not to mention the consumption of 'roly-poly pudding with avidity' attributed to the same Gilbertian figure.

The West Side of Torracorra never made up its mind as to its proper function. For household supply it had Catesby's linoleum; for decorations the famous wooden Highlander so prized of milling students on a 'rag' night; for piety White-field's great Tabernacle; this was religion's proper reply to the Shoolbred-Maple *massif* on the other side. There is still a nice shop towards the south end of the West Side: it specialises in catering and public-house equipment and there I bought the best cork-screw I ever had, one of the few labour-saving devices that has really continued, year after year, to save labour. If you are giving a party and feel need to warn your guests about small matters of behaviour, you can—or could—buy there notices for hanging up; these gave all the usual public-houses imprecations about adjusting one's dress before leaving or refraining from spitting, and so on. I specially liked the one which said

'Please do not ask for credit as a refusal often annoys.'

'Often' was perfect, allowing, as it did, for those so accustomed to a dusty answer when suggesting one or two 'on tick' that they would never be moved to any state of surprise or vexation by the expected negative.

The bombing dealt hardly with Torracorra. The gaps abound: the desolation remains. It is easy to cultivate melancholy here-abouts and such cultivation has long been a popular human exercise. How happy were the Elizabethans exclaiming, 'In sooth I know not why I am so sad.' Sir John Squire once sent some copy about *A Midsummer Night's Dream* to the printer: Hermia came back set as Hernia. Squire left it, adding a pleasing footnote to explain that he could not bring himself to interfere with his printer's first, fine careless rupture. I myself have made allusion in an article to Shelley's ' Stanzas Written in Dejection Near Naples. For Naples the printer substituted Maples.' If you know the area, especially in these days, you will understand why he did it—or at least agree that his unconscious error was inspired. Some of London's ruins seem to attract rare birds and flowers to nest there or dig themselves in. I cannot imagine this happening in the dismal blanks and chasms of this hard-smitten region.

The Road, still trailing some relics of its solid, Shoolbredian respectability, is like a ridge between two sea-coasts of Bohemia. To the East is Bloomsbury in whose chipped and blasted squares, once the proud examples of ducal and intelligent planning, all sorts of invaders have arrived. Gordon Square was once the Keynesian Academe, with Lydia Lopokova its coryphée and various Stracheys its sages; Duncan Grant, Clive and Venessa Bell, and, round the corner, Virginia Woolf made a remarkable muster. The tall, unworkable houses could then be somehow worked: now they are mostly offices or headquarters of scholastic and ' welfare ' bodies.

Those with a friendly feeling for ghosts may still feel in that air the sagacity and wit, the cultivation and hard, shrewd sense of Maynard Keynes who could always turn from the higher economics to discuss a question of painting or of ballet: he was an exacting man, who died too soon because he worked too hard, and he asked as much of his colleagues in energy as he gave to them in energy and instruction mixed. Bloomsbury of the nineteen-twenties had its lunatic fringe, but its central and splendid feature was an urbanity of which Keynes was the epitome. The definition of civilisation as the art of living in towns was here justified. There was no art or form of intelligence which was not being practised in a masterly way by some inhabitant of two or three London squares: and something of that glory lingers, but not enough. When you turn off Torracorra to sniff the Bloomsbury air, it is for the shades and not the substance of greatness that you must mainly seek.

On the other side of the Road there is the rougher artistic community of beard and corduroy. A flat-owner in the area who wished to obtain a profitable tenant might well advertise 'hunting with the Fitzroy,' for reputations are chivvied and killed with gusto in the tavern-disputations of the district. Here was the site of syllabub Tatnam and now of advanced painting and poetry and their frantic palaver. The restaurants are either as cheap as may be in dear times or as dear as may be when rationing exists—and is discreetly evaded. Charlotte Street, running parallel with Torracorra, is worth a stroll: here may be seen what eating-house is coming into fashion or what cut is modish in the beards of bards. Here, I am told, you may hire a hurdy-gurdy and take a chance as street-musician, provided you have the necessary licence and are on terms with the police so that you will not be 'run' for causing obstruction. The barrel-organ is now a scarcity in London and the Bank Holiday crowds who used to dance to them in the street go indoors to the 'pallies' instead. I am told that a pound a day is the hiring-fee for an organ and that you can make a profit on that outlay if you are prepared to chance your arm—and hard arm-work there will be. One thing is obvious: that if the barrel-organs are still to have stabling in London, Charlotte Street and its odd, continental environs are the right address.

The architecture of Torracorra is a matter more for amaze-ment than for admiration. At the Oxford Street end it achieves confusion's masterpiece where the Corner House confronts the Horseshoe Tavern and Dominion Cinema with Horne the haberdasher in all his glory, and Frascati's wondrous façade just round to the right. It only needs night time with Montague Burton's emporium Neon-lighted in blue and orange for the complete ravishment of the eye, the final delicacy of optical *tutti-frutti*. It would be a close match between this corner and the surroundings of Leicester Square were there a London Championship for hideousness of structure and contradiction of design. There are some kinds of ugliness that fascinate. Leicester Square, with the monstrous pile of the Odeon, appals and stuns me: but Torracorra leaves me alert and laughing. There is nothing to be done about it short of demolition; no neighbouring goodness is spoiled; no open space, no historic site is smirched, as it is in the case of Leicester Square.

There is abundant time in which to study this medley of modern styles—if styles they can be called. For the traffic is always congested here. Your bus from the north may linger long in Torracorra, moving but a yard or so at a time, all the way from Shearn's to Burton's, before you squeeze past the Dominion and ' make ' the Charing Cross Road. It is customary to use the term bottle-neck in this connection; but in this case there really is no bottle, only one prolonged, inadequate neck.

Once across Oxford Street you touch a more unified ugliness. The lower reaches of the Charing Cross Road were long known for their second-hand bookshops and thereby carried with them an air of rather musty culture and a passenger-load of questing students, fossicking in the old-time penny box or scrutinising the sixpenny and shilling shelves. But above this merchandise of the mind there was, and is, a striking monotony of anonymous gloom. No architect could ever have signed such a document in bleakness: some nameless builders must somehow have dumped it there. Contrasted with this dreariness of brick Torracorra is at least a variety entertainment.

In the centre there is a cool (but rather top-heavy) assertion of dignity by Heal's and at the north end the pillared massiveness of Maple's, sensibly symbolising the solid worth of a business fully meriting the title of ' firm.' There is an eye-taking modern Gothic public-house called The Rising Sun on the west side at whose ecclesiastical elegance I gaze in reverence. To increase the assortment of odd features there is, as I write, a convoy of motor-caravans awaiting customers on a site conveniently provided, I think, by a flying-bomb. These aids to a rural ride restore to some extent that holiday quality which it was the original function of Tatnam Gardens to emphasise.

Many London streets have their own particular smells. Perfumery works its way into such zephyrs as blow in Bond Street: the gross overcrowding of Oxford Street by domestic shoppers afflicts the ' woman's mile ' with a perceptible aroma of perspiration. Behind it Wigmore Street is disinfected by its famous chemists: a big shop for medicaments and antiseptics always seems to me to extend and scatter its studied cleanliness and stringency of atmosphere. Coming away from the pulsing heat of Christmas shopping round about Selfridge's I give thanks to John Bell and to Croyden, to Allen and to Hanbury, for the influence they rain upon their region.

If, in the press to the south, you feel that you can no longer breathe, there is respite in Wigmore Street. Here you can hold your own on the pavement without meeting aggression, here collect your thoughts and ruminate on literary pleasures by sticking your nose against the windows of The Times Book Shop, admire the majesty of Debenham's, a palace of commerce which can afford to stand back from the milling myriads of ' the mile,' and here, above all, you can sniff the bouquet of drugs and doses and curative appliances emerging from the doors of the renowned chemists. Sometimes in industrial England you find yourself in a town which has one governing smell, possibly a clean and bracing one: I think it was at Oswaldtwistle—Wigan's under-study as the joy of music-hall comedians—that I once seemed to be plunged into a disinfectant bath by contact with the odour of the place. To a less degree I feel this immersion at the southern extremities of Harley Street and Wimpole Street.

Returning to Torracorra, I remember very clearly the keen smell of vinegar coming from the huge, gloomy-looking Crosse and Blackwell fountain of pickles and condiments; as mighty of

stature as melancholy of air, it loomed, prison-like, at the top
end of Charing Cross Road between that road and Soho Square.
But its odour had a fiercely penetrating power and, with the wind
in the right quarter, would come seeping right up into Torracorra.
So strong was it that I still think of pickles as I pass by the site
now occupied by a dance hall, music shops, shoemakers, and
haberdashers.

But that is a memory only. The Tottenham Court Road
ought now to smell of furniture polish, for oak, mahogany, and
walnut are still its tutelary trees. The call of the ' Suite ' begins
away up in Camden Town with Bowman's and works down
through Oetzmann's of the Hampstead Road. I salute the latter
for maintaining its name unchanged through two long and bitter
wars; especially in the first war anything alien in nomenclature
was a source of suspicion and even of violence. Once into
Torracorra it is furniture most of the way on the east side. How
many of London's myriad children owe their origin and arrival
to Torracorra beds!

The firm of Maple, founded in 1841 at the sign of the Hen
and Chickens—for shops as well as inns had their signs—offered
in those years Mahogany Four-Posters at Two Pounds and
Brussels Carpet at 2s. 6d. a yard.

Petrol and furniture, with a breath of fruit and flowers out
of Shearn's—these are the local aroma of to-day. Yet one need
not be immensely old to think of horses there, the sharp smell
of their urine and the steam mounting from them in the cold
air after a brisk journey down from the northern suburbs. At
any rate the public-houses are faithful to the coachman. At the
corner of Oxford Street the vast Horseshoe Tavern still proclaims
the Smithy where the buses came rolling in and, as you motor
up Haverstock Hill to Hampstead, you pass the Load of Hay
(not the Gallon of Juice) in order to end between the Nag's Head
and the Horse and Groom in Heath Street.

It is just inertia or is it some instinctive fidelity to an equestrian past that keeps the titles of so many English inns unaltered? In London at most of the bus termini, now afume with oil, you will see a ' White Horse '—or a Black one. Streets roaring with motor traffic are still haunted by the hay-bags and the grooms. Nobody gets a ladder and paints ' The Sparking Plug ' or ' The Accelerator ' across the old, horsy lintels and sign-boards, although both these titles would fairly sum up the effect of alcohol upon physical fatigue or drooping spirits. Nowhere in the country has the otherwise all-conquering motor engine forced itself into the lexicon of tavern titles. Still you may discover the Four Alls, but where are the Six Cylinders? Still the Rose Reviv'd, but never The Tank Recharged. Still the Hark to Melody, but never the Step on the Gas.

So there is my sentimental note on the scents and savours of Torracorra. It was a horse-track when the lovers took chariots and went spanking along to the Adam and Eve and its botanic as well as gastric pleasures. It was a horse-track when I came to Hampstead as a little boy and sat aloft in blissful passage to the Hippodrome or Coliseum. I can still hear hooves by the Horse-shoe and see grooms emerging from the Load of Hay. Our theatre had once a Ghost Train for its thrills, but Torracorra for me has a Ghost Bus, a smell of stabling in the air, and the power to evoke a spectral ostler in December's dusk.

CHAPTER III
Poets' Corners

RELICS IN GLASS CASES may be interesting as specimens of period taste, as examples of craftsmanship, or as triumphs of the jeweller's or haberdasher's fancy. But they do not, for me, reach further than that. The personality of the owner is not to be thus apprehended. If you are a Bonnie Prince Charles man, you will seize your hero better on the western hills than amid the reverential storage of his napery in a Highland museum. Does Garrick's shoe-buckle stage Garrick in your ear and eye? Does the lock of a poet's hair set his words dancing in your mind? I must confess myself impervious to the emotional pressure of a snuff-box, a tie-pin, or a clouded cane, much as I may admire them as things in themselves.

So I cannot find Keats under glass. The manuscript of an ode whose phrases are everlasting echoes in the heart of man should bring one reasonably close to the writer: yet even something so private to an author as his own writing on his own paper does not greatly stir me. Could it be proven beyond all doubt that we have found the very quill and the tables with which and on which the text of *Hamlet* was set down, even if the whole manuscript were there with Shakespeare's scribbled corrections and after-thoughts, I should be happy to let them all go to America for the millions of dollars they would command, so long as we had good fair copies to examine and enjoy. Give me a nicely printed and well-covered book, apt to the hand, and I am careless whether it be the first or the five-hundredth edition. As for Hamlet, the stage is his place. With all due obeisance to such happy and persuasive Shakespearean commentators as Logan Pearsall Smith, who loved the texts and hated a theatre, you will find Hamlet in the grease-paint: there has been too much thinking about his cast of thought. Shakespeare lives in the Avonian water-meadows and on the boards at Stratford far more than among the exhibits of the Birthplace. This is probably a minority opinion, but it makes me a poor attender at museums, theatrical and literary exhibitions, and the like. Of course there have to be glass cases for preservation's sake; the scholars need them; but the sight of the snuff-box and the locket, labelled in such exquisite script, does not snatch at my fancy and put me in the company of the mighty dead. Perhaps I was frightened by a glazier in my infancy.

Places, on the other hand, do carry associations for me even though they have been radically altered on the surface, hewn and hacked and covered with new buildings. Admittedly a poet's authentic desk was nearer to the work you cherish than is the garden round his house, a garden in which there may now be only a single tree, or none, of those standing there when he wrote. But the lawn and the flowerbeds are much more to me than the furniture and the devoutly tended bric-a-brac. At Haworth in Yorkshire, where the old vicarage is a complete and unassailable Brontë museum, with the gloom of the old graveyard round about it, I find the spirit of the sisters much less approachable than I do on the moors at the back, although they are far from the finest and fiercest of Yorkshire scenery. I know many a Pennine steading which better deserves to be called Wuthering Heights than does the hinterland of Haworth. But in the moorland air personality, for me, survives: in rooms it vanishes. This is a paradox, since a house ought to be more tenacious of ghosts than any wind-swept garden with its mutable trees that soar and shrink with the years, that are in leaf and then are naked again with the seasons.

On a sunny morning, when spring is round the corner and the peeping blossom of an almond tree or prunus may be crying salutation to the better deeds of March, it is refreshing to turn into Downshire Hill and then to take the right fork past the prim, neat evangelical church of St. John which holds up its Puritan finger to all artists, pagans, and revolutionary scallywags who may be living thereabouts, as often they have been. For Hampstead has always mixed property and decorum with radical journalism or even philosophic anarchy. Recently it provided a far stronger Communist vote than did Poplar in the East End. For me Henry Nevinson is still the abiding spirit of Downshire Hill where people of Liberal views live in such agreeably conservative surroundings; many an essay and a pamphlet denouncing the tyrannies of domesticity has, I fancy, been written in this very domestic street.

What is now Keats Grove used to be John Street and what is now the Keats Memorial House used to be Lawn Bank and before that Wentworth Place. Before you reach it, going downhill, you pass the house where Robert Lynd so long reviewed other people's books and omitted to write enough of his own: the long application of authorship did not suit him: he was essentially the journalist, waiting for the starter's orders, a last-minute writer who always somehow got his copy to the printer. And what copy it was! Belated but enchanting, there came the most readable of reviews, the most happily scrutable of all essays—and compiled in a hand that only some gifted specialist in the printing-house could possibly decipher. It is simple truth to say of this gay and gracious man that he deserved to live in Keats Grove; for this brief avenue of the Muse has the fairground of Hampstead at its base and the Freemason's Arms adjacent. If not a Mason with a capital M, Lynd belonged to the masonry of Fleet Street; he loved public pleasures and public-houses, the

gossip of the race-course as much as the tattle of the book-world.
If the dead could choose their subsequent tenants and neighbours
John Keats should have voted urgently for having Lynd beside
his plum-tree. Yet Lynd chose his own grave in Belfast, his
native place and his first allegiance. But as ' John o' London ' he
often wrote and Robert o' London he essentially was.

The Keats House was once two semi-detached villas, Brawne's
and Brown's. We enter by way of the Brawne's (no charge) and
pass through into Brown's; the partition was removed long ago.
The Keats Museum is in a new building on the site of some old
stables and sheds: it is a part of Hampstead Public Library. So
miniature a house for two households was Wentworth Place
that Keats and Fanny Brawne were bound to fall in love, if only
from such proximity of two warm hearts. If there was a fence
or a garden wall it was only for looking over, the kind of barrier
that is a temptation. There certainly were mulberry and plum
in front of the two houses. When these were in hue and the
weather in good heart, the garden with its view out towards the
Hampstead Ponds and the still unsullied heathland reaching over
to Highgate, must have been idyllic. There was only one other
house adjacent. When Keats was living in Well Walk and
later at Wentworth Place, the total population of the whole
Hampstead area was just over 5000. It is now over 100,000.

The legend has it that Keats wrote his ' Ode to a Nightingale '
under the plum-tree. It may be so, but the link was snapped in
1949 when the withered tree was removed at last and a youngster
planted in its place. The aged mulberry remains. The two
houses were reduced to one by Miss Chester, a Victorian actress,
who naturally wanted to entertain in premises so precious; she
built out a long room which was damaged by enemy action
during the last war. Inside you will discover that both Keats
and Leigh Hunt worked at little narrow, school-roomish desks;
this suggests a certain discipline of tidiness—or were their papers
just thrown on the floor? The modern author prefers the liberty

of a huge writing-table: this creates, simultaneously, happiness and chaos.

I find it very hard to believe that Keats could compose an Ode on the confined surface of the desk you see, with his elbows out over the floor like a distraught schoolboy at his algebra. Perhaps he wrote in bed: it was not an age remarkable for large and comfortable furniture. Byron's horse-hair sofa, on which I have sat, was a hard and prosy article that few of us would enjoy or even tolerate to-day. And there was, of course, in summer time, the garden at night, with the May-time music of the birds piping in the dusk.

> *I cannot see what flowers are at my feet*
> *Nor what soft incense hangs upon the boughs.*
> *But in embalmed darkness, guess each sweet*
> *Wherewith the seasonable month endows,*
> *The grass, the thicket, and the fruit tree wild*
> *White hawthorn, and the pastoral eglantine,*
> *Fast-fading violets covered up in leaves*
> *And mid-May's eldest child,*
> *The coming musk-rose, full of dewy wine,*
> *The murmurous haunt of flies on summer eves.*

No, after that, I cannot relish the glass cases or stay long in the little back room which was the poets' study. Even though it be winter, let us walk in the garden.

Not long after the death of Keats in Rome a fictional figure was to be seen ' in the bushes at the bottom of the garden ' of Wentworth Place. The figure was of such superb actuality and so vividly enduring that we can almost view it as really there. Samuel Pickwick was collecting material for the paper which he contributed to the Transactions of the Pickwick Club. On May 12, 1827, it was unanimously agreed by the members that

That this Association has heard read, with feelings of unmingled satisfaction, and unqualified approval, the paper communicated by Samuel Pickwick, Esq., G.C.M.P.C., entitled " Speculations on the

Source of the Hampstead Ponds, with some Observations on the
Theory of Tittlebats: ' and that this Association does hereby return
its warmest thanks to the said Samuel Pickwick, Esq., G.C.M.P.C.,
for the same.

To gain this lore Mr. Pickwick had prosecuted his lacustrine and
tittlebatian studies in Hornsey, Highgate, Brixton and Camberwell. But Hampstead, after all, was the heart of his research and
the most easterly of the Ponds lies close to the garden where
Keats held hands with Fanny Brawne and out-sang in verse the
local nightingale. It must have been past those ponds that Keats
had walked when he met Coleridge in Millfield Lane, beyond
the farther chain of the Highgate Ponds. This was early in 1819.
Coleridge knew of the youngster's likely doom. Their fingers
joined in greeting and Coleridge reflected, ' There is death in
that hand.' We could surely have saved Keats had he lived to-
day. We have saved his house—or rather the refuge that Brown
provided, the house where Fanny was courted, where Severn
painted, and where Keats poured out his rare fund of verbal
beauty and some of his life-blood too. Many notables have
dwelt in and around this watery pleasaunce. Its fauna have been
made immortal. To have shared Keats's bird of night and Mr.
Pickwick's tittlebats is fame enough for any corner of London.
If Keats had turned up Highgate Hill after that sad meeting with
Coleridge, he would have walked over a piece of ground whose
history is aromatic with great names and rare personalities. It
still is a fascinating area and amply deserves a visit. Since descent
is preferable to ascent in the matter of walking, even in winter,
I suggest beginning at the top, the opposite end from Millfield
Lane. A bus running frequently from Golder's Green to Finsbury
Park goes right through Highgate Village and can be caught en
route at Highgate Tube Station.

The Grove where Coleridge lodged in a house more recently
owned by J. B. Priestley, and one of the best workshops of the
latter's quick wrist and multifarious mind, is the proper flank of

a charming village. Highgate remains nearly rural and obstinately parochial. Hampstead is, or was, until Progress arrived in its usual destructive way, a suburb of high status, but Highgate, though for administration it is in Hornsey and for a living sends its citizens down the hill to London, has a hamlet at the heart of it. There is now an enclosed reservoir where a village green with cricket and football ought to be, but the Flask Inn at the centre of things is a village tavern with benches outside and an air of easy spaciousness. You can sit on a bench in the open on a sunny March morning and think yourself away in the shires. John Drinkwater, whose poetry is sadly out of fashion, lived for a while in the Grove; he had an ear attuned to the ordinary scents and noises of rural England, especially of the Midlands and the Cotswolds. The mists rise among the grey stone in his verse and the owls are heard by the blink of the moon; his successors on the English Helicon mostly hate that kind of avian and landscape pensiveness.

As you walk down Dick Whittington's hill you can reflect on that mayoral figure who sang no songs himself, but at least had an ear for church bells and has since evoked a myriad rhymes and ballads from the composers of pantomimes. Whittington's City home was in College Hill, close to Cannon Street, and there he built St. Michael's Church, later to be buried in it. Not long ago a sort of mummified cat was found during excavations; the wretched animal must have somehow got into an airless, damp-proof niche and there died—unless, of course, this was one of Whittington's household cats honourably embalmed, as was suggested at the time of the discovery. It can hardly have been the original cat that went with him from Highgate to Morocco, since he was a boy then and the fortune had yet to be made which in turn made the church. The Whittington Almshouses, built by his bequest, were moved out to Highgate in 1808, as a salute to that hill of chimes on which Richard made his wise resolve and doubled on his tracks. There is no need to bow to the Whittington Stone, lower down the hill, however much you venerate success. It is somebody's memorial after-thought.

Before you get to the Stone, there is much on which to think. Cromwell House has been written off as ' good period ' but not Cromwell's own. It is a fine sight still, commands wide views and carries a nice impression of country-town spaciousness. Howitt, writing of 'The Northern Heights of London' in 1869, commended its brickwork and then broke out into a fierce attack on the rubbishy workmanship and jerry building of his own day. Yet the construction of his period was infinitely sounder than the stuff we have had lately. Is any age ever content with its own standards of craft? Must we always look back for the best? Apparently even the Romans were lamenting the age of Saturn in which all was peace and plenty.

This section of the hill was notably inhabited during the seventeenth century. In Cromwell House were Cromwell's son-in-law and daughter, General and Bridget Ireton. Opposite them—and this brings us back to the poets' corners—lived Andrew Marvell. His small, half-timbered house was still there when Howitt wrote. The picture of it, taken from a photograph of 1848, shows a pleasant, low, rambling building of no great size and therefore of immense potential value in these times. But it was not to survive. Howitt wrote while it was threatened: he thought the building rather mean and moralised on the poor rewards of honesty and poetry, matched with the glorious mansion of the unscrupulous Lauderdale just opposite, the mansion often warmed and decorated by the presence of Nell Gwynne.

Marvell makes a fascinating figure. This is Aubrey's picture of him :

He was of a middling stature, pretty strong sett, roundish faced, cherry cheek't, hazell eie, browne haire. He was in his conversation very modest, and of very few words: and though he loved wine he would never drinke hard in company, and was wont to say that, "he would not play the good-fellow in any man's company in whose hands he would not trust his life." He kept bottles of wine at his lodgeing, and many times he would drinke liberally by himselfe to refresh his spirits, and exalt his muse.

'Exalt his muse' is charming. Some of the best of his poetry was written when he was tutor to the Fairfax family at Nun Appleton in the Vale of York. There the flowers and trees were his exalting elements. His Highgate writings were more political and satirical. He was M.P. for his native town of Hull and sent thither a weekly letter on the proceedings in Parliament. So serene in a garden, he could be savage in polemical poetry and lampoons.

What Aubrey said about Marvell's drinking habits and his fear of losing his grip in a boisterous company may surprise us, but Andrew had made many bitter enemies. The politics of the age were those of persecution as well as of persuasion and the road to Highgate from Westminster was dark and lonely. Aubrey reports the rumour that Marvell was 'poisoned by Jesuites,' but does not confirm it. Augustine Birrell prefers to believe the account of Richard Morton, a student of fevers, who in 1692 laid it down that the poet was killed by the ignorance of an old, conceited doctor who would not administer Peruvian Bark, against which he 'raved excessively,' and seems instead to have sweated the poor patient to his death. This is Morton's account of the passing of the poet who lodged so long—and presumably happily—on Highgate Hill. After copious bleeding

. . . a great febrifuge was given, a draught, that is to say, of Venice treacle, etc. By the doctor's orders, the patient was covered up close with blankets, say rather, was buried under them; and composed himself to sleep and sweat, so that he might escape the cold shivers which are wont to accompany the onset of the ague-fit. He was seized with the deepest sleep and colliquative sweats, and in the short space of twenty-four hours from the time of the ague-fit, he died comatose. He died, who, had a single ounce of

Peruvian bark been properly given, might easily have escaped, in twenty-four hours, from the jaws of the grave and the disease: and so, burning with anger, I informed the doctor, when he told me this story without any sense of shame.

We need not absolve modern medicine of all follies and blunders if we assume that it could have lengthened the life both of Keats and Marvell and extended, as well as exalted, their Muse.

It was from this retreat in Highgate that Marvell set out on a strange, wearisome, and dangerous journey which has a special interest for us to-day. In June 1663 he apologised to his constituents in Hull for proposing to take a year's absence; as secretary to Lord Carlisle, 'Embassadour Extraordinary to Muscovy, Sweden, and Denmarke,' he was to accompany his lordship to those countries in the interests of British trade. They left Gravesend on July 22 by frigate and went by way of Archangel, reaching that port on August 19. Once landed, they met trouble all the way. Discourtesy was rampant. The Russians failed to supply the expected sledges. Carlisle had to hire his own, no less than two hundred of them, and it was not till February that most of the party at last reached Moscow. Six months of sledging and quarrelling through a North Russian winter! Marvell must often have thought of his home comforts on Highgate Hill. Was there vodka to 'exalt his spirits'?

On February 19 the Tsar gave the English party a dinner which began at two, included five hundred dishes, and only ended at eleven because the Tsar's nose had begun to bleed. The visit lasted till May and the trade negotiations, long and futile, yielded nothing whatever. Carlisle in pique refused a gift of priceless sables, the Tsar handed back the gift of plate sent by Charles II, and Carlisle snapped that up as his perquisite. His secretaries got nothing and the whole business of going to Moscow was, from the nations and Marvell's point of view, completely barren. It is a tedious common-place that history repeats itself; but in this case one can hardly refrain from such comment

upon the Molotovian negativity of the proceedings. Doubtless a good time was had by all as they came back through
the far more mannerly and hospitable cities of Stockholm
and Copenhagen. Marvell was out of Highgate for eighteen
months. If he murmured his own verses to himself, he might
have thought of his garden in Highgate as poignantly as Rupert
Brooke sighed for Grantchester and its meadows while he sat
among the ' temperamentvoll German Jews.' Dutifully attending
the trade talks with Russian officials who would talk interminably
but never trade, he could reflect that diplomatic laurels were
hardly won. How sweeter far the herbs on Highgate Hill or in
the Yorkshire garden of his youth.

> How vainly men themselves amaze,
> To win the palm, the oak, or bayes,
> And their uncessant labours see
> Crown'd from some single herb or tree,
> Whose short and narrow-vergéd shade
> Does prudently their toyles upbraid;
> While all the flow'rs and trees do close,
> To weave the garlands of repose.
>
> Fair Quiet, have I found thee here,
> And Innocence, thy sister dear?
> Mistaken long, I sought you then
> In busie companies of men.
> Your sacred plants, if here below,
> Only among the plants will grow;
> Society is all but rude
> To this delicious solitude.
>
> Here at the fountain's sliding foot,
> Or at some fruit-tree's mossy root,
> Casting the bodie's vest aside,
> My soul into the boughs does glide,
> There, like a bird it sits, and sings,
> Then whets and claps its silver wings;

> *And, till prepar'd for longer flight,*
> *Waves in its plumes the various light.*

On return he was once more in 'rude Society,' once more
neighbour to the loathed Lauderdale, once more beneath a king
whom he savagely assailed. Marvell's poetic personality shows
a sharp division of tempers and style. There is the metaphysical
hedonist of the green thoughts in green shades: there is the
angry Puritan who could write like this of the King and his
companions. Britannia cries of Charles II (in the rhymed
imaginary dialogue between Raleigh and Britannia)

> *Like a tame Spinster in's Seraigl he sits,*
> *Besieg'd by whores, buffoons, and bastards chits;*
> *Lull'd in security, rowling in lust,*
> *Resigns his crown to angel Carwell's trust;*
> *Her creature O(sbor)ne the revenue steals;*
> *False F(inc)h, knave Ang(le)sey misguide the seals.*
> *Mac-James the Irish bigots does adore,*
> *His French and Teague command on sea and shore.*
> *The Scotch-scalado of our Court two isles,*
> *False Lauderdale, with ordure, all defiles.*

Presumably these lines, like so much of Marvell's work, only
came to light after his death. It would have been safer so.
Journeys for a poet with such fangs and with Lauderdale, so
venomously attacked, his neighbour on the hill, would have been
risky on black nights. Better even Russia, 'when nights are
longest there,' than certain passages and conduits round the court
of a Stuart King reviled and of his cronies thus dung-spattered.

Lauderdale House has lived on, with a notable irony, to serve
democracy with tea and buns. The ducal home of stratagems
and surfeits has dwindled to be a park waitress, as Millamant
talked of dwindling to be a wife. The twenty-nine acres behind
the house were given in 1889 by Sir Sidney Waterlow to be
the pleasant, well-timbered, well-watered Waterlow Park. Sir
Sidney, like Sir Richard Whittington, was Lord Mayor of

London in his time. So, if you pause during a poetical pilgrimage to admire the March foliage and coquetry of the mating mallards on the pond and turn in for a cup of tea, you do so at the remains of Lauderdale House where Nell Gwynne rusticated. (But not with the Duke. The careful King sent her only to Highgate when Lauderdale was on his Scottish visits.)

Highgate is a history of literature whichever way you turn. St. Michael's Church, facing the old green, stands on the commanding site of Arundel House. It was there that Bacon died. The great lawyer, philosopher, essayist, and man of science was taking a winter drive to Highgate. Snow had fallen and Bacon paused to indulge the innate curiosity of a man of learning. Could natural refrigeration work in the larder? He procured a fowl, stuffed its carcase with some of the available snow, and was prepared to await results. But he caught a sudden chill, was taken to the Earl of Arundel's and there foolishly and fatally placed in damp sheets, a warning both to over-enthusiastic scientists and to neglectful wardens of the house-linen. At least this is Aubrey's version of his end. If Bacon was also Shakespeare, which some pertinaciously maintain, then Highgate Hill is more than ever England's Helicon, since Bacon-Shakespeare came to his demise where Coleridge, Marvell, and A. E. Housman actively practised the poet's craft. It makes a powerful team.

Housman lived for close on twenty years at Byron Cottage, North Road, Highgate, exercising his scrupulous scholarship to the glory of London University and his English muse to the abiding enrichment of our minds and book-shelves. The author of *A Shropshire Lad* was born in Worcestershire of Lancashire and West Country parents and educated at Bromsgrove and Oxford; he worked in London and Cambridge, and was never for long in the shire now linked with his name. ' I had,' he wrote, ' a sentimental feeling for Shropshire because its hills were our western horizon. I know Ludlow and Wenlock, but my topographical details—Hughley, Abdon-under-Clee—are some-

times quite wrong.' He states that he was brought up in the
High Church, was attracted to paganism by Lemprière's *Classical
Dictionary*, became a deist at thirteen, and an atheist at twenty-
one. He wrote verse at eight or earlier. At fourteen he composed
a school-prize poem on Sir Walter Raleigh in which he said
of James I:

> ' *A King who sought the land to bind*
> *Down to the meaness of his mind,*
> *A man to coming times exempt*
> *From every feeling but contempt.*'

Could Marvell have thrown more acid? The Stuarts certainly
caught the tail of the whip from one Highgatian of their own
time and from another Highgatian to be.

His Oxford career was astonishing. (First in ' Mods.,' ploughed
altogether in ' Greats,' and a failure in the Newdigate Prize
Poem.) He could do no better after the plough than get a
routine job in the Patent Office, and it was this that first took
him to Highgate where he lodged, an obstinate bachelor, for
two decades. His landlady's cook claimed to have worked for
two poets already and to be shy of the breed, since they demanded
stimulant, poem-producing dishes at two in the morning.
Housman, according to his brother Laurence, whose book
'*A. E. H.*' is essential to the understanding of Highgate's Salopian
singer, loved telling this story because the two poets in question
were Swinburne and Watts-Dunton. Watts-Dunton a poet?
It gave scope to Housman's sardonic flair.

However the cook need not have worried. Alfred Housman
was taciturn, remote, and most unlikely to make a fuss in the
kitchen. In an autobiographical note to his brother he stated
briefly,

> While I was at the Patent Office I read a great deal of Greek
> and Latin at the British Museum of an evening. While at University
> College, which is not residential, I lived alone in lodgings in the

environs of London. *A Shropshire Lad* was written at Byron
Cottage, 17 North Road, Highgate, where I lived from 1886 to 1905.

A Shropshire Lad was offered to Macmillan, and declined by
them on the advice, I have been told, of John Morley, who was
their reader. Then a friend introduced me to Kegan Paul; but the
book was published at my own expense.

The friend mentioned was Alfred Pollard who did far more
for *A Shropshire Lad* than give an introduction. He gave that
great little book its admirable and appealing name. Housman
was going to call it ' Poems by Terence Hearsay,' which might
have killed it altogether. In any case it had to struggle for life.
At the end of the year the sales, at half a crown, were 381. First
editions subsequently reached £80 a copy—and may be higher
now. The elder generation of critics were cold to it, George
Meredith in particular. But gradually the young discovered it—
and rejoiced.

Housman was a good enough Highgatian to write letters to the
Press in defence of his adopted countryside. He protested, with
an irony which may well have been too acute for the ordinary
reader, against the thinning of Highgate Wood by its owner,
the City of London, so that the surrounding scenery became all
the more apparent; the said scenery being the railway to Muswell
Hill and the scarlet petticoats then fashionable in the Archway
Road and so hung out to dry after washing-day. His plea for
bigger and better undergrowth has been of no avail. The
Highgate Woods through which I occasionally walk are all
trunks and little else, the most naked of forests.

At any rate ' A Shropshire Lad ' is Highgate's own. Housman
has revealed some at least of the time and methods of his composition. He found an afternoon walk, with some beer taken,
to be the right stimulant. He was extremely modest about his
English verse (but not so about his Latin scholarship) and he
would scarcely have claimed that his malted Muse did more
than Milton could. Housman's arrogance, in certain matters,

was of a size to destroy any charge of pettiness. 'You should be welcome to praise me,' he wrote of his rival Latinists, 'if you did not praise one another.' He rejected the frequent compliment of honorary degrees because he despised other men who held them. He even turned aside the supreme honour awarded by his nation, the Order of Merit, because it had been accepted by John Galsworthy, of whom he had small opinion. This was his reply to the King's Secretary:

> With all gratitude for His Majesty's most kind and flattering wish to confer upon me the Order of Merit, I humbly beg permission to decline this high honour. I hope to escape the reproach of thanklessness or churlish behaviour by borrowing the words in which an equally loyal subject, Admiral Cornwallis, declined a similar mark of the Royal favour: "I am, unhappily, of a turn of mind that would make my receiving that honour the most unpleasant thing imaginable."

His brother adds:

> In the official reply, he was assured that His Majesty would appreciate his reasons for this decision, which, considering the final phrase of the quotation defining them, indicated a remarkable power of sympathy on the part of His Majesty.

Perhaps it is natural that Housman's first poem should have been in praise of Sir Walter Raleigh, that aloof man, 'damnable proud.' I am myself continually fascinated by Housman's English poetry and do not doubt that his classical scholarship was as profound as his criticism of rivals was devastating: but I cannot approve the doctrine that to be offered a high honour which must be shared by one or by some of whom you do not approve is an insult. Such conduct may not be vanity, but it is grotesque intolerance.

Let us return, however, to happier matters, Housman, Highgate, his poetry, and the source of it. Passing by the Flask Inn on Highgate Hill I have often wondered whether a pint absorbed there before a stroll towards Hampstead (pause at The Spaniards for another?) released for us one of those lyrics about Ludlow that will hold their place for ever in the English treasury of mournful and melodious balladry. From this hill, at any rate, came the word-music, which sighs like the wind in the trees, so exquisite in cadence that its melancholy becomes in the end more dulcet than dismal.

Housman was a connoisseur of wines and his life was mainly lived in the civilised era when even scholars could afford to drink them and so, ruminating on their respective merits, could exercise upon the vintage at night some of that discrimination applied by them in day to the niceties of verbal style. He liked to spend some of his vacations in a sampling progress through the notable wine-countries. So he might have attributed his inspirations to a noble Claret or a spritely Hock. But when he came to tell the origin of his minstrelsy he proclaimed himself a native drinker and a maltworm. England and hops are the more honoured by this man of Highgate.

There is, however, little of London in his verse. The strong emotion on which it drew, the recurring theme of soldiery and passion, of the dead comrade and the bitter parting, may have been, in essence, country matters. ' Very little in the book,' he said of *A Shropshire Lad*, ' is autobiographical.' At another time he stated:

> I did not begin to write poetry in earnest until the really emotional part of my life was over; and my poetry, so far as I could make out, sprang chiefly from physical conditions, such as a relaxed sore throat during my most prolific period, the first five months of 1895.

Well, we can be thankful to that tonsilitis or laryngitis which set the bells ringing on Bredon and the winds bending the saplings double upon Wenlock Edge. It is my belief that physical health is often a hindrance to mental activity: there is such a thing as feeling too well to work. The sun is up: one absorbs it gladly; and then, after the exercise it provokes, there is the glory of a basking idleness. The sick man is not so tempted: his bodily limitations throw him back on mind and feeling: his athleticism is of these faculties. The history of our literature is enormously indebted to invalids. From the evidence of terminology, metaphor, and simile, it is arguable that Shakespeare's best work was done when illness was very much on his mind. My own experience has always been that good health and fresh air and days in the sun are a menace to mental activity. Out of a sick-bed may come strength: out of a temperature the cool steel of argument acutely phrased. Out of a Londoner's sore throat and his Shropshire visions came the ' blue, remembered hills.'

> That is the land of lost content,
> I see it shining plain,
> The happy highways where I went
> And cannot come again.

We can salute Byron Cottage, as we salute the site of Marvell's Highgate home.

Where Paddington meets Maida Vale on the banks of the Grand Junction Canal, Robert Browning lived for sixteen years after the death of his wife. The address was 19 Warwick Crescent. Despite much battery of that area by bombing, the house is still there. It has a pilastered front which, though merely an architectural pretence, gives it some kind of classical authority. So passionate a friend of ' ingenious Italy ' as Browning could reasonably live behind such a façade. Time and two wars have smudged the region where they have not blasted it. Warwick Crescent is not attractive in a winter drizzle: one sees too keen a point in Blake's lugubrious line about ' mournful, ever-weeping Paddington.' For Blake, however, Praed Street must have been still pastoral and should have smiled.

The Crescent faces quite a broad sheet of water, for the Canal

Browning's House, Paddington

here widens to a small, triangular lake on the far side of which the artist Feliks Topolski has a Bankside studio. Canals lie as a rule in trenches that hold the haze and on a bad day it can be thick in this area. (' Fear death? To feel the fog in my throat, the mist in my face?' Browning must have known the ' London particular' well enough in his prime.) But, with a spark of winter sunshine to gild the painted barges moored hereabouts or plodding on their way to the Midlands, the scene kindles. Our artists nowadays are not eager to be Canalettos, though London offers them scope enough. But painting, as well as poetry, is invited from the windows of No. 19. During Browning's tenancy the view was almost rustic as well as aquatic and his son would row him up between houseless banks as far as Kensal Green. But we have said good-bye to all that. It is brickful, evil-smoking Paddington now.

After losing his wife Elizabeth, Browning lived by the Canal with his father and sister as well as his son. But he was a constant traveller with his head and heart deep in the Apennines. To one accustomed to the hill towns of Italy neither the climate nor the prospect of Warwick Crescent can have been alluring, especially in the dark, wet months. Yet, in all but his poetry, Browning was a complete Londoner. His mother came from Peckham, he was christened in Walworth, spent his youth in Camberwell, married into Wimpole Street, was twenty years a householder in Warwick Crescent, ended up in Kensington, and was buried in Westminster Abbey. He was born in 1812, the same year as Charles Dickens, three years after Tennyson, and he outlived Dickens by nineteen years. Browning wrote from scholarship and travel as well as from himself: Dickens from self and observation. One feels, standing by the placid, murky water of the Canal, that Paddington was a convenience to Browning, but uncongenial and uncreative. He could so easily have found a theme for an English epic of popular life had he pottered with any affection about the taverns of the bargees or of the newly

massing railwaymen. And had Chelsea nothing to offer so keen
a poet of the arts and their makers? But he chose the path to
Rome, not the Harrow Road. The gondola, not the barge,
glides through his verse. He justified his eagerness for escape,
if ever a man did.

Yet little though Browning was rooted in Paddington, the
district might do more for him than it has done. The local
heroine is Mrs. Siddons, who was buried in the North End of
St. Mary's Churchyard, and has a statue by Chavalliaud on
Paddington Green. It has been thought right, also, to name a
block of flats after her; but there is much less honour for a
man of words than for a tragedy queen. So the nation or the
Browningites—how many of the old Browning Societies are there
left?—might get something done. Among the best preserved
Memorial Houses are those of Dickens in Doughty Street
and of the Carlyles in Cheyne Row, Chelsea, a National Trust
property. Both are very well worth visiting. It would be well
if the National Trust held more of our literary properties, not
dispossessing them of tenants, but finding, when vacancies occur,
the right appreciative, affectionate type of occupant and guaran-
teeing the fabric of the building. Browning's home, as well as
Charles Lamb's in Colebrooke Row, needs vigilance. We must
not allow any more of such finely ghosted properties to crumble
or be broken up. There has been too much of that already.

I have alluded to Blake's watery view of doleful Paddington.
He was a Regent Street man, though Nash's noble thoroughfare
had not, of course, arrived to greet his birth. Born near Golden
Square, Blake later sold prints in Poland Street. He was, later
still, in South Molton Street, but he is mainly associated with the
practice of the arts (and nudism) in Lambeth where, like Mrs.
Siddons and unlike Robert Browning, he has immortality in a
block of flats. In the vast, strange spaces of his visionary poem of
'Jerusalem,' there are apocalyptic glimpses of a London transformed. (Blake could not stop building new Jerusalems and

much of our London was for him still green and pleasant arable.)
In his mind's eye,

> *Pancrass and Kentish-town repose*
> *Among her golden pillars high,*
> *Among her golden arches which*
> *Shine upon the starry sky.*
>
> *The Jew's-harp-house and the Green Man,*
> *The ponds where Boys to bathe delight,*
> *The fields of Cows by Willan's farm,*
> *Shine in Jerusalem's pleasant sight.*

What melodies, I wonder, came out of the Jew's-harp-house and
where did Willan farm? Was it in Willesden? Despite such
snatches of tranquillity, what a strange, minatory poem that is,
with its mixture of Old Testament and Old England!

> *Battersea and Chelsea mourn, London and Canterbury tremble!*

Blake can hardly haunt the Lambeth Walk of these days: but,
as I take my London strolls, he makes a glorious rumbling in
my memory.

Number Two, the Pines, still stands sedately where the busy
shops of Putney end and the residential solemnity begins. There
is indeed, something very solemn and not at all suggestive of
Bacchus, Apollo, and the Nine in the grey brick and the spiky
towers of Victorian Putney Hill. Over the window of this
famous house, where Swinburne was triumphantly deflected into
sobriety of mind as well as of body, there is the head of a bearded
gentleman who might be Zeus, the First Gentleman of Olympus
—if gentleman he can, in view of all his conduct, be justly called.
That gives a slightly classic flavour to what is otherwise English,
Londonish, and bourgeois to the last brick. It must have been a
much quieter house when Swinburne was fetched there by
Theodore Watts, later Watts-Dunton, in 1879, and even when
he died there thirty years later. Now there is a multitudinous

roar of traffic grinding up Putney Hill to the heath, on which the poet went for his daily and, it seems, his delightful walk.

Sir Max Beerbohm's well-known essay on visiting Swinburne at The Pines describes a man not only enraptured with his lunch-time ration of bottled Bass, as it were a stoup of the old Samian, but ecstatic, too, about the pleasures of promenading in Putney. 'Max' makes it plain that Swinburne thoroughly appreciated the local amenities. He may, at times, have cast a lingering mental glance at the Bloomsbury in which he had played the Bacchanal to the peril of his life, but, on the daily parade ground of his new regimen, when the strict Watts-Dunton had got him under control, he walked enchanted. 'Max' relates that, when questioned concerning his outings, Swinburne cooed like a dove. Then 'rapidly, ever so musically, he spoke to us of his walk, spoke not in the strain of a man who has been taking his daily exercise on Putney Heath, but rather in that of a Peri who had at long last been suffered to pass through Paradise.' This utterance of bliss, was all 'as spontaneous as the utterance of a bird-song.'

So if we stroll on Putney Heath and the confines of Wimbledon Park to-day or visit the tavern where Swinburne is supposed usually to have rested in mid-ramble, we need not think of a caged lark. No doubt Watts-Dunton was a solemn owl, but what he did was indeed necessary if a great man were not to die young: what he threw out from The Pines was a life-belt as well as a leading-string. The substitution of a little Bass for a lot of brandy greatly prolonged Swinburne's years, though it certainly did not enlarge his genius. Housman, although a devoted Swinburnian, regretted that he kept 'clattering on' when he had nothing left to say. But 'Max' makes it plain that when Watts-Dunton resolved to save Swinburne's life by combing the vine-leaves out of his hair he by no means reduced him to a languid melancholy.

The poet's old enemy, John Morley, lived near by in

Wimbledon Park.   Honest John's slashing attack on *Poems and Ballads* in the *Saturday Review* had been one of the heaviest cannonades in a bombardment directed from the Right at the supposedly libertine Radical and red-head. Algernon Charles Swinburne—how well the name befits a Victorian Admiral's son with a literary bent and Eton and Balliol behind him! But the boy never stayed the educational course and the under-graduate was restless too. He took up with all the wrong things, from an Admiral's point of view, agnosticism not belief, lush hedonism not dutiful asceticism, the ringing poetry of revolution instead of the decent prose of reform. Morley, as an agnostic might have been expected to blow a kiss to the young recruit for his camp. But British secularism has often been extremely austere and even purer than the Puritans; Swinburne's morbidities—he was assailed, from his school days, by sadistic and masochistic fantasies—and the voluptuous doctrine of his verse were altogether too much for Morley, who might spell God with a small ' g ' but for whom Propriety had a very big ' P ' indeed.

Mr. Humphrey Hare's excellent book on Swinburne has recently analysed the psychological complications in a way neither fussy nor pretentious—rare virtue when such analysis is made—and is the right preparatory reading for a walk past the Pines and on to the adjacent commons. Here the sight of the many birch-trees, whose silver lights up the heathland on a winter day, may, with their whisperings of pain, have been exciting and disturbing to the poet's maturer years: but he settled down to compose critical prose and to voice Conservative and even Imperialist politics. The hand that wrote ' Faustine ' and ' Anactoria ' had abandoned the cognac and the company that went with it. Unlike Housman, Swinburne did not burst into his best poetry on a basis of hops. He was quite happy, as ' Max ' has said, with his small beer, ' ultimate allowance of one who had erst clashed cymbals in Naxos,' but he was rather like the Sherlock Holmes whom Conan Doyle was compelled by public pressure to resurrect, 'not the man he was before.'

When death came in 1909 it was in Putney, not Rome or Missolonghi, not Lesbos or Spezzia Bay. Arnold Bennett wrote a valedictory article which I vividly remember: he described his personal shock and loss and told of the enormous emancipation that had come to a young man in the Potteries when he discovered the poetry of Swinburne. Here was both a new Eldorado of the senses and a new republic for the radical mind.

Swinburne was buried in the family grave at Bonchurch amid the Victorian respectabilities of the still very Victorian Isle of Wight. After such a youth of riot and rebellion and the handing of such torches of revolt to the runners of the younger generation, it may seem the wrong conclusion. But he is better there than in the vast sepulchral assemblage of Putney Vale. He lies close to the sea; and the sea, from which Aphrodite rose, was almost as much to Swinburne as Aphrodite herself. His lines about seascapes roll like breakers and the salt sting of the hissing waters is upon them. In much of Swinburne the imagery is overwhelmingly oceanic and the metaphors marine. And sometimes there was a preoccupation with drowning as strong as that with whips and rods and blood.

> I will go back to the great sweet mother,
>   Mother and lover of men, the sea.
> I will go down to her, I and none other,
>   Close with her, kiss her, and mix her with me,
> Cling to her, strive with her, hold her fast;
>   O fair white mother, in days long past
> Born without sister, born without brother,
>   Set free my soul as thy soul is free.
>
> O fair green-girdled mother of mine,
>   Sea, that art clothed with the sun and the rain,
> Thy sweet hard kisses are strong like wine,

Thy large embraces are keen like pain.
Save me and hide me with all thy waves,
Find me one grave of thy thousand graves,
Those pure cold populous graves of thine,
Wrought without hand in a world without stain.

In Putney lived on a semi-Swinburne, which was better than none. Watts-Dunton has been called a gaoler of genius, but he kept alive half of that which would otherwise have been wholly dead. That half was happy enough, busy with his critical reviews, and his praise of poets long ago; he was felicitous and fecund in his prose, a contented surburban stroller, and refreshed, when his spirits wasted, with small tots of punctual Bass. He needed, for the fullness of his lyrical genius, the larger freedom of the grape. But Putney can be proud enough of its adopted son who for thirty years was consoled by the wind on this high, congenial heath, where the skyscape atoned for the absence of the sea.

CHAPTER IV

The Great Invisibles

——————⟨❧⟩——————

ONE OF the more bizarre facets of the English character is the
common passion for flocking, even at much cost and dis-
comfort, to view sights which are known in advance to be
mainly unseeable. Not only do we accept the familiar advice
of W. H. Davies to stand and stare when there is some possibility
of optical profit: we even do it where the fruits of observation
are certain to be as dry as dust or altogether absent. Nothing
gives us greater pleasure than, as Hamlet said of another matter,
to make mouths at the invisible event.

An obvious example of this is the Derby. Since this famous
horse-race is run in early June, it can hardly be cited as one of
London's winter pleasures. (It has, however, been run in a
snowstorm, is frequently run in a downpour, and is sited on
Epsom Downs which offer some of the draughtiest expanses
amid London's environs; so it is not altogether an æstival
outing.) Whatever the weather, hundreds of thousands will
crowd their way to Epsom to watch the competition of the best
three-year-old horses for a victory made valuable not only by
prize-money but also by the enormous stud-fees chargeable by
the owner of a Derby-winning stallion.

The Derby long ago became the Race of the Year, at least for
Londoners, an Annual Event, an Institution, and Everyman's
occasion for 'having a flutter.' Such dense masses of people

accordingly collect on the Epsom slopes that the grass is scarcely visible: to join the mob involves no payment, as it guarantees no view. The public is more allured by the right of free entry than discouraged by the certainty of not seeing. ' Oh, who will o'er the Downs so free?' inquired the old ballad with its invitation to a ramble. The answer, in this case, is half a million.

Some may see the start if they climb away up to the back-end of the course. Otherwise, unless you are well and expensively deposited on a grand-stand beside the winning-post, you may with luck and with binoculars observe during the first minute and a half of the race the caps of the jockeys moving along the skyline until Tattenham Corner is reached. After that, unless, by rising early and waiting long, you have somehow squeezed yourself into a front-row stance in the free part of the course and have not fainted in the process, you will get a long, steady, but unprofitable stare at the back-ends of motor-buses and motor-coaches or of your fellow-men. Never mind: there is a great deal of public clamour, from which you may discover, still gratis, which of the horses is leading as they thunder invisibly past and which horse is finally triumphant. You would, had you sat quietly at home with your informative radio-set, have received a good impression of the swaying fortunes of the race. By actually going to the Derby you get no impression of anything but humanity: nowhere, indeed have I seen more of people—and less of horses.

The same absurdity besets the Oxford and Cambridge Boat Race which is rowed from Putney to Mortlake about the end of March—and therefore ranks as a winter festival. The day may promise spring; the almond trees may be painting the suburbs with delight: the sun may be gleaming on the daffodils: the Thames itself may be sparkling and vivacious. In that case there can be great pleasure in attending a party in one of the riverside houses of Hammersmith or Chiswick. Or there may be an east wind coming fanged over Essex; there may be an iron-grey sky promising the attenders at riparian garden-parties nothing but pneumonia; there may be no joy in any place but a fireside. Yet, whatever trick the weather plays, the crowds will be on the river-bank; there they will wait for hours, defying the pneumococcus, or they will even climb on to trees, roofs, and other periculous perches, defying death by collapse, in order to see—not the race, but one meagre fragment of it.

Since the course is a meandering one, with curves occurring quite frequently, the boats soon vanish from the view, and since the course is more than four miles long the amount of it visible from any one niche on the curving bank is quite small. So, when the crews have gone swinging past, it is necessary for the spectators to wait as much as ten minutes or a quarter of an hour and then to find out from hearsay who it was that won. A more disappointing spectacle for the average looker-on I cannot imagine. Yet the Boat Race, like the Derby, is an Annual Event and an Institution: but it is not the excuse for a flutter. Only cads bet on the Boat Race. But the magnet perpetually works. The lure of the Invisible is supreme; so the millions, at Derby or Boat Race, enthusiastically follow Robert Browning's counsel and greet the Unseen with a cheer.

And what a roar of cheers may be heard around the rites at Twickenham! Alexander Pope's riverside suburb is now chiefly famous as providing London's principal match-ground for Rugby Football. No dishonour there; it is a noble game and might have evoked some classic couplets of the best from that ingenious hand.

Here, in a deep, dark arena, surrounded on three sides by sky-ascending, light-denying grand-stands, is a piece of turf, superbly cared for, on which the two senior Universities and the five nations of England, Scotland, Wales, Ireland, and France— not to mention the gaily bedizened players of the club called the Harlequins and the various Service teams—go into their routine of annual or seasonal combats. Rugby Football, with its handling of the ball and the fantastic ceremonial of the scrummage, is generally supposed to be more esoteric, more of a mystery than is the Association game. The latter is literally football, except when it is being headball, and has a pattern of play more easily grasped by the lay observer. Yet very large numbers of women go to Twickenham for the high occasions of 'Rugger,' bringing to the snell bitterness of a February afternoon a reassuring apparatus of fur coats, wool-lined boots, rugs, flasks, and what is called in war-time 'comforts for the troops.' Thus equipped they look cosy enough for the achievement, without frostbite, of an Arctic expedition.

The match which I never miss is the one least likely to be visible. Fifty thousand others support my view that even a glimpse of this is good enough to justify the journey. The Oxford and Cambridge Rugby match is played at the end of the autumn term on a date close to December 10. The daylight is then almost at its shortest and Twickenham, being a riverside spot, water-meadowy until the builders profusely scattered villas over its clay, is a natural haunt of midwinter mist.

As I said, what light there is the soaring stands do much to obscure. The University match begins about 2.15 and is played for two periods of forty minutes with a five-minute interval. There are usually a few pauses while men who have lost or, frayed and tattered, seem likely to lose their vests or trousers in the maul are decorously regarmented in mid-field behind a closed circle of their standing fellow-combatants; pauses also occur while the injured are being sponged or massaged into recovery or despairingly removed. Thus the affair will last 90 minutes and end about 3.45. And there is small chance of seeing in detail the final rushes that decide the issue; no chance at all, if there be much mist seeping up from the river to this dark canyon of contest. The players flicker in and out of darkness. One guesses the achievement and seeks information from a neighbour. Once more the great and grotesque truth of

London sport is made manifest; the less visible, the more pursued.

The later matches, which continue until April, are far less concealed. It is the Oxford and Cambridge match that most seems to vanish in the fuscous air. But its excitement is tremendous. Let me quote the view of the battle round the oval-shaped, egg-like, erratically bouncing ball given by that brilliant Welsh story-teller, Rhys Davies. He is describing the English and Welsh International match, played on England's home ground, Twickenham, in alternate Januaries. This brings thousands of Welsh miners from their valleys, accepting two nights in the train as the pain of their pleasure and considerable swilling of beer as the relief of that pain, as a celebration of victory, or as a consolation in defeat. (It is one of the major blessings of sport that, win or lose, there is always cause for a glass; it both marks the triumph in the mind and smudges out the memory of disaster.)

The Welsh bring their pride and symbol, the leek, to brandish, and their national songs, such as ' Mochyn Du ' and ' Sospan Fach,' to chant in sweet melancholy as they wait for the battle to begin. In Mr. Davies's picture you must alter red beetles and white beetles to the dark blue and light blue of the University teams and subtract fifteen minutes from his timing of the start. Otherwise what he says is exactly what the foreigner, innocent of these mysteries, would see if he went to Twickenham to watch Oxford versus Cambridge on a drooping day of mid-December.

At two-thirty, into a grey misty field surrounded by huge walls of buzzing insects stickily massed together, fifteen red beetles and fifteen white beetles ambled forward on springy legs. To a great cry the sacred egg appeared. A whistle blew. The beetles wove a sharp pattern of movement, pursuing the egg with swift bounds and trim dance evolutions. Sometimes they became knotted over it as though in prayer. They worshipped the egg and yet they did not want it: as if it contained the secret of happiness, they pursued it, got it, and then threw it away. The sticky imprisoning walls heaved and roared; myriads of pin-point faces passed through agonies of horror and ecstasies of bliss. And from a great quantity of these faces came frenzied cries and urgings in a strange primitive language that no doubt gave added strength to the fifteen beetles who understood that language. It was not only the thirty below the walls who fought the battle.

The huge banks of massed humanity standing on the lower tiers and seated in the stands above (our wonderful English language always calls a place where you sit a stand) make the most curious spectacle. The Rugby game itself, coldly considered, is curiously artificial, a rite of massed bodies, but the wild, individual dashes cause constant and infinite hope and fear. Then the eye may be ravished and the senses set tingling by the beauty of a passing movement at full speed, with the faster-running players ribboning across the field in order to get it to the fastest of all, who is on the wing, so that he may sprint round the defenders without being hurled to earth or driven out of the field of play. In the match of 1949 there was one brilliant frantic, last-minute solo dash by J. V. Smith for Cambridge: there was also one brilliant, frantic, last-minute solo tackle by Carpenter of Oxford, who came across with miraculous speed to throw Smith over the touch-line at the last second. That tackle saved the victory for Oxford. But it made a breath-taking, heart-hammering moment for fifty thousand lookers-on. I do not know whether any ageing partisan has ever died of ecstasy or agony in the Twickenham stands: I am always expecting it to happen and would it be such a bad end, especially if it were the ecstasy of triumph which snatched the last breath of some Methuselist devotee?

Twickenham, on a big day, provides one of the last sessions of the Forsytes. Here are the professional classes, the Anglo-Saxons, the Nordics; non-Aryans are scarce. Where else in London will you see such fidelity of type? Those politicians

who regard the middle class as vermin might tremble to enter
here; the rats—if so they be—are so many. But rats they
certainly do not look. The standard of middle-class clothing in
Great Britain has gone down, of course, as prices have gone
rocketing up and the overcoats are not the soft, rich, glorious
blankets that they were: yet the standard of looks, male and
female, is as high here as anywhere in England; I am told and
I can believe that Edinburgh, on an International 'Rugger' day,
marshals the best-lookers of all and adds to these a majestic
promenade of tweed and tartan. But London, at Twickenham,
is worth regard.

Winter's clothing endures longer than summer's: hence the
dwindling wardrobes of the middle class are more noticeable at
the cricket ground of Lord's in July than on the rugby ground
in December. The Universities' cricket match used to muster
considerable elegance, but I noticed at recent matches that
there was no shame at being shabby, which is honest and may
be well. What was so sad about the midsummer event was the
absence of the parsons.

Of old the country vicar made a mid-week trip to London to
see a couple of days' play and reverently clap (or mildly deplore)
the efforts of his old University. The Mound Stand was heavily
sprinkled with the dingy, parti-coloured straw hats much favoured
by the clergy who were thus further distinguished from the
light-strawed, gaily ribboned laiety. But on this last occasion
scarce a parson could I see. The railway fares have risen so
cruelly and his meagre, static income will not stand the hotel
prices of the day. Nor did I see much of his cloth at Twickenham
five months later. Seats cost as much as ten shillings, travel is
dear, and the clergy do not easily spend a pound or more
nowadays upon a day's outing.

Even though it occurs in the weeks of poorest visibility, the
University match is my choice for a Twickenham visit. 'Rugger'
is a young man's business (too old at thirty, as a rule!) and here

is youth, at its fittest, at its fastest. The game is fought hard
and the tackling is terrific. The crowd manages to combine the
ardours and agonies of the partisan with a regard for the decencies
of spectatorship. In an amusing short ' leader ' in *The Times* on
the morning of the match it was rightly written that nobody at
Twickenham to-day would be ' so miserably anæmic as to want
to see the best side win.' Yes, victory is what is wanted; no
nonsense about that. But the referee is never in danger of his life.

So, soon after one o'clock on the afternoon of the match, the
assembly begins. There are the old and bold and very masculine,
with their caps and check overcoats, their spats and their tales
of tackles long ago. There, with them, watching the parade
before seats are taken, are the young and fair and very feminine,
the sisters and the cousins of the present Undergraduates and
perhaps of the players themselves. They are furred and booted
for the shiversome and possibly mysterious occasion, whose
technique of play they may but poorly comprehend. But they
put a pretty, as well as a brave, face on it. The winter air is
thick with chatter and jostle and anecdotes and smoke. It is a
Tuesday: large numbers of busy men seem to have important
engagements out of town this afternoon.

Then after salutes to Royalty the teams emerge and then
begin the dance-movements—as Rhys Davies calls them—of
the thirty artists and acrobats caracoling round the egg and
collapsing on top of it in a pell-mell frenzy. There rise now the
bellowed imprecations of the fifty thousand worshippers while
the acolytes, locked in conflict, sway to and fro, dart, twist,
and are tumbled, rise and re-attack on the perfect turf, which is
so queerly, richly green in this great dim cavern of Twickenham
field. Should the sun shine the myriad faces opposite go pink:
the stand is in flower. If the light fails, every kindled match of
a smoker glitters like a spangle on a Christmas tree. Before the
game is over the whole of that bank of humanity before you will
be fretted with this twinkling fire. Then, as the fog works in

and darkness falls, with ten minutes to go and a match to win, two packs of dazed and desperate forwards go scrummaging again for the leather egg or plunging in loose rushes to drive it down the field. A small man hurls himself under the booted feet of this seemingly ferocious phalanx and by a miracle emerges with the egg, which he kicks for safety out of bounds. There is a moment's respite while the ball is rescued from the crowd. Back it goes into play. The reserved, Forsytish crowd have laid aside the decent silence of Forsytism. They no longer have stiff upper lips: they roar encouragement, they mutter curses, they call on heaven. Five minutes now. The ritual of the egg is on the boil. Darkness marches on. Only those with seats or stances near the actual play can see now. What was that? Hostile neighbours of the rival factions are colleagues now in straining of eyes or guessing at the news. What was that? A score? No, a penalty. No, nothing at all.

Oxford just lead. Cambridge is pressing, pressing, yes, right on the Oxford line. Players, battling for the ball, collapse on top of it in a vast pile of bodies. But out it comes and back a little, back. Oxford, hard-pressed, is holding them and hoping just to last out the allotted time. If it goes on much longer Cambridge will win. Four minutes to go, three, two, one. The minutes, like the players, are run to a finish. There is the last, long blast of the referee's whistle. Oxford has just endured. A colossal roar goes up. Those who must go home by train plunge for the road and are wedged in a slowly moving mass that is skilfully carved up by the patient railway officials and served in slices into the waiting trains. Served? Well, rammed in and patted down, eighteen to a compartment.

Meanwhile the motoring Forsytes are drinking tea out of thermos flasks as they wait for the car-parks to clear. It is black night now and celebration ahead. But 'Rugger Night' has ceased to be a rowdy night. No longer do huge packs of revelling undergraduates besiege Piccadily Circus and form scrummages round Cupid, with a policeman's helmet knocked off to be the sacred egg of these nocturnal rites. It was foolish and it led, quite often, to a brief incarceration in that extremely gloomy pile with the gaily Bacchic title of Vine Street. The revel could be a public nuisance and a cause of damage, with its violent ejections from music-halls and indignation meetings of those thrown out. The undergraduate of to-day, after his visit to Twickenham, must count his shillings and shillings go nowhere in the West End. He cannot dine and wine to the extent of lighting up the town. He follows up the match with a pint or two of negligible beer and a seat at the pictures. To this has descended the traditional wassail and tussle of ' Rugger Night.'

But the players are dining. They have earned it. And they are in their own niche of history. Years hence the Twickenham reunionists of December 10 will talk of Jackson's try or Smithson's tackle. That is immortality of a kind—and not the least.

CHAPTER V
The Borough

———— ⟨≈⟩ ————

Wɪᴛʜɪɴ a few hundred yards of each other Chaucer started his pilgrims on their Canterbury journey, William Shakespeare offered the finest of his plays, John Keats studied pharmacy, and Charles Dickens launched Mr. Weller on the great ocean of the *Pickwick Papers*. Here were the very streets which he had so sadly promenaded as a child. Can Athens or any of the proud Italian cities claim such distinction for an acre or two, such contiguity of glory? The old Bankside, now Southwark, the Borough, may not look much to-day, but this, for me, is holy ground. Man's inhumanity to buildings has slashed and smashed: the fire of 1678 was as ruinous on the south side of Thames as the great blaze of a decade earlier had been on the north. What the flames spared 'progress' removed. What this kind of development left alone, the German bombers further punished. Such squandering of London's tenements of fame has Southwark seen and suffered.

The Borough to-day is harbour and hop-market, maker of shoes and vendor of vegetables. Not one in a thousand of its citizens, I fancy, cares a jot for its star-lit chronicles or stops to envisage Will Shakespeare crossing London Bridge or hiring a waterman for passage before the first performance of *Hamlet* or *Twelfth Night*. Nor do many pause to picture the angry, hungry little boy who lodged in Lant Street, while his father was inside the Marshalsea, and went along the river-bank each day to his detested drudgery in Lamert's blacking factory at Hungerford Stairs. Charles Dickens was not long an inhabitant of the Borough and never a happy one, despite the kindness of the family with whom he lodged. But before the move to Bayham Street in Camden Town, that quickest of eyes had seen and that amazing memory had been at work.

> *A chield's amang you, takin' notes,*
> *And faith he'll prent it.*

Here he found his models for the Garland Family and the Marchioness, just as hereabouts Shakespeare may have found models for Pistol and Bardolph, Nym and Doll. 'In the south suburb, by the Elephant'—there is nothing in London to touch it, for the richness and variety of its ghosts. The Tower has its spectres grim and gallant. Westminster echoes with the challenges and word-battery of statesmanship. But out of the Borough has come the spring-song of Chaucer, the full diapason of Shakespeare, the still, sad music of Dickensian prison-thoughts, and the Cockney lyric that is the heart of Mr. Weller. No handful of acres could be asked for more. Nowhere is more genius in the air.

Southwark was on the road from Kent and the coast, the last halt before knocking at the gate of London city itself. A place then for adventurers, pilgrims, marauders, honest merchants, carriers, drovers, and observers of the pageant of things. When London Bridge was closed at night, there was nothing for belated medieval travellers to do but to stable and sleep at Southwark. Hence it became the innkeeper's suburb, site of the Tabard, the White Hart, the King's Head, the George, and other taverns less renowned. If things were nasty, rebellion suspected, and nerves frayed, the citizens of London could use suburban Southwark, beyond the water and across the bridge, as a kind of Ellis Island. The incomers might be sifted and detained.

Chaucer found his pilgrims outward bound upon an April day.

> *Bifil that in that seson on a day,*
> *In Southwerk at the Tabard as I lay,*
> *Redy to wenden on my pilgrymage*
> *To Caunterbury with ful devout corage,*
> *At nyght were come into that hostelrye*
> *Wel nyne-and-twenty in a compaignye,*
> *Of sondry folk, by aventure y-falle*
> *In felaweshipe, and pilgrimes were they alle.'*

Hither, inward-bound, came Jack Cade, Shakespeare's Jack—that is if Shakespeare wrote *Henry VI*, Part 2, as I surmise that he did. Cade swore to make all the realm common, have seven ha'penny loaves on sale for a penny, and would treble the measure of liquor in the pot. There was no austerity about Cade's Socialism; he distrusted print and parchment and all speakers of alien tongues, be it the Latinity of a grammar-school or the French of a courtier. Briefly victorious, he and his rebellious comrades swept through Southwark and over London Bridge into Cannon Street, but there followed ' alarum and retreat' with Cade roaring ' Up Fish-street, down St. Magnus' corner! Kill and knock them down! Throw them into Thames!' According to the dramatist he had made the White Hart his headquarters and railed at his broken ranks,

> ' Hath my sword therefore broke through London gates, that you
> should leave me at the White Hart in Southwark? I thought ye
> would never have given out these arms till you had recover'd your
> ancient freedom: but you are all recreants and dastards, and delight
> to live in slavery to the nobility. Let them break your backs with
> burdens, take your houses over your heads, ravish your wives and
> daughters before your faces: for me, I will make shift for one;
> and so, God's curse light upon you all!'

And so, defeated, he marched away down the Old Kent Road to die, famished and unfit for fight, in unfair combat with

Alexander Iden into whose garden he had gone to seek the paltry nutrition of a salad.

It was in this same White Hart that Mr. Pickwick first met Sam Weller working with his brush and blacking on the Wellingtons, Hessians, Painted Tops, and other species of boot then to be expected in the galleries and corridors of a Southwark tavern. This establishment had two tiers of balustraded bedrooms running round the court where gigs, chaise-carts and wagons collected. Old London had a habit of getting burned down, if it were not knocked down. Jack Cade's White Hart vanished in flames in 1676: its successor endured drastic alterations during Victorian times and closed in 1904.

Dickens put Bob Sawyer into lodgings, *chez* the sharp-tongued Mrs. Raddle, in Lant Street, which runs a little farther south and close to the Marshalsea Prison. He described it as a thoroughfare of repose and gentle melancholy, its residences not of the ' desirable ' kind, but yet

> If a man wished to abstract himself from the world—to remove himself from within the reach of temptation—to place himself beyond the possibility of any inducement to look out of the window —he should by all means go to Lant Street.

Its population included

> a few clear-starchers, a sprinkling of journeymen bookbinders, one or two prison agents for the Insolvent Court, several small housekeepers who are employed in the Docks, a handful of mantua-makers, and a seasoning of jobbing tailors. The majority of the inhabitants either direct their energies to the letting of furnished apartments, or devote themselves to the healthful and invigorating pursuit of mangling. The chief features in the still life of the street are green shutters, lodging-bills, brass door-plates, and bell-handles; the principal specimens of animated nature, the pot-boy, the muffin youth, and the baked-potato man. The population is migratory, usually disappearing on the verge of quarter-day, and generally by night. His Majesty's revenues are seldom collected in this happy

valley; the rents are dubious; and the water communication is very frequently cut off.

For the boy who was, as they say, 'all eyes,' here was a quarter of the town most lavish in human spectacle. Around him were the river with its traffic and its incursion of watermen and sea-going men, the incoming coaches and chaises that rattled up from Kent on to the cobbles of the inn courtyards, the chattering of the Borough market, the high spirits and the rattling cynicism of the medical students at the great Hospital which Mr. Guy had founded a hundred years before, and the astonishing company in the Marshalsea, that mixture of Bastille and Liberty Hall, half gloomy, half-gay, where a strange law left debtors to moulder in a modest kind of comfort and even of petty affluence, if they were capable of earning at all. Dickens himself used the phrase 'the key of the street' to signify power of observation. And what streets were these of which to have the key!

As one wanders about Southwark nowadays it is natural to speculate on the effect that our new Welfare State will have upon the artist. Art thrives on contrasts and contrasts are created by inequality. Art needs the unusual; romance has been defined as strangeness with beauty. The old Borough abounded in the queer, the diverse, the picturesque, the savagely cruel, the gently charitable. So did all London, but the Borough, because of its history and because of its plentiful assortment of trades and traditions, of lodging-keepers and of lodgers, was a particularly rich mine of raw material for the artist with pencil or pen.

It hardly seems so now. The debtors left long ago, in 1842. Medical students grow steadily more studious and less colourful. Little riot is possible now on their allowances and Bob Sawyer's reliance on credit is unlikely to bring in such results to-day as he achieved with the rough-tongued but fairly patient Mrs. Raddle. The poor are less poor, better educated, and drenched daily and nightly, with the fun (or culture) of the B.B.C., safe stuff, the same for all.

All this has its manifest advantages. There is far less malnutrition: rickets are less frequent on the hearth of Borough householders: there is more cleanliness, more hygiene, and the Mrs. Gamps of the Bankside have had to bring themselves and their clinical methods up to date. Excellent, no doubt, for the Leveller, whose century we know this is. But not so excellent or so easy for youngsters burning to write. Life on this level is inevitably flat: there may in these days be the money about and better spread, but there is not the whimsicality, the madness, that belonged to the Dickensian world of the ostlers, the watermen, the gentlemen's gentlemen, and the crumbling, incarcerated mismanagers of personal income. It is not diminishing the genius of Dickens to say that things were a good deal easier for him then than they would be for a worker in his school to-day.

Norman Collins took fiction back to the South side of the river with *London Belongs To Me* and there were crime and punishment in that. But ordinary Dickensian human nature broke in, too. The public much liked that return to the natural man with all his oddities and humours about him. But abnormal psychology of a criminal type, rather than workaday behaviour, is at present the fashion in fiction and in films: it may be the age of the Common Man, but we prefer to be entertained by uncommon neuroses. I cannot see Mr. Graham Greene surveying the go-to-market types of the Borough with much satisfaction: go-to-Black-Market would be much more in his line. Such fellows, no doubt, can be found. But Southwark to-day is no longer the London gateway where all types loitered, a treasure for the novelist.

Lant Street is still there, with a modern school and modern housing of the tenement kind. But green shutters, lodging-bills, brass-door plates, and bell-handles are not to be seen and I doubt whether muffin-bells are still to be heard, since London hears them no more. The old houses are solid, deep-basemented, and dark; one of them has a bit of sculpture over the lintel to give it style. There are a thousand such streets in South London; but here the Pickwickians supped and Mrs. Raddle, infuriated by the kind of noise made when Pickwickians supped, refused to serve hot water for the later bowls of punch. Here, hot water denied, Jack Hopkins inquired, 'Shall I step up stairs and pitch into the landlord or keep on ringing the bell or go and groan upon the staircase? You may command me, Bob.' But Bob, with much rent overdue, commanded prudence and retreat. Not even 'groaning on the stair,' a simple but superb suggestion, would appease or terrify Mrs. Raddle. Immortal Lant Street where such nights occurred!

There are no plaques in Lant Street, but the L.C.C. has remembered its Dickens. So neighbouring Lombard Street—a very minor cousin of the City one—has become Leigh Hunt Street and Little Lant Street has been given the honourable title of Weller Street. Leigh Hunt is there because of his imprisonment: incarceration was long one of the local staples.

Southwark's early prison was the Clink—a name that has lived in slang ever since. It was on the Bishop of Winchester's ground by the Bankside and it was maintained, according to Stow, for such as 'should brabble, frey, or break the peace on the said Bank or in the brothel-houses' for which the Bishop's estate was notorious. Shakespeare's mention of 'Winchester geese' in *Troilus and Cressida* refers to the light women of that shore renowned in Tudor times for its chambering and wantoning. Of about the same age was the Old Marshalsea which had, in its earliest form, been assaulted by Wat Tyler and his rebels who came swarming through Southwark as Jack Cade was to do later. It had many illustrious inmates in its time, including George Withers the poet, who thus adds another link to the Borough's chains of union with Parnassus. There was also the King's Bench Prison in Southwark, where John Wilkes was detained for two years and Smollett 'went down' for libel. Benjamin Haydon was one of its regulars in the eighteentwenties. Life there was not necessarily dull or confined. The prison had a coffee-house and two public-houses to meet the needs of the occupants of its two hundred and twenty-four rooms. There was much liberty allowed and the King's Bench was rather oddly described as 'the most popular debtors' prison in the country,' much as though it had been an hotel, which indeed it was for debtors with enough means and the will to defy their creditors by staying there.

Horsemonger Lane Prison, demolished in 1879, was on a site now in Union Road and housed murderers, including Mr. and Mrs. Manning who had a short way with one of their lodgers. They were publicly executed in 1849 and Dickens denounced the scenes of horror at this open and repulsive spectacle. The Borough has had traffic enough with death in its time, being the rebels' gateway to their prize, the rich City, as well as a nest of gaols, when capital sentences were frequent and the execution of them a raree-show for the rabble. Leigh Hunt spent two years in Horsemonger Lane for describing the Prince Regent as a fat Adonis scant of breath.

The Old Marshalsea was succeeded by a new one and it was thither that John Dickens was sent, there that his son imagined old Dorrit. The second Marshalsea was made deathless by the story of *Little Dorrit*. 'Whosoever goes into Marshalsea Place, turning out of Angel Court, leading to Bermondsey, will find his feet on the very paving-stones of the extinct Marshalsea gaol: will see its narrow yard, very little altered if at all, except that the walls were lowered when the place got free: will look upon the rooms where the debtors lived: will stand among the crowded ghosts of many miserable years.'

Thus Dickens ended his preface to *Little Dorrit*. You may see a section of those walls still: even Goering and his airmen failed to blast them, much as they damaged the Borough itself, which was once more the gateway to the City and the neighbour of the docks and so was battered on the way in and the way out as well as being in the path of the later flying-bombs hell-bent for London. Angel Court, or Angel Place, seems to have been wiped out or to have otherwise vanished. When I asked for it in the Borough High Street there were negative shakings of the head. But one elder said, ' You mean Harding's? ' I vaguely agreed that Harding must be the Angel and he directed me to a big warehouse just north of St. George's Church. Part of it was behind a long dark wall with barred windows. So here dwelt old Dickens for some months, visited by his boy Charles, and here little Dorrit was born amid a reek of spirits and a buzzing of the special Marshalsea insect-life. (' What between the buryin' ground, the grocers, the waggon-stalls, and the paunch trade the Marshalsea flies get very large,' observed Mrs. Bangham who fetched Dr. Haggage's brandy—and her own— while Mrs. Dorrit lay in child-bed on a stifling summer day.) But existence in the Marshalsea had its compensations, convivial meetings of ' collegians ' in the Snuggery and a game of skittles in the yard.

Standing beside the dreary menace of the wall, and wandering back to St. George's Church, which is fairly enough labelled ' Little Dorrit's Church,' because the infant gaol-girl of the story, having survived the attentions of Mrs. Bangham and Dr. Haggage, was christened there, I could not help wondering about those Southwark prisons, which loomed so long over the Borough. They were dirty and insanitary: they were madly illogical, especially in their treatment of debtors. The prisoners were allowed to earn money, if they were able to, and this they could spend on liquor and minor comforts. Nobody seized it and put it by for their creditors. John Dickens was drawing good money every week while in the Marshalsea. Within a year he bought his creditors off by means of a legacy: otherwise he might have stayed there for life, earning enough for his keep in prison and for some mild dissipation too, and never paying his debts at all.

What good was done by putting debtors into this mild, unprofitable and often unending sequestration it is hard to see. But the process had a kind of humanity which was later driven out of the prison system. There was none of the torture by solitude which is so intense an agony to people coming out of crowded homes and workshops and so being utterly unused to any kind of solitude. There were comradeship and even conviviality. There was privacy when wanted, in a room of your own. There was the cruelty, it is true, of the indeterminate sentence. But there was not the regimentation and the beating down of personality which came later in the penal methods of this country. Dickens certainly saw misery enough in the Marshalsea: but would he not have been more aghast at our practice of solitary confinement with cells locked in the late afternoons and then kept shut throughout the steely duration of the night?

There was, moreover, family life. Your wife might go with you to the Marshalsea instead of seeing you at stated periods through a grille. Inside the place there was the Christian charity of some most unchristian people, the decency of the downcast, and the clemency of officials who would now be remote and suspect of 'irregularity' if they gave a prisoner their friendship. It was something of a miracle that Little Dorrit ever clung to life after conditions of birth as septic and after medical attention as bibulous and clumsy as the mind can imagine. But when the baby did grow into a child she became the Marshalsea's own daughter and the turnkey's pet. In reformed and scientific prisons there is no petting—and, of course, no conjugal relations, no children pattering to and fro.

It is a fair guess that John Dickens, when in custody for debt, had a considerably better time amid the humane squalor of the Marshalsea than he would have done in Brixton to-day. This is not to say that prison was pleasant: but at least it was free from the damnable cruelties which reformers inflict because they see everybody from the same hygienic, methodical and moralising point of view. Freedom to be genially squalid is not within their bill of liberties. They cannot comprehend that for an illiterate man from a crowded home solitude is an entirely different thing from what it is to a reading and reflective type. To the one it is hell, to the other the only heaven that prison can afford.

Mr. Hesketh Pearson in his life of Charles Dickens points out that his father in the Marshalsea was drawing for his family six pounds odd a week from the Navy Office—quite a fair sum in those days—and that ' as they could not be worried by creditors in prison their existence was far more comfortable than it had been for some years. It practically amounted to a fresh start in life and the head of the family made no attempt to pay the debt for which he had been arrested.' It was a general gathering: Mrs. Dickens and some of the children were in this odd mixture, shabby but friendly, of hostel and lock-up, while little Charles and his sister, who was working at the Royal Academy of Music, came in on Sundays. Young Charles had a ' third floor back ' in Lant Street and a good landlady. But prison, whatever its kind, strikes at pride and bitterly sears the memory.

Looking at the glum façade of Harding's warehouse one can begin to imagine the old life behind the bars: but one need not work fancy hard. The picture is there. Charles Dickens wrote *Little Dorrit* and out of that monumental and uneven book step shades sufficient to give you ample and eerie company while walking in the Borough. Why did not my own country of Scotland have its own Dickens to begin where Scott and Galt left off and record for ever the new teeming life of the industrial revolution, the upthrust of the Victorian Caledonia, the spawning of the towns in Scotland's middle belt, the new Clydeside industry and the types of Scot that it created? There was great wealth there for a novelist. Dickens exaggerated for effect, no doubt. (Art has been well called 'exaggeration à propos.') But he is the grand historian of London; rather less of England. There is usually something 'Christmas-cardy' in his winter-landscapes or too vernal to be true about his April scenes. His countryside is a convention. But for comprehension of the Borough, a drab, bomb-dented Borough now, as for comprehension of Camden Town or the river, go to Dickens. Guidebooks can be useful for the facts. Dickens transcends the chronicles. Chesterton said that he was not a man, but a mob. It is also true that none has written history more authentic, if by authenticity we mean the revelation of essentials and universals below the beavers and surtouts, the bonnets and mantuas of a particular age.

CHAPTER VI

The Bankside

W HAT IS LEFT of oldest Southwark lies mainly underground and is revealed in occasional and accidental process of excavation. The Romans, coming up from Kent to Londinium, had cross-roads here and recent digging on the site of the original Marshalsea has found evidence of that junction. While I was looking at the walls of the second Marshalsea the site between it and Guy's Hospital was being cleared for the Southwark that is to be, working-class flats of decent equipment, most necessary building but made possible only by large subsidies whose burden the ratepayer will long be carrying. The official in charge of this clearance kindly showed me a bagful of bits and pieces, recently upturned, of Roman ware, delf, the pots and crocks of many centuries: there were large numbers of clay tobacco-pipes found. Did the Collegians of the Marshalsea throw these about when in funds and therefore, almost inevitably, in their cups?

Scholars, working on old manuscripts, employ the Greek term palimpsest. This means a parchment that has been written over more than once; when writing materials were scarce it was natural to use the same surface two or three times. A discerning eye may scan the surface of these documents and descry, at the foundations, the original script. So it is with London, as it was with Troy, where the archæologists delve down through various layers of deposit, allotting one kind of civilisation to each. Dunbar, the medieval Scottish poet and singer of London's praise, referred to the old tradition that England was the final refuge of Aeneas. So Dunbar called London ' Troy Novaunt,' the new Troy. London is certainly, like Troy, a city of layers: the builders can hardly sink foundations anywhere in the central region without discovering old walls, cellars, pots, pans, pipes, ornaments, and bric-à-brac of all kinds. Anybody who starts turning earth at any depth in the Borough soon strikes history with his spade.

A thorough overturning of the soil beside the river would almost certainly yield all sorts of treasure. At Beck and Pollitzer's wharf they have a case of bones and such in the office: among them are the skulls of hounds and bears. These must be the débris of Paris Garden, the baiting-ground and bear-garden of Tudor times. It was close to Shakespeare's Globe Theatre on the Bankside, and the roaring and baying of the tortured animals must have been a rival to the voices of the actors as they delivered to the open air the most beautiful lines of poetry ever written in the English language. Shakespeare himself makes plentiful reference to the head-lugged bear and the chained victim of the dogs' attack.

> *They have tied me to a stake; I cannot fly*
> *But, bear-like, I must fight the course*

cried Macbeth in his extremity. The ' big name ' among the Paris Garden bears was Sackerson, who is mentioned in *The Merry Wives of Windsor*. Master Slender asks ' Why do your dogs bark so? Be there bears i' the town?' Anne Page replies that ' there is talk of that.' Slender, declaring his affection for the sport, asks Anne if she is afraid of bears loose, to which timidity she confesses. Slender retorts

> That's meat and drink to me, now. I have seen Sackerson loose
> twenty times, and have taken him by the chain; but, I warrant you,

the women have so cried and shriek'd at it, that it pass'd:—but women, indeed, cannot abide 'em; they are very ill-favour'd rough things.

Hearing of a bear's skull dug up on this very spot, one cannot help musing over such bones in the way that Hamlet mused over the grisly relic of the jesting Yorick. Where be the bear's antics now? Where his pawings and bellowings as he faced his tormentors? Alas, poor Sackerson, that was wont to set the Garden on a roar, quite chap-fallen now; to this favour he has come.

Nothing can be less romantic in these days to the immediate glance than the dark canyons between wharves, warehouses, and breweries through which one meanders in search of the old Bankside. The site of the Globe Theatre in Park Street (with a plaque and a rather attractive head of Shakespeare set on the wall of Barclay and Perkins's Brewery) is no beauty spot, and Rose Lane, leading thence to the river, is about as roseate as the dingiest wynd in a Scottish manufacturing town. But here was the Rose Theatre where Ned Alleyn thundered in rivalry against Dick Burbage of the Globe. Gloomy it may be now, and the great voices have gone into the air. But what they uttered is on paper and it is speech unparagoned. On this now scarred and shabby shore the immortal stuff was born; for Bard's sake—and possibly for the beer's too—we can bow to Barclay and nod in reverence to Perkins. To theatre-people this is consecrated ground. The entry to their brewery, incidentally, is courtly, almost baronial, and merits its place, upon this bank, where magic haunts.

In the Borough High Street itself the obvious and genuine antique is the George Inn, with a fragment of its galleried courtyard still existing. It is now owned by the National Trust and administered by the house of Flower, brewers in Stratford-upon-Avon, a proper circumstance in this Shakespearean nook. Thither go the hop-merchants and ' medicals ' for lunch. It is a maddening place by reason of its mutilation. What a glorious memento

of old London it must have been! The original George and
Dragon, which we can assume to have thriven mightily in the
great days of the Bankside and its sports and plays, was burned
down in 1674: what we can still see was built soon after that,
but in 1873 the authorities of Guy's Hospital, who then owned
it, sold it to the Great Northern Railway, which tolerated this
notable antique for sixteen years and then smashed away two
sides of the courtyard in one of the most damnable bits of
vandalism ever suffered by London. The place was, when in
its entirety, a perfect example of the coaching inn and still, for
a few yards, remains so.

I am not maintaining that galleried inns are the best for comfort. On a windy day the draughts invading the open court and
beating on the bedroom doors must be fiendish. I prefer,
myself, to have a proper front door and not to sleep up against
the weather. But Guy's should never have sold the place without
conditions and the railway company should never have
destroyed what it bought. For this kind of inn was the kernel
of English society for centuries, when life flowed with the coach
and the coach clattered into the yard, almost into the heart of
the inn itself. The type cannot have varied much since Chaucer
lay at the neighbouring Tabard and Sam Weller varnished the
boots at the equally adjacent White Hart. Some relate the
original George and Dragon with the Bastard's cry for guidance
in sword-play in Shakespeare's *King John*.

> St. George, that swinged the dragon, and e'er since
> Sits on his horse-back at mine hostess' door,
> Teach us some fence!

This may be a reminiscent allusion to the tavern close to London
Bridge and the Bankside. There was doubtless some such sign
outside it, as there is to-day. But whether the dramatist had this
particular tavern in mind must be only a guess.

A lady who took an American student for an afternoon's walk

through the Borough complained to me that the George is closed in the afternoons and serves no teas. This might be remedied, but we have a thing called the Catering Wages Act which makes it highly uneconomic for innkeepers to keep staff on duty unless there is a considerable amount of business to reward them. The visitors took tea opposite at Ye Olde Delta Café which claims to have been founded in 1650. That may be so, but Ye Olde should go; the new Tabard Inn is also Ye Olde. Southwark is genuine London and needs no aids of Ye Oldeismus.

The young American had not far to look in the Borough for a link with his own country—and with his own University if he happened to be a Harvard man. Inside Southwark Cathedral he would find a Harvard Chapel with the Stars and Stripes modestly displayed therein. The Harvard family were in trade, as fleshers, in the Borough while Shakespeare was most busy there. It is a curious coincidence that Robert Harvard had the same profession as Shakespeare's father, who may have been a butcher as well as a merchant of leather and gloves. Robert Harvard must have visited Stratford-upon-Avon, for there he met and married Katherine Rogers; the wedding took place in the Parish Church of Stratford in April, 1605. She was the daughter of Alderman Thomas Rogers, butcher and maltster and, according to Fripp, the greatest authority on Shakespearean Stratford, ' the builder of at least one beautiful house, a devoted Borough Councillor, " gentleman," and a father of a very notable family.'

How did Robert Harvard come to marry into Warwickshire? Southwark was then a small place, though busy and much-frequented for its pleasures. It is not being fanciful to suppose that Shakespeare was a friend of Harvard's and took him down to Stratford for a holiday on one of his journeys home. And there, as they say, ' boy met girl.' If that is so—and I cannot see why it is not a likely explanation—the great University of Harvard is directly linked with the greatest of English poets and playwrights. Indeed, William Shakespeare, if this assumption be true, was directly responsible for its parentage.

John Harvard, the second child of Robert and Katherine (née Rogers) was christened in St. Saviour's, Southwark, in November, 1607, a month before Shakespeare's brother Edmond, the actor, was buried in the 'forenoon there on Thursday, December 31, with a knell of the great bell.' This, with interment in the church, was expensive. The entry in the burial-register of St. Saviour's states that the cost was 20s., which would be worth £20 to-day. Edmond was only twenty-seven, but perhaps a victim of the year's extreme cold. He had lost an illegitimate son, buried at St. Giles, Cripplegate, earlier in the year. Did William pay the costs?

Master John Harvard had a chilly start in the world. Just before Christmas, 1607, the Thames was frozen over above London Bridge. The bitterly cold weather lasted for many weeks; there were sports of all kinds on the ice, wrestling, running of races, and sliding; stalls were set up and there was much consumption of ale, sack, and victuals. The author of The Great Frost: Cold Doings in London even mentions usquebaugh (whisky) as one of the cordials on sale. 'Stage players, Inglisch' had been as far as Aberdeen; they were entertained to supper by Provost Cullen and the Burgesses in October, 1601. They may have brought back the usquebaugh habit. At any rate supplies were available at the improvised bars on the ice, while John Harvard was taking his mother's milk. It had never occurred to me, until I started reading about this Southwark of 1607, that Shakespeare may have been a whisky-drinker. As one myself, I would like to believe it.

John Harvard survived that dreadful winter, when the Thames watermen, their boats out of action, had perhaps to live by selling wine and whisky, if they could get it. The players, in an open theatre like the Globe, must have lacked audience, but Shakespeare's own troupe were kept busy at Court. Young John went later on to school in Southwark and thence to Emmanuel College, Cambridge. He survived the heavy plague of 1625 which killed his father and nearly massacred his family. He was eight years at Cambridge and was perhaps ordained. Emmanuel was then a Puritan stronghold and the reason why John left England in 1637 may have been, as his Southwark biographer, Canon Stevens, suggests, that a High Church England, dominated in matters of doctrine and discipline by Charles I and Archbishop Laud, was no place for him.

It was a challenging adventure to cross the Atlantic in those days. Harvard certainly had no economic motive for going: the plague, by thinning out his family so drastically, had left him an heir to a fair amount of property, including the Queen's Head, a Southwark tavern. But his mind was not on such worldly things. According to Canon Stevens, ' he was brought up in an Anglican home, went to an Anglican College, signed the 39 Articles more than once, married a clergyman's daughter and became a religious teacher.' He arrived in America in August, 1637, and found much religious controversy across the Atlantic as well as the desire for a college providing ' the untarnished wisdom of heaven.' His qualities of mind and conduct must have been immediately recognised, for he was appointed teacher; but he died of consumption at the age of thirty-one.

The new institution benefited by the books and money he left to it: the name of Cambridge was given to the place and of Harvard to the College. So Harvard men, when they come to London, should cross London Bridge, and enter the Harvard Chapel of St. Saviour's, which is now the Cathedral. The British owe much to American endowment of their educational work through the Carnegie, Rockefeller, and Pilgrim Trusts: it is pleasant for us to remember that Harvard owed something of its earliest sustenance to the little fortune carried overseas by this pious Southwark citizen. That fortune was originally derived from money earned in a tavern and garnered from retail

trade within a few yards of the Globe Theatre. So the great
University of America's Cambridge is linked with Shakespeare
both by Robert Harvard's marriage in Stratford-upon-Avon and
by commerce in the Borough of Southwark, Shakespeare's own
'quick forge and working-house of thought.'

Southwark is most easily approached from the City by way of
London Bridge. It has its own Southwark Bridge, but this is
one of the least used of the Thames bridges. London Bridge
separates the water which is London's river from the water
which is 'Port of London.' I know that the Port of London
Authority has a dominion reaching right up to Teddington, but
it is on London Bridge that you first see big sea-going vessels
docked and loading right below you. The Tower Bridge to
your left may, while you dawdle, split gracefully to admit a
newcomer from the Baltic or the Sound. At London Bridge
you begin to reach out from London to the world. The nation
of shopkeepers merges with the nation of sailors and of merchant
adventurers.

My own access to Southwark—from Fleet Street and its
tributary lanes—is by way of Blackfriars Bridge and an excellent
stroll it is, taking some twenty minutes or half an hour according
to the time devoted to standing and staring or to deviating into
the bricky chasms amid the warehouses. One needs a sunny day
for it, with a light that relieves the melancholy muddiness of the
once silvery Thames and will play on the Portland stone of
Wren's spires on the northern bank. St. Bride's, the fane of
Fleet Street, was justly called by W. E. Henley 'a madrigal in
stone' and, though the body remains broken by bombs, still
does the head go flickering to the sky: the tower seems to tinkle,
you might say, if the sun be on it and the river is making what
Wordsworth called eye-music. Blackfriars Bridge is 'probably
the widest bridge crossing any river in Great Britain': it
supplanted in 1869 an earlier bridge of 1769. It gives you a
good view to the west, but the eastward prospect is ruined by

the railway bridge running parallel to it. Once across you turn left under the railway and make for the Bankside. But to gain that you pass a neat pattern of almshouses, the Charles Hopton Charity. This was there before the first Blackfriars Bridge and it still whispers the last enchantments of the Age of Reason, so sane and seemly and composed do the little houses look amid the metal forest of cranes and gantries into which we are moving.

The Bankside now consists of wharves on the one side of the road and large, gaunt storehouses on the other. The largest structure of all, the new Southwark Power Station, is beginning to rise as I write. There was bitter controversy as to the rights and wrongs of putting this monster just opposite St. Paul's: into that battle of amenity and utility it is useless to enter now: as I write, the great scoops are shovelling up the soil and the huge girders begin to climb the sky. The wanderer passes among lorries on the rough, foot-testing cobbles that are here the substance of the riverside road. Almost at once Cardinal Wharf is reached and here one charming fragment of domesticity remains: the little house of Cardinal Wharf, with Cardinal Cap Alley beside it, and a tiny high-walled garden behind, is as lonely as a jewel on a stony beach. Anna May Wong, the actress and film-star, once chose to live there. But the new Power Station, when it is completed, will not increase the pleasures of the place. The Cardinal, I take it, was the great Henry Beaufort, Bishop of Winchester, who was made Cardinal-priest of St. Eusebius. His niece Joan married royally, going to Scotland as the Queen of James I: the Cardinal was at the trial of Joan of Arc and may have seen the Maid burn. The Bishops of Winchester were for long grandees of the Bankside. The great Christopher Wren is said to have lived on this shore while giving glory to the other.

The Cardinal Wharf offers a superb view across the river to the slopes of the City. I say, 'the slopes,' because, once in the City, you easily forget that it was owing to its fortifiable eminence that the town ever grew there. The nobility of the church spires, towers, and domes adds to the sense of a city surging up from the waters and brings to mind the exquisite justice of John Davidson's familiar lines written as from Primrose Hill but easily applicable to the south bank.

> Oh sweetheart, see! How shadowy
>   Of some occult magician's rearing
> Or swung in space, of heaven's grace,
>   Dissolving, dimly reappearing,
> Afloat upon ethereal tides
>   St. Paul's above the City rides.

It is best to look across the river here on a bright day flecked with light cloud, a gentle breeze, and a dancing light. Then you will see St. Paul's as Davidson saw it, launched into air, majestic yet floating, and curiously evanescent for all its solidity of weight and power. Very often the best praise of London has come from the Scots, beginning with Dunbar who hailed the New Troy as

> Gemme of all joy, jasper of jocunditie,
> Most mighty carbuncle of vertue and valour.

' Carbuncle,' cried Scottish Dunbar in praise. ' Wen,' snapped English Cobbett, in despair. Scottish Davidson, so often in melancholy, felt ' the heart of London beating warm ' and it is the Scottish journalists of our own time, James Bone in *The London Perambulator* and *London Echoing* and Ian Mackay, columnist of the *News Chronicle*, who have shown the sharpest ears for London's music and the keenest eyes for London's oddities and secrets.

On the river are the useful barges and the decorative swans. Swans retain their faintly absurd, yet always captivating, grace even when their plumage is smudged. The Thames swans sail down the poetry of England and the fouling of the waters has not driven them away even now from London Harbour: you would think that with all the cleanly beauty of the river from Richmond upwards at their full disposal they would desert the kingdom of coal-wharves and of grimy barges. But birds do not share our sensibility in such matters: I have seen swallows nesting in numbers in the dirtiest of industrial villages when ' veritable beauty-spots,' as the guide-books say, were awaiting them a mile or two away, with everything clean and handsome about them. So, pausing, as you will do, at Cardinal Wharf, where there may be an artist with easel and palette ensconced by the parapet, you will probably see some less than radiant swans afloat in the Pauline foreground; I take it that the swan is not a pernickety feeder.

Then eastward again. Culture is restored to our attention by Emerson Street. The old site of the baiting-pits is commemorated by Bear Gardens and that of the Globe's rival by Rose Alley, up which you may thread a murky way to find the Globe Theatre plaque, already mentioned, set upon the brewery wall in Park Street. Frankly, modern London seems to have done its worst for ancient London in this historic terrain, but there is some humanity left at the Anchor Inn, facing on to the river. Its history is uncertain, but it is certainly old, probably a Georgian replacement of a Tudor or Stuart tavern.

It has been claimed that this was ' the little ale-house on the Bankside ' where Pepys watched the great fire of London grow in 1666, but there were probably many other taverns then. The famous Falcon ' on the Stewes ' has gone, but there is a Falcon Dock. This area, the environs of the Bishop of Winchester's Palace, was long the suburb of sin. Lust and sadism were amply catered for in a busy market. Now it is a wilderness of dark and soaring brick threaded by a few narrow channels of road or opened and left desolate by the German airmen. It has a frightening quality: as I look upwards to the openings in the warehouses whither stores are lifted, I expect to see Daniel Quilp emerge, pouring his vituperations from the odious deformity of his body and mind.

Clink Street brings us right up to the Winchester Palace, of which I understand it is possible to find a bricked-up window and a doorway if you search carefully. But almost nothing is here to be seen from the street but warehouses. However, if your imagination is sufficiently morbid, you can picture the Tudor bucks of London ferried over from the City and the Inns of Court to drink and fornicate and indulge their taste for blood in Paris Garden. The Clink Prison was presumably first used by the Bishop for the cooling of hot youth in the Bankside's licentious past, but it was given general purposes, housed victims of religious persecution, and finally shared the principle trade of the Borough by becoming a gaol for debtors. It was burned down by rioters during the ' No Popery ' insurrection of 1780. The Clink, as I said, was one of the Borough's gifts to English slang: ' in clink,' was common vernacular for ' in prison ' at one time and would still be widely understood.

We have now reached Southwark Cathedral, alias St. Saviour's, alias the Church of St. Mary Overie. The last name was the earliest: it probably means St. Mary Over-the-river. The Reformation removed the offending name of Mary and substituted St. Saviour's. But modern sentiment is less sternly anti-feminist and anti-Marian. In 1937 it became, officially, the ' Cathedral and Collegiate Church of St. Saviour and St. Mary Overie.' Our old climatic friend St. Swithun established a college of priests here, but the early Norman church was burned down in 1206—fires, plagues, gaols, as well as plays and poetry, are the Southwark staples down the centuries—and so the first Gothic church in London was established on its spot. Some say it is the finest after Westminster Abbey. It is the sole remnant of medieval Southwark and it is one of the very few buildings in London which our eyes share with those of Shakespeare. It has had a history of vandalism and gross misuse: as in the case of Jerusalem's own Temple part of this house of prayer became a den of tradesmen, if not of thieves. It has lost windows and been badly shaken by recent bombing. But there it is, now

Clink Street, Southwark

carefully looked after, open to all Londoners for devotion, if
they have the faith, and for meditation, if they prefer reflection
to devotion. A lunch-time walk by the road that I have described
must end in the Cathedral. I am one of the meditators and like
to sit awhile by the Harvard Chapel, Gower's tomb, or the
Shakespeare memorial before going across to the George to see
whether the hop-merchants and the medical students have left
a scrap of lunch for the belated.

Gower has been called the Father of English Poetry and was
a friend of Chaucer: he lived in Southwark within the precincts
of the Priory, being accepted for his virtue as well as for his
verses. Thus the Borough provided the fountain not only of
England's greatest poetry, when it housed Shakespeare and his
players, but also of the earliest English creation in this kind when
it took in John Gower to lodge upon its holy ground. Greatest
and earliest—it is no small combination of superlatives for this
small corner of London to possess.

Shakespeare is honoured with an effigy of himself in alabaster.
He is, as the literary gentlemen say, 'recumbent.' Behind him
is the Southwark of his day with the Cathedral, Winchester
Palace, and the Globe Theatre lined up on view. He might be
gazing at the City whence came the wealthier members of his
public: but he appears rather to be slightly comatose and gently
'dropping off.' It is not an inspiring figure, but it seems to me
a fair tribute to a poet who sang the praises of sleep and the
horrors of sleeplessness with a poignant intensity of feeling. One
of the best guesses about Shakespeare is that he had bad nights
when sleep did not knit up his cares or prove to be sore labour's
bath.

Here he seems to be seeking compensation for one of those
torturing vigils by having forty winks to the lullaby of water-
music. No doubt the artist, H. W. McCarthy, intended to imply
that the Master was brooding deeply and was pregnant with some
sounding passage. But to me the Bard seems to be dozily

tranquil and I like to think of him so, at least for one summer day, instead of as being haunted by two pitch-black eyes and the white hands of a maddening and heartless beauty or agonised at the thought of a play-ending that just would not come—and there was Burbage screaming for the script. If a title is needed I should call it Will's Afternoon Off or Early Closing Day. It is agreed that of Southwark's playwright-poets John Fletcher and Philip Massinger are buried here and there are stones in the choir with their names, next to that of the short-lived actor Edmond Shakespeare. It is not known exactly where they were buried. Nor surely does it matter. Fletcher and Shakespeare were of the same fellowship and the former, with no mean powers, took on the cloak that Shakespeare had put off. The scholars will argue eternally about the attribution of *Henry VIII* and *Two Noble Kinsmen,* and certainty will not be found. But when in the latter play we fall upon such lines as

> *Oh great corrector of enormous times,*
> *Shaker of o'er-rank states, thou grand decider*
> *Of dusty, and old titles, that heal'st the blood*
> *Of the earth when it is sick, and cur'st the world*
> *O' th' pleuresy of people. . . .*

we can either decide that Shakespeare's hand was strong in this play or that Fletcher's hand was powerful in Shakespearean *pastiche.* I am myself distrustful of textual attributions based on the use of words, for one man can very well be so much influenced by another as to want to copy him. And who would not want to copy Shakespeare, foolish though the effort seem? I leave the argument alone, content to know that the poets are well remembered on the stones of this single choir, since Southwark was itself a nest of choristers who sang, in drama, for their supper and earned it as few singers since: whether they always got it is another matter. Shakespeare, at least, in this new-found prosperity which had come to him as he moved across the river, was unlikely to go hungry or thirsty.

Southwark has been a great importer of brains. In that it is true to the City of which it is a part. The eminent dramatists of Bankside, remembered on the stones and in the statuary of their St. Saviour's, were not London-born or London-schooled. William Shakespeare and his brother Edmond came from Warwickshire: John Fletcher, his colleague with the King's Men and in some sort his successor, was from Rye in Sussex. Beaumont, Fletcher's frequent partner (buried not here in the Borough, but in Westminster Abbey after an early death) had come up from Leicestershire. Massinger, honoured beside Fletcher at Southwark, was from Wiltshire, where his father was one of the stewards to the great—and play-loving—house of Pembroke. All these worked at one time for the royal company, Shakespeare's own ' fellowship of players.'   Of their rivals and coevals, Marlowe came from Kent, Chapman from Hertfordshire, Marston from Oxfordshire, Heywood from Lincolnshire, and Ford from Devon. Ben Jonson is the chief asset of the capital in this school of glory, and rather a lonely one.

England then was much less centralised than now and London a smaller section of the national fabric than it is to-day. The noblemen's houses in the country were often considerable fortresses of the arts as well of arms. But, even so, it is curious that London has had to keep on enlisting its brains from outside. The exceptional men whom London unceasingly attracts live, work, breed, and die in their city of adoption and you would think that their children would supply an ample stock of London-born brains. But still Scotland, Wales, and Ireland as well as the English counties pour in their talent, for which there appears to be ample scope. These incomers meet at County and National reunions; the Society of Rutlandshire Men in London will dine in full fig or a Scots night will evoke the tartan. Somebody once suggested, I think, a similar organisation for the Middlesex men in London: but, when he looked round, he could not find any. On the ' Jacobethan ' Bankside the situation was somewhat similar; the county men could out-number and out-write the natives. But London has always been a hospitable, accommodating place, a considerable melting-pot in its own tolerant way.

Shakespeare was living in Southwark in 1596. Malone (1741-1812) asserted that he was resident close to the Bear Gardens, but there is no existing evidence for this. Yet it is probable enough, for the Bankside suburb was not extensive. Fripp says that he moved away to lodge with Mountjoy, the tire-maker, in Silver Street, Cripplegate, in 1602, ' for quiet, we may believe.' Southwark certainly was likely to be ' full of noises ' and these often less musical than were to be heard in the air on Prospero's island. Moreover the temptations to squander time and health by accepting excessive hospitality, temptations which John Aubrey said that Shakespeare resisted, would have been stronger for those living in or near the town's chief centre of revel and dissipation.

If Shakespeare was a Borough man from 1596-1602, then Southwark has reason enough to be proud. For those were the years of his richest mixed achievement. The bulk of the great tragedies was still to come, but the comedies were to cease. Into the Southwark years we pack the greatest of the comedies and the one supreme tragedy *Hamlet*. For a single borough to have seen the birth of *Twelfth Night* and *Hamlet*, not to mention the creation of Rosalind and Beatrice, is glory enough. Were I a jealous South London patriot, I would claim that when Shakespeare left Southwark he stopped laughing. Cripplegate gave him *Othello*, *Macbeth*, and *Lear*, no doubt, but his mirth was never to be the same again.

I have stressed the dismal inadequacy of modern Southwark in architecture and its utter failure to be a spectacle worthy of its past. But the Cathedral, after all its vicissitudes at the hands of the vandals, the restorer, and the bomber, is not only a direct link with the richness of Southwark's history but an extremely beautiful building in many of its aspects. Whether you are a disciple of T. S. Eliot and wish to honour the memory of his hero Bishop Lancelot Andrewes, whether you are a Chaucerian or a Shakespearean, or should you feel that Fletcher has been under-honoured and Massinger too much neglected, Southwark Cathedral has something to show you and a word to whisper in your ear. For City people it is reached by a walk over a bridge —and a bridge with what a view! From Ludgate Circus you may make the Bankside walk that I have outlined, a stroll of rare variety according to the season, the weather and the light.

The Tube station and the buses at the south end of London Bridge bring you from almost anywhere into the streets where Bob Sawyer contemplated his debts and arranged his pleasures, where Old Dorrit dwindled, and where Sam Weller brushed up his worldly wisdom as slickly as he brushed the boots.

In corners Southwark is the old parish still. Just before you reach the Cathedral, coming in by my way along the Bankside, you may see a tiny creek called St. Mary Overy's Wharf. Squeezed in between the warehouses of Winchester Square, it does not seem to be of much utility, so narrow and obstructed is it, nor does it seem to be much used. But it carries a notice that the dock offers 'Free Landing of goods for all Parishioners of St. Saviour's.' There are to be no tolls on local men, unless of course they live outside the parish. What happens in that case I cannot think, for if I rowed in with a boat or 'huddled' a barge into the creek with a cargo of taxable stuff, it would be fairly difficult to land the cargo at all and I have never noticed any official to whom the dues could be handed. But there the notice remains, breathing that pleasant conservatism of the English which refuses to take down notices when the need for them has long past. Just as in august and modish Albany you can still read the hansom-cab fares chargeable for various journeys to and from the courtyard, so here, where the muddy water laps up against the bleak houses of the Bankside wharves, you can ponder on parish affairs and wonder whether some extra-parochial scoundrel from Bermondsey has been running cargoes into the midget dockyard of St. Mary Overy's.

Here is a queer fact suggesting that Shakespeare haunts the Bankside and spreads his influence on the water. When I was last surveying this docklet, if so we may call it, there was one vessel moored there. It was a Thames barge in some state of age and decay and due, I fancy, for retirement. One expects barges to be called Martha or Nancy Jane. But the name of this venerable senior was—believe it or not—*Prospero*.

CHAPTER VII
Christmas, Body and Soul

THERE IS the mighty wave and then dead calm. Pre-Christmas London is a cauldron lashed by a hurricane: the day itself is doldrums. Take a walk on any of London's open spaces on Christmas afternoon and there is nothing but vacancy, nothing but silence. It is probably a mild, grey, dampish day, —the Christmas of 1949 was marked by a tepid, greenhouse warmth, and a temperature of almost unknown height—and you will not feel inclined to go far. But this dead vast of noiselessness is worth sampling in a city that normally grumbles and screeches and roars. When Wordsworth composed his sonnet on Westminster Bridge the town was 'bright and glittering,' which it usually is not on Christmas Day. But take a turn on the Embankment or in any of the Bankside gardens.

Ne'er saw I, never felt, a calm so deep!
The river glideth at his own sweet will,
Dear God! the very houses seem asleep;
And all that mighty heart is lying still!

Wordsworth still applies.

Mighty heart—yes, but we cannot omit the other organs. The stomach has been, or is about to be, appeased. Into this tremendous tacitness of the Christmas streets steals, slightly but universally, the odour of sage, onions, and other garnishings of goose or turkey. Most windows are closed or nearly closed and so no large rattle of the radio, no overpowering scent of stuffing seeps out: but there is a profound sense of bodily satisfaction in this uncanny calm. If you are strolling at three o'clock, there is a slight rift in the numbness and dumbness of the City. Through such chinks as emit any sound comes, universally, the King's voice as he gives the Christmas greeting and address to his myriads of ocean-sundered hearers. There is never, I think, any lessening of the audience for this. Going down a suburban street on a Christmas afternoon when it was warm enough for open windows, I have heard virtually the whole of it as I moved past the houses, so many were the listeners.

I wrote of the wave before the calm. What of that surge? There is a frightening onslaught of the shoppers on the shops, an attack which reaches its most furious point when the Boarding Schools have closed, about December 20, and ejected some hundreds of thousands of boys and girls in the high excitement of release on to the platforms of the great termini. When sorted out, those not redispatched to the country go shopping. So do swarms of their elders. To approach a counter is then a football-match matter. The heat and hustle of this spending tumult makes the recession into calm more astonishing. The peace comes a little earlier than you expect; some of the shops are reasonably empty on Christmas Eve. This reminds me that I have never walked through the City itself on a Christmas afternoon: I herewith resolve to do so and am willing to bet that between Ludgate Circus and the Tower I shall not meet a dozen people on the pavements.

Christmas church-going fills pews that are usually empty. This applies especially to the Anglican congregations, which have the largest proportion of intermittent attenders. Many people like to go to church on festal days, when the flowers are in full display and familiar hymns are sung. This, I cannot help thinking, is cheating. It is using the church as a convenience.

Those who believe should believe every week in the year and not only when sentiment stirs them, as at Christmas and Easter, and when the service has traditional appeals. To look in now and again is like using the church to get christened, married and buried (with more beauty of language and of rite than a secular treatment of the occasion provides) and then never going near the place again. Such exploitation of the church seems to me discreditable. Those who will not take the discipline should not snatch at the privilege. If the Faith is not worth their attention on the dull Sundays—not to mention the week-days— what right have the perfunctory worshippers to share in the attractions on the festival days?

As I am not a Churchman it may be said that I have no right to speak. But I cannot be forbidden to comment on the logic of those who treat the benefits of religion in such an arbitrary way, occasionally using them, but generally passing by. What reason can be given for seeking a Church marriage and then giving no further heed or service to the Church and to its modest demands? To stay away from church altogether, to have a civil marriage, and to end with a secular cremation, is within the rights of any citizen now that, after centuries, we have defeated the old bigoted persecutions of the independent. It is also perfectly logical. But what is not within the bounds of right thinking is to admit a Sacred Mystery by occasional genuflections and then to forget all about a matter so supreme for fifty Sundays out of fifty-two. If religion, any religion, is what it claims to be, then it is something so tremendous that you must either reject it with due reflection or accept it with due devotion. To potter about with it, like the Christmas Day church-goer, is to be both illogical and insensitive.

Surely the Church of England should be far sterner with what may be called the play-boy Christians: marriage in church should be limited to regular attenders and not open to any who put up the banns and the fees. Sometimes it is so limited, but not always. Now that even the hierarchy admits that Christianity has become a minority faith in this country, not because of declared agnosticism, but because of a ' stay-away ' kind of apathy, a careless, shrug-of-the-shoulders secularism, it is natural, I suppose, for all sects to seek supporters. But religion would surely be far stronger in the possession of a passionate minority, who denounce the casual, in-and-out or absentee member of the Church and insist on full acceptance of responsibilities as the condition of enjoying Christian rights. That a faithful congregation should have its carol services and other seasonal pleasures is fair: but to coax the waverers or deserters with appeals and ' attractions,' as though the Church were part of the entertainment industry, seems to me fatal. During the Christmas of 1949 I received from my local parish church an invitation which struck me as really lamentable in its tone.

> ' Christmas Day is the Birthday of our Lord Jesus Christ—Will you let Him share it with you at one or more of these services? '

Will I let Him? Should not I be told, firmly and even fiercely, that, if I believe in the facts of the Christian story, then it is a supreme privilege to be allowed to share in this grandeur of spiritual opportunity, and that I am committing unpardonable folly if I miss the chance of sharing such communion? Will He of His mercy let me, not will I of my kindness let Him, is the only dignified, indeed the only reasonable, approach. Will we let Jesus Christ share His birthday with us? It is like the appeal of a petty salesman, asking whether we will give his vacuum-cleaner a chance.

If I am an unbeliever, then I frankly reject the invitation of religion and I risk the consequences. That is honest enough. But, if I am in any way a believer that Christ the Lord has lived and died for man and made man's salvation possible by His suffering, then I should be awe-struck at the splendour of this mystery. I should be advised solemnly of my privilege, and strongly commanded to attend the services as part of my duty and my discipline. To put such wheedling leaflets under the door a few days before Christmas is certainly not to command the respect of any intelligent person. Will I let Him? This is the last word in Christian defeatism. I do not believe that the Church will bring people to their knees by going on its knees to them.

Do I sermonise? My excuse must be a Presbyterian ancestry and a philosophic present which makes me see Christianity as a thing so tremendous and so exciting that it must either be accepted or denied to the full. It must be friend or foe: it cannot be a nodding acquaintance. To treat it in such a casual and patronising manner seems to me both foolish and rude. But enough of scolding. Back to the happy secularities.

Boxing Day, named not after pugilistic festivals but after the boxes once put out for the collection of tips and money-gifts, is not so quiet in the open spaces. The new toys are on trial and they can be as noisy as the things of which they are the miniatures. Here is a model Diesel-engined aeroplane, kept captive by a wire lest it vanish across the Park, as it certainly would, so powerful does it seem: thus confined, it circulates screaming its indignation at restraint: its menacing din will certainly not encourage normal bird life in these parts. There on the pond are half a dozen motor-vessels, puffing and growling, and completely disregarding the mannerly example of tranquillity set by the old-fashioned sailing yachts which lie suavely on the water, seeking a breeze, or gently taking the wind when it comes. A fellow-walker, passing me, nods his head sadly at the raucous aeroplane and asks if the whole of our public spaces are soon to be made horrible with this uproar. I cannot reassure him. I presume they will.

The world of mechanisation and of science has given to the Christmas present a new significance in the schoolroom and even in the nursery. The toy industry follows the industrialism of the outer world. It continually improves the model: its mimicry is ever more exact. Its railways are more like railways, the aeroplanes are more nearly the real thing, its yachts and battle-ships are more seaworthy and self-sufficient. The Toy Department, especially at the Seniors' end, is a carnival of realism. Just as the old Wooden Soldier, stiff and rosy-cheeked, was supplanted by the miniature army in tin, complete now with Bailey bridge and bull-dozer, so the simple sailing-boat or the old kite are made to look sad fogeys by these engined corvettes and roaring sky-masters which the more prosperous lads carry off to common and to lake. This machinery needs cunning to work it: and the cunning is there. The new technocracy is in our homes and schoolrooms.

So Boxing Day brings out the young mechanics, the engineers, and the pilots of to-morrow. (On whose playing-fields was the Battle of Britain won, beyond those of the indomitable heart? The toy-shop, as well as the school workshop, played its role.) Now there are ugly fumes on the pond in the Park: there is a hideous reverberation in the air on the Common. This might be any actual dock or aerodrome. There is no longer any need of fancy in the handling of a toy: imagination wilts amid such authenticity. I strongly suspect that it is the poorer boy who gets most pleasure in the long run. Regard that captive aero-plane whirling on its wire, circuit after circuit, buzzing like some mechanised cockchafer, demonic, deafening. Even with all this din it can do no more: its zenith of achievement is immediately reached. Round and round: nothing else. That battered craft, which electrically snorts across the little lake, can only repeat the voyage which it makes so easily and triumphantly.

But to the imagination there are no such bounds. The boy who has some make-believe left in the temper of his play, the boy who has turned his room into a fortress or a coral island with a table and two chairs and has a poker for his rifle, has no limits to the warfare or the hunting in which he can indulge. To those with the gift of fancy every copse is a continent and every rivulet an Amazon: to those with an accurately-engined model aeroplane there is only one advance—to a bigger and better engine.

That Christmas should mean festivity is natural and universal. That it should mean presents is a recent happening. It is also a happening which continually piles up those 'records' so dear to newspaper paragraphists. 'The money isn't there' has been the continual cry, when a restaurant or a theatre was doing less than well or a shop found goods lingering on the shelves. But, when Christmas came, the demand for goods was most abundantly there and an extra fifty million pounds worth of paper had to be issued from the Mint in order to provide sufficient ammunition for this great onslaught on the stores. What proportion of that gigantic outlay went on actual Christmas presents nobody can say; but it is a fair guess that a very large proportion of the extra currency did pass from hand to counter in that way.

Yet the Dickensian Christmas, now always accepted and sometimes rather acidly derided as the classic example of Yule-tide merriment, was not, in fact, a present-giving occasion. At Dingley Dell there was a pre-nuptial dance and then the annual games, story-telling, and a punch-drinking party in which staff and all joined during Christmas Eve. Mr. Pickwick and his companions properly took with them a gigantic codfish, which to us sounds strangely dull, and four barrels of oysters, which sound extremely attractive. But that was a contribution to the common larder at Manor Farm, such as any visitor may well make to-day in these rationed times. But there was no bringing of separate gifts and there is no mention of any Yule-tide presentations inside the Wardle family and household. The young lady with the fur-topped boots who so fascinated Mr. Winkle was not further enriched, as far as we know, with fur-tipped gloves or a pair of satin dancing slippers. Nor did Mr. Pickwick hand Mr. Wardle, on behalf of the Pickwickians, a piece of silver or a gold watch. When the Muggleton coach set out for the holiday jaunt it carried the supplies of 'sea-food' which have already been mentioned, but the travellers did not bring with them for presentation purposes, as would have happened nowadays, a batch of the latest books in vogue or half the contents of a fashionable haberdasher's shop.

To students of that period, and especially of Christmas, two points not commonly noticed are worth observation. One is that the spree came before Christmas; there was no Boxing Day jollification. The party left Dingley Dell on the morning after Christmas, which in those days was much less of a general and prolonged holiday than it is now. Scrooge's clerk Bob Cratchit had no statutory right to absent himself from the office on December 26. Mr. Cratchit was to be there on that morning at nine o'clock sharp and no nonsense about it. The Cratchit Christmas was a very short one and the Londoner of his type had to seize it and make the most of it while it was still there.

The other, and quite different and to us almost incredible, feature of the Dingley Dell occasion is the performance by the gentlemen of the party on Christmas Eve. They attended a wedding-breakfast in the morning at which there was enough toasting to put 'the poor relations' under the table; the Pickwickians were harder metal, no doubt, but they had not failed to do their best by the wine. Then 'the males of the party,' at Mr. Wardle's recommendation, took a *twenty-five-mile walk* to get rid of the effects of their lavish wining at the wedding. The country was frozen and snow-covered: it was skating weather. Twenty-five miles! Could Mr. Pickwick have carried that paunch of his through a march which would be considerable for a young and trained soldier to execute? The males of the party could hardly have done more than three miles an hour in the difficult going, which would account for eight hours and twenty minutes of walking time without any space for a 'breather.'

When did the wedding breakfast end? By noon? If so—and it might well have been later—the party had just four and a half hours before it was dark. So the last twelve miles must have been covered in darkness, or by such moon as may have happened to assist them. Then came the dinner and the household revels. Mr. Pickwick turned out without his gaiters 'for the first time within the memory of his oldest friends'; he sported speckled silk stockings and smartly tied pumps; he danced briskly through the night, and he was up for breakfast the next day. I am afraid that I do not believe for a minute in that ramble of twenty-five miles. Did the pen of Dickens slip or did he really fancy that such a route-march could have been endured and even enjoyed as part of the Christmas revels and within the schedule of time?

It has been an old-established habit in our own time for groups of moderately active men to get into the country on Boxing Day and walk. But a ten-mile stretch with a good pull-up at midday was amply sufficient for those sociable excursions and I fancy that the call of the golf links has recently made an end of, or at least considerably diminished, that custom. Our Christmas ambulations are generally brisk turns on the London heaths and commons and, in such modest strolls as I have taken myself, I have noticed very few doing anything more than meander in that gentle fashion. We have a much longer period of idleness after Christmas Day. In 1949 there were two Bank Holidays on Monday and Tuesday after Christmas, which fell on a Sunday. (Scrooge would have died of a frenzy had such things happened in his day.) I noticed, during my outings on those days, some horse-riding, but few walkers. We evidently lack the energy and stamina of the marching Pickwickians.

Returning to this matter of gifts, we find no mention of presents, outside contributions to the larder, if we examine the matter lower down in the financial scale. Take the case of Mr. Cratchit. True, there was not much chance for Scrooge's clerk to buy much for giving away: his income was fifteen shillings a week and his family, living in a four-roomed house, consisted of self, wife, and six. But Bob could somehow run to a goose and a half-quartern of brandy for the proper firing of Mrs. Cratchit's remarkable Christmas pudding: there were also warm potations to follow. So he might have contrived, if such had been the social habit, to buy a penny toy for Tiny Tim: and penny toys in those days would have been ' quite something.' Mr. Cratchit did pass on one of his collars to one of his boys so that the lad might be presentable at dinner, but there was no more a general ceremony of present-giving at that home than there was at Dingley Dell. The concentration was upon good will and good feeding; the ingenuous shopkeepers have since turned the lights on all the other kinds of good spending.

Again at Joe Gargery's Christmas Dinner, that agonising occasion for little Pip, there were contributions in kind. Uncle Pumblechook, being a well-to-do corn-chandler who rode in his own chaise, brought a bottle of port, a bottle of sherry, and a pork pie to amplify the catering of his poor relations. The pork pie was consumed at the close of the activities, that is after the Christmas pudding which came after a leg of pickled pork and two roast fowls. It was this curious ordering of events which drew from Mr. Hubble the superb decision that ' a bit of savoury pork pie could lie a-top of anything you could mention and do no harm.' This grave, dietetic judgment, which might have had wide support at the time, inclines one to believe—and dozens of other Dickensian meals confirm the belief—that progress has sadly weakened our stomachs.

A modern Christmas is strategically prepared for and tactically met by liberal doses of digestive powders. The public journals of the Pickwick era do, indeed, carry many advertisements of salves for dyspepsia and constipation. But I do not remember that the Pickwickians habitually carried a medicine-chest on their journeys and were cautiously equipped with salines, anti-acid capsules and draughts, and all the defensive preparations raised by ourselves against heart-burn in the night and headache in the morning. Yet if ever a country gentleman's house deserved the alternative title of Hangover Hall it was Mr. Wardle's Manor Farm at Dingley Dell. The science of the chemist and the ubiquity of his establishments have lowered our resistance, I fancy, while relieving our pain. Christmas has become a feast both of more moderation and of greater medication.

The child of prosperous parents has to-day a lavishly equipped toy-cupboard and Christmas brings its elaborate additions to what is really a workshop. In some cases I have noticed that the play-room has become a combined garage, railway terminus, and airfield. Of course these various masterpieces of mechanism in miniature do bring their appropriate pleasures. They suit the realistic temper of the time and the boy-mechanic can be a happy realist as he equips himself for a mechanised world with neat-fingered manipulations of the engine-power at his disposal. But the more he uses his knowledge, the less does he employ his fancy. The old fun of 'lets pretend' was genuine fun and made much of little. It is not sentimentality to suggest that the fancy-free of juvenile masquerade was a happy and a healthy possession. Daphne du Maurier in her fine novel, *The Parasites*, made the point through the mouth of one of her characters, the maternally-minded helper of others, Celia Delaney.

> They are different from what we used to be. Our world was one of fantasy. Theirs is reality. They don't pretend. An arm-chair is always an armchair to the modern child, never a ship, never a desert island. They are sweet and have honest, carefree eyes. But they have not any magic in their day.

Magic and machines do not naturally mix, and Christmas con-tinually brings more of the latter to the young recipients of the seasonable gifts. Moreover the very young are accustomed to seeing in full detail, at the pictures, the adventures about which their parents used to read and dream. The Redskin romances have become technicoloured realities. Children from all kinds of homes have their cinema clubs and may see any Saturday morning a ' Western ' in all its glorious hues. This, with its visible and audible actualities of the rodeo, the stampede, and the pursuit, supplants the excitements which once came only in words. Playing at soldiers has been developed into mechanical warfare with models true to the munition factory. Now television comes to many thousands of homes, and brings the cinema to the hearth. The great processions and ceremonies and the athletic events of real life happen in front of myriads of young eyes. Why dress up, why make a forest wigwam out of two chairs and a rug in the nursery, why bother to pretend and to indulge in a play-boy's dream? The facts are before us and every Christmas the toymaker's catalogue takes us closer to the actual factory and farther from the kingdom of fancy.

I am not, I hope, to be regarded merely as a growling old codger if I call attention to this change. The mood and tastes of childhood must alter in this altering world of the technocrat and much happiness comes to the young talent which can master and ' service ' the model aeroplane that has been buzzing so infernally on the heathland this Christmas morning. But I did notice a group of boys, coming from what were obviously poorer homes, nimbly climbing trees, at some risk to themselves, and conducting a lively form of skirmish with no more weapons than they could improvise from fallen branches. No doubt they envied the privileged amateur mechanic with his aeroplane; but they were deeply absorbed in their own pretences and, I could swear, happily too. Christmas can still make do with a simple flight of fancy as well as with a complicated flight of the power-driven hardware, which, on London's oases of land and water, now screams ' Buzz, buzz, here come the play-boys.'

The trough of the Christmas wave lasts until New Year. The shops have an after-the-party look. 'The Sales' used to be the great January magnet for housewives and turned Oxford Street into a bee-swarm of busy bargain-hunters. But surplus stocks were insufficient for a while to restore this terrific clatter and flutter in its old intensity. The sales, if they occurred at all, were shorter, and fewer and the bargains, if discoverable, were immediately snapped up. But there has been considerable activity of late, with the queues re-forming as of old and stampedes for the treasures. But for five days the great Yule-tide tranquillity lies blanket-wise upon the town; Mother has catered the household into a coma and Father's purse and cheque-book can manage no more. Those who have to pay the bills have taken cover and are licking their wounds. It is just then that the Income Tax demand, in its hideous, jaundiced envelope, floats in through the front door.

There is some hubbub, it is true, in Shaftesbury Avenue and thereabouts. Big parties come in from the suburbs for the plays and pantomimes and queue for tea, after the matinée, at the Corner Houses, where there is value for money as well as gilt on the gingerbread and music while you munch, About six o'clock the matinée crowds are going home and the evening crowds are streaming in and to find a niche on the pavements round Leicester Square or Charing Cross is as much as the most able-bodied can manage. Decoration is supplied by the barrow-boys, whose massed fruits glow beneath the lamps; a well-lit bank of oranges puts Christmas cordiality into a misty evening.

The barrow-boys are abused for 'fiddling' and diddling and certainly one has known the fruit below the surface to be a very odd and shabby replica of the imposing specimens on top. But time and again I have lifted up my eyes unto the spivs (and street-traders are not all to be dismissed as that) and, seeing a livid splash of colour in the greyness of a winter day, have felt a great relief of the senses. What the fashionable flower-shops do in the West End for the eye and spirits of the passers-by, the barrow-boys do in a more obvious and flamboyant way: they have no magic casements, extravagantly orchidaceous, but they do spill a box of paint in the gutter where they flaunt the golden tangerine or kindle an optical blaze with ' orange, orange, burning bright.' This heartening spectacle is one of London's ' free-for-alls ' and, when no sun shines, the colour-hungry are indebted to the parade of barrows, whether they stop and buy or stand and stare.

The habit of ' going-up West ' and then wandering about vaguely increases to a curious extent. I do not pretend to understand the fascination of the melancholy mooching and milling which goes on round the pubs, milk-bars, and garish 'snackeries' of the Leicester Square district every Saturday night. I suppose it is the case that we are all fidgets nowadays and that one of the patron saints of the new social democracy is St. Vitus. When petrol was plentiful people of the car-owning class used to dash fifteen miles into the country (in twenty-five minutes) in order to buy themselves in a crowded, smoky saloon-bar a few gin-and-whatnots which they could perfectly well have done at their own ' local,' with the same frowst, in their home town. They never looked at the country through which they were hurtling, and they cared nothing about it. But it was the thing to use the car, to show its paces, and to ' go places.' Anywhere would do, so long as there was speed and dash in the getting there.

In the same way a family now living and working in the industrial suburbs and having a bit of money in hand thinks it dull or *infra dig* to do the Saturday junketing in the local ' centre ': so its members pack into tube and bus in order to eat the same ice-cream and drink the same bottle of beer, at rather more cost, amid the Neons and the elbowing mobs of ' Up West.'

New Year's Eve is the end of the after-Christmas calm and

on that night this species of mass-meandering comes to its climax. The police reckon on having 100,000 strollers in the Piccadilly area by midnight. The statue of Eros has to be protectively boarded over lest the love-god be a casualty amid the exuberant salutes to the New Year or knocked about by the enthusiastic mountaineers who on these occasions like to treat London monuments as ' needles ' in the mountains and to establish themselves on a beetling eminence above the pedestrian mass. Those psychologists who believe that a crowd has its own subconscious, which is different from the aggregate of the ' subs ' of all its members and is an entity on its own account, may find some good material for observation in these great urban mobs which besiege Broadway or Piccadilly on nights of special significance. Because one piece of the calendar's arithmetic has ended and a new figure has come in I am not inclined to get into a gigantic huddle with some hundreds of thousands of strangers: but that process does seem to yield considerable satisfaction to the great majority. Great bliss apparently comes to those couples and families who have been steadily strolling and standing for hours in the damp or chilly night.

Another mystery of New Year's Eve is this. Why, both in large and public or small and domestic assemblies upon this occasion, do the English insist on joining hands, somewhat self-consciously, and singing, somewhat out of tune, a series of Scottish verses, which, if put to it, they could hardly translate? But are the English to blame for believing in 'willie-wauchts' when on my desk there is an edition of Burns *printed in Edinburgh* which actually hyphens it so? Of course the phrase is guid-willie waucht, a good-will drink, but most people think of a willie-waucht as some outsize or superbly potent draught.

When, why, and how did the genius of Robert Burns for simple, melodious statement of universal sentiments so impose itself upon the huge, un-Caledonian world that circling groups of perspiring City gentry and their ladies, having sufficiently dined, wined, and danced at the Grand Nineveh Hotel or the Balshazzar Night Club, must then greet each New Year with solemn swinging of arms bejewelled in cuff or bracelet and with the chanting of lines out of Ayrshire about gowans, stoups, and wauchts?

CHAPTER VIII

Pantomime

—◄◦❧◦►—

CHRISTMAS IN LONDON means, for all classes, Pantomime.
Whether you sit augustly, for fifteen shillings, in the stalls
at the Palladium or have two shillings' worth in the farther and
higher reaches of a suburban or East End music-hall, which is
housing Dick Whittington for the season, the feast is the same:
the trimmings differ. Of two things you can be certain. A
mature masculine comedian will be impersonating with ringlets,
feather-boa, and Jemimas (elastic-sided boots) a peppery or
plaintive female, while a young woman chosen mainly for the
delicate contours of her legs will be displaying those charms in
the role of Robin Hood or Prince Charming.

This transmigration of the sexes is not so much old as eternal.
It is part of the age-long Saturnalia or midwinter revels celebrated
all over Europe. The eighteenth-century Pantomimes, which
chiefly derived from the Italian comedians with Harlequin their
captain, may have dropped the primitive practices for a while:
with them Harlequin was man and Columbine was woman. But
when Pantomime had become thoroughly well naturalised and
was mixing British music-hall with foreign fairy-tale, the old
custom of a sex-changing masquerade soon re-established itself.
Mr. A. E. Wilson, an affectionate historian of pantomime, dates
the introduction of the feminine Principal Boy at 1853, so that
the prince in tights, pivoting on the highest of heels as a-hunting

or a-courting he will go, is, at the time of writing, very nearly a centuriañ.

But that affair of 1853 was not an innovation; it was a revival. And if, as is highly probable, the colleagues of the Principal Boys and Girls and their comrades in the knock-about part of the business, now arrive with a cat or a horse—the cat being one man in an animal's coat and the horse a joint effort under similar cover —then here too is a return to primeval mummery. For the popular midwinter masquing did always contain these two elements, both sex-change and the wearing of animals' skins. A professor of social psychology and an analyst of the popular subconscious may be able to explain why this urge exists: for the moment it is enough to show that it has—and does.

There was always a general topsy-turveydom about the December Feast of Fools in which man expressed his delight that the shortest day had been reached, that the light was returning, and that the plough could move again. Anarchy, as well as fertility, has been the essence of the matter and anarchy is still the essence of pantomime. The lowly trip up and beat their lords and masters; forlorn maidens get the better of bullying Ugly Sisters; Dick the cast-out apprentice returns as Lord Mayor of London. If there is a comedy scene in a schoolroom the teacher is sure to get the worst of it and the whirling cane descends upon the wrong posteriors. Even in a severely Socialist paper, *The Tribune*, I found a Christmas acknowledgment that in pantomime ' the sword, the magic lamp, the glass slipper, the magic phrase are all agents of reversal, either unparliamentary instruments of social justice or symbols of the might of private enterprise.' ' The pattern of rebellion and change ' has always to be maintained. ' The Government in office is always the target just because it is the Government.'

Let us see how this modern riot compares with ancient practice. Dr. Enid Welsford, historian of *The Court Masque*, which was the lordly entertainment of the English kings and

milords for two or three centuries, has delved into the origins of
masquerade, as indeed have many others who bring back much
the same report. Here is her picture of the Feast of Fools, a
medieval New Year festival in which the Church gave license
to most unclerical doings and did so with a liberality which
seems astonishing nowadays.

> 'The inferior clergy, who for the time being took precedence
> over their superiors, elected one of their number as Bishop or Pope
> or Abbot of Fools and celebrated the occasion by drinking bouts,
> riotous masquerading in beast-heads or women's clothes through
> church and street, and by burlesque celebrations of the Divine
> Office when the censing was done with pudding and sausages, and
> the priests played dice upon the altar.'

The Feast of Fools had descended from the Roman Saturnalia,
more anarchic rites in which servants were allowed to be masters.
The uprising menials took part in mummeries whose performers
wore skins, beast-masks and women's clothes. The English
rural ceremony of Plough Monday—the Monday after Twelfth
Night—was also celebrated with a similar ritual of altered sex
and clothes. 'The Plough is accompanied by music and by
one or more grotesques, the Bessy, a man dressed as a woman,
and the Fool, a man adorned with skins, hairy cap, and animal's
tail.'

Wherever we turn in time and space we come back on those
enduring features of the winter mime: the fun must release
man's urge for the breaking of laws and the flouting of authority:
and it must also satisfy the curious impulse for 'let's pretend'
in a way that will turn men from their proper selves into the
likeness of women and animals.

Contemporary pantomime is doing that still. The tenacity
of tradition in this matter is remarkable. Most aspects and
elements of the world of entertainment alter considerably. A
prominent actor once said to me that the theatre changes radically
every five years; he exaggerated, but the theatre does markedly

and rapidly alter. The musical comedies of my boyhood, as then acted, would be yawned off the stage by the young addicts of the contemporary American ' musicals,' which are so much more highly organised, so much more vigorous in attack. ' Strong ' plays inevitably turn weak as their themes and problems, once so pressing, fade into triviality. The whole force and pace of acting are a matter of shifting fashion. But the pantomimes that I have been seeing in recent winters are in general the same that I saw when I was a small boy. The change in a few details is trifling compared with the similarity of the whole routine.

There are always the spectacular pantomimes, expensively exhibited in large theatres, and the cheaper pantomimes relying on rough knock-about, traditional drollery, popular songs, and sentiment. I could point out minor fashions that come in and go out, but, on the whole, the British pantomime is a form of entertainment quite amazingly rigid. It is manifestly unreasonable, even preposterous, in its medley of a possibly delicate fairytale with irrelevant clowning, fantastic acrobatics, ambitious ballet, sentimental ditties and topical allusion. But this medley refuses to budge under pressure of progress. It turns up every winter and, owing to public demand, it is apt to stay so long that some regard it as a loitering nuisance and an obstructive tenant of stages required for loftier matters. In some way it appeals, as the old Feast of Fools and Revels of Misrule, the Roman Saturnalia and the English Plough Monday used to appeal, to a deep-driven instinct. Without some such foundation in the general mind, will and feeling, an institution so unreasonable and so inexplicable could not be so firmly rooted nor could it go on flourishing as it does.

Yet Christmas and conservatism do not necessarily go together. The Victorians, for example, brought in an entirely new and somewhat Germanic midwinter ceremonial: this we have modified in some ways and expanded in others. A Londoner of

1850 would find our Christmas junketings so long drawn as to be evidence of national laziness and he would be puzzled by our extravagance in the matter of Christmas presents. Most of our plays, except the classics, he would not understand at all and the classics he would find interpreted with a speed and a lack of declamation that might baffle him completely. But our panto-mime, since in his day the masculine Dame was already leering out of his (or her) ringlets and the feminine Principal Boy was just about to arrive, would seem to him natural, intelligible and satisfactory.

Fashions in clothing change radically outside the theatre; the best dressed woman of one decade is the frump of the next, as skirts lengthen or shorten, broaden or slim down, and as hats diminish from the vast cart-wheel to the tiny saucer. But in the Pantomime there is abiding uniform. I remember a Dick Whittington of many decades back. Until Highgate Hill was passed the lady wore a brown leather jerkin, a brown leather cap with a pheasant feather, and long brown suède boots, slender-heeled, and laced up the side. Visit any of this year's manifesta-tions of Master Richard and you still find exactly the same rig-out, complete with the pheasant-feather and the side-laced thigh-boots.

Robinson Crusoe has, to my regret, disappeared from the Pantomime rota. (Mr. Wilson explains that children dislike this yarn on the stage because the librettist has to introduce characters strange to Defoe, carrying Ma Crusoe, Polly Flinders, and Will Atkins, V.C., to the desert isle: but I do not see children objecting to the Widow Twankey and Wishee-Washee in *Aladdin* because they are the product of un-Arabian nights.) If *Robinson Crusoe* had been one of the London pantomimes this year I should regard it as disgraceful if the dashing girl in the hero's part had not come on parade with white rabbit skin about her middle. Everybody knows that Cinderella's Prince Charming will be a glittering eighteenth-century beau, sporting, at least on one occasion, a very white wig over a black silk essay in Gent's Court Wear, with silver-buckled shoes.

Most of the items and characters remain, with equal obstinacy, as the years roll by. But I notice a certain tendency to shed the Demon King and Fairy Queen who introduced the plot and defied each other in snarling tones (masculine) and silvery song (feminine). They should, I think, be retained and listed, as of old, in the programmes under the caption Immortals. We cannot have our Immortals made subject to mortality.

Another regular feature was the Food Song. It was ever the custom for the more robust of the Comedians to sing in praise of mince pies, treacly pudding, boiled beef and carrots, or some other popular constituent of the general menu. The public were invited to join in and heartily accepted the invitation. I presume that the meagre rations of wartime and after gave to this kind of communal dithyramb the semblance of a somewhat dreary mockery of the consumer-goods available. Would even the most acceptable, the best beloved of comedians dare to suggest that his audience join him in songful praise of some recent additions to the larder? 'I do like a s'nice snack of snoek.' 'A whale of a lump of whale-meat.' No, they will not do. So the Dame or Idle Jack have to cajole us into melody with less succulent themes. It is a pity. The Food Song was once indispensable.

I remember how that eager theatrical pioneer, Alfred Wareing, when manager at the Theatre Royal, Huddersfield, found to his dismay, even to his disgust, that a pantomime company which was visiting his house for the Christmas weeks had brought no Food Song in its luggage. Wareing was a genial ' all-brow ' and was concerned with introducing, to somewhat reluctant audiences, foreign novelties of the highest intellectual class: he was the first in Great Britain to put Chekhov into a repertory programme and he both honoured and puzzled the citizens of Huddersfield by offering them a new play by Pirandello for the performance of which he lured Mrs. Max Beerbohm out of Italy. Max himself came too. (I use those names as this was before Max's beknighted days.) A more incongruous spectacle than Max, fresh from sunlit Rapallo and forlorn upon the grey steps of an hotel in Huddersfield, I do not remember. But Wareing, at one moment ambitiously Pirandellian, had always a great sense of theatre ritual and propriety and the idea of a Pantomime with such an essential feature as the Food Song missing was odious to him. So he sat down and wrote one himself and not a bad one either. 'I do like a doughnut with jam in the middle, That's a lovely fruit.' Possibly in these narrow years the articles of food available for such minstrelsy have all been worked through. In that case we might start all over again, returning to mince pies and treacly pudding. There is no reason why plum-cake and stomach-ache should not continue to be linked in rhyme for many years.

Pantomime texts were and still are, but insufficiently, a salute to poetry. The British have an instinctive feeling that rhymed verse has ' something about it ' and is a better vehicle than prose, for the conveyance of deep emotion. Hence the proletarian habit of composing rhymed epitaphs for their dear ones. Local papers carry columns of farewells to the dead and of death-anniversary notices: these are paid for by the authors at advertisement rates. They show that the mass of the people have a somewhat faulty ear for scansion, but a considerable respect for rhyme:

> You left us, Mum, for a happier lot,
> By Grace, Bert, Daisy, and Dad you'll never be forgot.

That is typical of these simple and sincere tributes to the hand that rocked the cradle. The fact that rhyme is nearly always preferred to prose is a symptom of some instinctive reverence for the poet's craft. Even the crudest composer of popular ditties gives evidence of the same conviction by continuing resolutely to rhyme his moon and his croon, his eyes and his skies, his trues and his blues. Cockney rhyming slang, i.e. plates of meat for feet and trouble-and-strife for wife, is, in my opinion, a tedious form of ingenuity on the whole: but it is another aspect of deference to the magic of rhyme.

The Victorian pantomimes were full of rhymes and of far-fetched puns. It was the art of the librettist to pile up as many assonant syllables as possible. The result might be fearsome schoolboy doggerel packed with no less fearful schoolboy humour. Dick Whittington, having breasted Highgate's heights on his flight from unjust accusations, would pause to remark:

> Here somehow on the summit of this hill
> I sum it up that I feel somewhat ill.

Rhyme was at one time employed for most of the dialogue in pantomime: but now the comedians' gags are a more or less separate matter and rhyme is usually limited to the observations of Fairy Queens and Principal Boys in the development of the plot. I would like to see it restored more thoroughly, but am glad to see (or hear) that it has not by any means disappeared so far.

At the Princes' Theatre in London in Christmas 1949 the Dame's part in *Dick Whittington* was played, with a gentle melancholy and a nice touch of confidential 'low-down,' by Barry Lupino. These Dame parts, so pertinacious a feature of the sex-changing ritual, are rendered either as great bullying creatures, massive of figure, beetling of brow, cross-examining their victims with a fierce, arms-a-kimbo stance, bridling and leering; or else they are presented as unlucky creatures, shamefully put upon, getting the worst of all worlds, but taking disaster philosophically and, as a rule, alcoholically too. They explain their sorrows and their little ways of dodging the harsh laws of man or the injustice of fortune.

George Robey in his prime was the grand master of the Dame

Domineering. I suppose Dan Leno, the idol of Drury Lane, who died in his early forties, was the prime example of the Dame Pathetic. I never saw him, but have read much of him and can see in the photographs of his large-eyed, elastic face both the sadness of the ' lone, lorn crittur ' and the mischief of the un-biddable ' old faggot ' that the ' lorn crittur ' may become when she has been stirred to action by proper indignation or a nip of ' mother's ruin.' Nellie Wallace, who broke the rules by being a Female Dame and proved that all rules are the better for an occasional breach of them, was another of this kind. So is Barry Lupino. Susan the Cook, as he presented her in this pantomime, had a sad, withered gentility. She never bullied; she appealed.

I have mentioned Mr. Lupino because his name is an enduring testimony to the traditional nature of Pantomime. If the essence of this entertainment be, as we saw, primeval, if the fun is set deep in human impulse and represents, century after century, subconscious longings, then the performance of it should be a hereditary profession: and so it is.

The Lupinos have been traced back, in their function as entertainers, to St. Bartholomew's Fair in 1642, when a Signor Lupino would present ' Bel and Dragon, newly arrived, besides several Jiggs, Sarabands, and Country Dances.' A. E. Wilson in *Christmas Pantomime* has traced the Lupino history in the circus rings and on theatre stages from Civil War to World War. It runs continuous, with dancers, clowns, harlequins, and, most recent, a film star in Hollywood. One of the great Lupino features was ' trap ' work in which they have set up records for athletic and acrobatic ingenuity and daring. Barry is the son of George Lupino, a great Pantomime veteran. Of him Mr. Wilson writes:

In the Drury Lane pantomime of 1889 he turned a triple pirouette out of a 'star' trap, winning a wager of £50. The only other members of the profession who have repeated this feat are his son Barry and his nephew Lupino Lane, and perhaps Arthur Conquest has come near it.

This trap work subsequently became one of the great assets of the Lupinos, and resulted in an epidemic of copyists—but none approached the family in this form of acrobatics, although Arthur and Fred Conquest, sons of George Conquest, the original inventor of the ' star ' trap, ran them closely.

The Conquests, Vokes, Leclerqs have been other great families in the craft. But none have persisted like the Lupinos, whose connection with our Saturnalia, the Christmas Feast of Fools and Revels of Mad Misrule, has spanned not the decades only but the centuries and drives right back into the epoch of the Stuart Masque.

When I was young the prevailing notion was that Principal Boys should be proper Amazons, tall, powerful women who, once in Prince Charming's tights, would slap a thigh like a thunderclap as an introduction to a heartening song of amorous or patriotic sentiment. My earliest diva of this kind was the great Queenie Leighton whom I saw in ' Sinbad ' at Drury Lane: Mr. Wilson, by including her photograph, reminds me not only of the glorious uniform, which is still in use, but of a fine and formidable figure. Unfortunately my memory does not go back to Harriet Vernon of whose ' ample, Junoesque figure ' there was general praise.

In a volume by James Agate called *Fantasies and Impromptus* (published in 1923) there was an eloquent essay called ' In Search of Prince Charming,' the upshot of which was that His Royal Highness was no longer to be found, save possibly in the person of a Miss Ouida Macdermott, discovered in Kennington. Agate's opinion was that the great days of Principal Boydom were over.

Some talk of Dan Leno and some of Herbert Campbell, but for me pantomime has always centred in such artists as Harriet Vernon, Ada Blanche, Marie Loftus and Maggie Duggan. Youngsters sometimes ask with wonder in their voice: " And did you then see Maggie plain;" In the mind's eye I see these "principal boys" as though it were but yesterday that they trod the boards, golden visions with their cockades and their diadems, modish riding-whips and jewelled garters. I loved them all, without distinction or faithfulness; captivated now by a bunch of lace pinned at the throat by a diamond the size of a pheasant's egg, now by an elegant phrase of the hand, now by a particularly handsome turn of the heel. About comedians there could be dispute: tot homines quot funny-bones: All principal boys were adorable in their own right.

And then a change came over them which it is hard to define—a leaning to circumspection is, perhaps, the nearest. At any rate, the boys became less dashing. They lost the art of slapping their thighs, and executed that spanking manœuvre, when indeed they did not omit it altogether, with diffidence. They became introspective, sicklied o'er with the pale cast of thought; and one I encountered who was positively morose.

I am surprised that Agate made no mention of the truly princely Queenie, Miss Leighton of the Lane, but I agree that the slapping of a thigh, as the expression of high spirits or as summons to a chorus, is a lost art. In the matter of inches, too, there has been decline. Surely it was once assumed that no young lady could hope to be cast in the male role at Christmas without having some of the bulk and big assemblance of a man upon her side. (Vesta Tilley may be cited as the adorable exception who broke this rule.) I am sure that Harriet Vernon majestically o'ertopped her Cinderella. This is not to imply any clumsy excess of size, merely that, when boy met girl, girl could look up into boy's eyes before both broke into song on the subject of the lovelight in those orbs softly shining. In our own time I see Pantomime Princes of the most meagre dimensions: even on the highest of high heels they can hardly overlook their partners in the fine, upstanding manner of a periwig-pated gallant. And as for ' that spanking manœuvre,' it is nowhere.

But recently I have observed a young lady called Hy Hazell. (Hyacinth, I gather, is ' the long ' for this Hy, which

abbreviation more often springs from the masculine Henry.)
She played Dick Whittington at the Prince's Theatre and wore
the uniform, complete to the pheasant's feather, with conviction.
Massive she was not: but manly she was—and an actress too who
seemed to relish the role and play it with a proper faith that the
story is a true one. One really began to take the plot seriously—
an occurrence almost unthinkable in Pantomime. And then, when
all were aboard the lugger and Morocco-bound, she paused amid
a patriotic ballad of the Navy in order to recite most of John o'
Gaunt's swan-song about our blessed isle, demi-Eden with a
moat defensive, this happy breed of men, and the rest. Moreover
she did it remarkably well. Shakespeare in these quarters! What
would James Agate, seeking his slap-happy Prince of the old
school, have thought of such proceedings? They will be demand-
ing tax-emption for Pantomime next, on the ground that it is
' partly educational.'

Another difference is the absence of Songs of the Year. There
used to be a good, catchy song that was composed for sale to as
many pantomimes as possible and was later on included in the
shilling albums of these favourites, albums discoverable near every
family piano in the country in days when people did play the
piano and sing (out of tune) instead of having it done for them
(in tune) by gramophone and wireless. Whether to be an unskilled and active amateur is better for the soul than to be a
passive recipient of the most skilful professional talent is a nice
debating society point into which I shall not digress. Suffice to
say that we all chanted, after the Pantomime, that we were afraid
to go home in the dark and echoed (more or less melodiously)
similar statements of policy pronounced by Principal Boys.

The tunes had to be obvious and easy and the words were
often of the most banal kind. The Principal Boy usually had the
privilege of exploiting this popular number. So with him we
all went the same way home or down the Strand or out in the
beautiful twilight. That sort of ditty faded when mashing and

spooning faded from the popular lexicon. It was sportive, amorous, encouraging, and optimistic; the mood changed and Pantomime, so conservative in the essentials, can always take a change of fashion on the surface and modulate the beat of the song in its heart. Hence Dick Whittington took, in time, to the blues and Aladdin to croonery-moonery lamentations.

But, if new kinds of melody may come in, new characters very rarely do. Dick Whittington is unthinkable without Idle Jack, Cinderella is eternally accompanied by the prancing Dandini, who sounds like a hair oil, and by the sympathetic page-boy Buttons. Robinson Crusoe, on the too rare occasions of his re-appearance, is partnered by the mysterious Will Atkins, V.C., while Aladdin is for ever the son of the Widow Twankey. The provenance of the Widow has puzzled many. But it has to be remembered that the scene of this story is in China and that, during the great formative period of our modern English panto-mimes, tea was more associated with China than with Ceylon and Assam. Twankai was a brand of tea, as Bordeaux and Burgundy are species of French wines. A ' pot of Twankai ' was a familiar order in Thackeray's London and so, with Twankai passing into Twankey, the ever-recurring Widow of the laundry is simply the old tea-swiller in Victorian language.

Tongue-twister songs have been great favourites. To me they recall Wilkie Bard, a sad, sly droll. If classical recitation, now practised by Hy Hazell, had been then in vogue, this glumly philosophical clown might have appeared as one of the melan-choliacs so dear to Shakespeare and spouted, as Idle Jack, some such Elizabethan self-introduction as ' In faith I know not why I am so sad.' He was the master of these scarcely pronounceable ballads in which all had to take part. Their difficulty was well accompanied by his wry diffidence. ' She sells sea-shells by the seashore, and the shells that she sells are sea-shells, I'm sure ' was his masterpiece in this kind. At the beginning of the 1914 war Jack Norwood popularised at the Hippodrome (but not in

Pantomime), ' Sister Susie's sewing shirts for soldiers.' He ended
with the line ' the saucy soft short shirts for soldiers sister Susie
sews.' Also there was a telephone song which inquired, ' Which
switch is the right switch for Ipswich? It's the Ipswich switch
which I require.' These were not so easy to hurl back correctly
in reply to his request for a chorus.

The animal impersonation, so essential a part of the whole
primeval Christmas revel, is carried out by specialists. The
Brothers Griffith reached the highest status and were even
included in a C. B. Cochran-Noel Coward revue owing to the
brilliance of their combined antics as the fore and behind sections
of their spirited nag, Pogo. The Whittingtonian Cats frequently
display a very sharp comprehension of feline movement and
carry out their gambols in a most life-like and amusing way.
What becomes of this mimetic talent after February? I presume
that in many a seaside concert party or touring revue there
lurks a potential or frustrated Whiskers or half a Dobbin that
will be on the tiles or in the traces when Pantomime returns in
December.

The pantomimes visible to-day are the old mummery, but
they are cut to a new size. In the great days of Drury Lane the
mere bulk and duration of the business were overwhelming. The
matinée began at one-thirty; the audience would be there till
six or later. At seven-thirty the huge machine began to revolve
again and the second audience would be there till midnight.
Two great wars, especially the second, put limits to that. Earlier
hours were the rule and remained the rule. Transport stopped
earlier and people had longer and slower journeys to make. So
four and a half hours were cut to three and a half; and wisely.
The London pantomimes of to-day, running from two to five-
thirty and from seven to ten-thirty, are amply long. Even the
happiest and most absorbed child is beginning to yawn and
fidget before the end. The rush on the lavatories becomes urgent,
a queueing matter. Any more of this would be torture.

The cuts have been made at the expense of the vast Transformation Scene, which occupied the end of the first half. With the present cost of materials and labour we cannot afford the many layers of scenery which were deployed in these gigantic and sumptuous approaches to Aladdin's Cave or the Enchanted Castle. Such garish wonderments were contrived with more cost than taste. Now we have to mix our paint with more brains and less ' brass,' which is all to the good. One frequently sees Pantomime trimly decorated, with fresh, clean, simple colourings instead of the old bizarre elaboration. There is less parade of womanhood. Once huge troops of unskilled ladies paraded in tights with cage-like upper-coverings, representing flowers, shells, jewels and so forth. Their miming was elementary, their movements gauche, and the whole thing a considerable bore. It suited the Edwardian sense of splendour: the public felt that here in this multitude of gauze-divided scenes with their caverns, castles, and fairy grottoes, real value was being given for real money. To-day neither value nor money is so real. So we get less tonnage and poundage of ' production,' less spread of canvas, and on the whole, a far more pleasant, or at least sufficient, view of the Baronial Hall or the Moroccan Palace.

Well, there is a cant of Pantomime and a cant of anti-Pantomime. With a couple of good acrobatic clowns, unsparing in bloodless battery and with the rough-and-tumble which they can so cleverly contrive as to break no bones, the customary scenes of violence may be very amusing indeed. I am an impenitent lover of parlours papered amid oceans of paste and of kitchens prolific in custard-pie. The spectacle of tumblers tumbling is made the more acceptable not only because they are funny fellows; since they know their craft down to that last-second somersault, they also work in comparative safety.

The circus crowds, on the other hand, who watch trapeze-artists and tight-wire walkers and pole-balancers executing their miracles of poise or hanging on by their teeth eighty feet above

the ring and with no net below them, are, I think, fairly chargeable with an innocent kind of sadism. If the wire and trapeze
were only just off the ground, the actual feats performed on them
would be no less difficult. But the risk of a broken neck or back
would have dwindled away and the public would regard as
trivial, because unrisky, just those expert moves which they
relish when a life is at stake. What is the point of a man entering
the tigers' cage, unless there is at least some chance of his being
savaged?

I do not say that the circus crowd is deliberately waiting for
an accident, but the possibility of the disaster gives spice to the
turn in which it may occur. Even the most violent knock-about
in Pantomime contains little danger of serious damage and that
is one reason why I prefer it to the circus. The spectacle of a man
throwing knives all round his lady partner's head and only
missing by millimetres gives me no joy at all. But that sort of
senseless accuracy on the man's part and of incredible gallantry
on the lady's part does delight millions, just as millions can be
made to twitter at the sight of animals, normally possessing some
beauty and dignity, turned into conscript clowns, shabby captives
or exploited pets with a routine of inane tricks. I regret to
notice that kind of animal ' act ' creeping into Pantomime where
it has no business at all. Pantomime has its own bestiary of
composite horse and cow and of man-into-cat. These are in the
direct succession from the transformations and wearing of animal
skins in the old Saturnalia; the Cat of Fancy should not be made
to rub paws with animals of fact.

If I were to bet on anything concerning the year A.D. 2000
(should our civilisation ever reach so far) it is that the British
people will be making their midwinter trip to see *Cinderella*,
Dick Whittington, *Aladdin*, and the rest on a bedizened stage where
girls will impersonate men and young men will embody old
women, where lads will be cats and horses will be human and
bi-partite. All this will occur in a huge packed house with a

huge orchestra making a huge rumpus—the music of Pantomime in a big theatre achieves din unparalleled—and with a general and intense aroma of perspiring bliss. Of the young Fenton in *The Merry Wives of Windsor* it was said, ' He speaks holiday, he smells April and May.' The English patron of Pantomime speaks, and will ever speak, holiday. And he smells, in his rapture, December.

CHAPTER IX
Marx and Marble

T O WALK amid the tombs of London is to be a historian
willy-nilly. You are forced to notice the names and perhaps
the professions and callings of the buried; geography comes in
too, so often have those lying here been strangers to this land
and city, feeding upon alien corn, and finally ' rotting to flowers
and. fruit, with Adam and all mankind.' Of course in a close-
packed urban cemetery there is not much room for apple-trees
or for the flora natural to the environs of a country church. The
main crop is man-made of stone, nowadays chiefly of marble: it
is usually hideous, sometimes moving in its tributary style,
scarcely truthful in its letterpress. But that is understandable. As
Dr. Johnson remarked, those who compose lapidary inscriptions
are not under oath. They would not traduce and so may
exaggerate. It is a failing on the right side.

All sorts of noticeable history is to be seen in many a London
cemetery. You may watch, for example, the complete collapse
of taste that occurred rather more than a century ago. Till then
the lettering on the memorial stones was usually of a nice Roman
cut and the sentiments gravely, not floridly, expressed. But
with Victoria came vulgarity: it was not her fault, of course,
but something happened in the mood of man which made him
lose natural modesty and crave the exotic, the over-emphatic, the
heavily picturesque. The florid humbugs whom Dickens drew

with such happy loathing could not be buried as though they were mere children of God, being so large among men.

So it was that shiny imported marble replaced the decent greys of native stone: this is most hatefully visible in country churchyards. Restraint in valedictory speech, as in sepulchral material, was discarded and death was no longer described as death, but as various forms of celestial passage into the holy arms or sacred bosom: the merits of the deceased were proclaimed with a too glib, almost a greasy, liberality. The unctuous style of Chadband had replaced the witty and candid epitaphs of previous centuries. The lettering, in all sorts of bogus Gothic, was there for effect and not for the simple, honest statement of a last salute. No flowers, we say now: and flowers of speech we also try to avoid. Not so the Victorians; their plumed, processional funerals led to flights of angels, in marble, and to flights of speech in lapidary rhetoric.

For a winter walk I often wander into Highgate Cemetery, which climbs steeply, a vast expanse of tombs and mausolea stretching from the base of Highgate Hill nearly to the top of it, bordering almost on Hampstead Heath at one corner and marching with Waterlow Park to the north-east. W. Howitt, author of *The Northern Heights of London* (1869) was even in those days commenting on the over-population of these marbled slopes:

> 'In fact, in situation and in tasteful laying-out, it is one of the most attractive cemeteries in the kingdom. The vicinity to London has in a few years densely crowded it with graves and enormous loads of monumental marble, so that a great extension of it has been necessary. Such a cemetery in a popular suburb is but a questionable institution for the deposit of the London dead, which, continually carried thither in hearses, is neither a very cheerful object, nor would it be very satisfactory in a sanitary point of view, were it not that the ground is a deep stiff clay, which must effectually prevent any exhalations from the mountain of decaying mortality accumulated there.'

Highgate Cemetery

Though much added to since Mr. Howitt's day the cemetery has not, as far as I know, detracted from the pleasures and hygiene of living in Highgate. Much virtue, I suppose, in that ' deep, stiff clay,' a pall insisting that the dead shall indeed lie down.

My stroll moves by way of Well Walk in Hampstead, where Constable looked out upon the galleon clouds above a landscape which is still blessedly open to all-comers and remarkably deserted except on Saturday and Sunday. In this small row have lived in my time, E. V. Knox, the Editor of *Punch*, Leslie Banks the actor, and Sturge Moore, the poet. J. B. Priestley wrote *The Good Companions* in a large red house of later period just opposite and Professor Joad emerges from hereabouts to perform on a hockey-pitch on Sunday afternoons. I have loved nearly all games except hockey, which I detest. The spectacle of the Professor, bearded, plump, and spectacled, trotting about as Master of the Ceremonies among a bevy of fleet youngsters, who invade Hampstead Heath with hockey-sticks after Sunday dinner in winter, is not one which persuades me to a new judgment on this particular form of athletic caper.

It happens to be a fine December afternoon. There has been some sticky weather, but that was washed away by a deluge last night and now the sky is a great clean bowl of blue; a strong south-wester briskly dispatches any sign of mist: no doubt there is rain to come, but for a space London has been deliciously sluiced and brushed up. The air is clean stuff again, well worth the gulping. Both heath and houses have a scoured, shining look. So it is the right day for crossing the stripling River Fleet and climbing the ridge which gives the pleasant view to woody, towery Highgate, fronted with ponds, crested with a green copper dome and backed with a nice, undisciplined spread of large, well-timbered houses. A spacious, easy-going spot, it reminds me of those spa towns with large Victorian villas hidden behind their zarebas of laurel and rhododendron.

In such places, withdrawn from the world, there used to live in prosperous amenity numbers of solid merchants or pensioned servants of the Empire, a class which just manages nowadays to keep the roof on while the garden runs wild. But now and again an old lady dies in one of these genteel coverts and it is discovered that she was worth half a million pounds. None of her neighbours knew it; possibly she did not know it herself; she spent little and worried little, leaving all things in the care of a sedate firm of family lawyers in Lincoln's Inn Fields. Many charities benefit; her maid gets £250, her 'companion' £500, and some fortunate, bewildered nephews and nieces acquire such balance as the Death Duties permit. The house is sold, split into flats, and the old party herself is carried to one of the big family vaults or cata-combs, as they still call them, in the famous cemetery upon the hill.

When you have dropped off the Hampstead ridge and are breasting Highgate Hill, you will be amazed at the size of the shrubberies and gardens surrounding the hundred-year-old houses. Only five miles from Charing Cross! Surely the land would have been too precious to be given to over such acres of unprofitable boskage. But no, Highgate is old and grey and full of sleep. It is less developed, altogether less Londonish than Hampstead. Wandering there I might be back in Cheltenham, where I lived as a boy, in the Victorian outskirts of that spa, not the trim Georgian centre. Highgate, too, is a region of stucco mansions set amid thickets, domestically unmanageable now but once the last infirmary of many a minor nabob, back from 'John Company' or the I.C.S.

If I am to enter by the lower gate of the vast burial-ground I must pass through a little of the new Highgate with its notable pile of Tudor-style mansion flats, and its broad roads of neat, new, workable houses. Reaching the rustically named Swain's Lane—Highgate will be pastoral ever, despite those mansion flats—one realises that here are the Northern Heights in stern reality. Drivers are warned that the hill is too steep for traffic after passing the cemetery gates. The hearses, aiming no higher, can just manage it: ' Set down, set down your honourable load.' After that the way up is for pedestrian mountaineers only.

Swerving round to the south entrance I see at once the grave of Fred Billington: he was for many years the Heavy Comedian of the Doyly Carte Opera Company, a monstrous Yorick, the huge, gruff joy of our countless Gilbertians and Sullivanians, a potentate among Poo-Bahs. He was, I believe, great company if in the vein and made merry, when in towns, at the Great Eastern Hotel at Liverpool Street Station, famous in meatier days for its chops and steaks. No lacrimose pietism is written over Billington: the sentiments are pagan and poetical.

> *Lo, some we loved, the loveliest and the best,*
> *That Time and Fate of all their Vintage prest*
> *Have drunk their Cup a Round or two before,*
> *And one by one crept silently to Rest.*

Apt words. These acres of Highgate are not of the Christians' God only: pagans and Bohemians lie here and many who had no faith at all or were even strong enemies of the Church. Not least Karl Marx.

It is not easy to find the narrow grave of that world-shaker who has lain so humbly for nearly seventy years among the English who gave him refuge and so close to the London merchants with their grandiose tombs, the capitalists of his indictment. Lenin lies in perpetual state in the Kremlin, a mummified god, if a scientific materialism will admit that word, the ' g,' of course, being kept suitably small. But Marx the master-thinker has never been exhumed; one would expect the coffin to have been removed in scarlet pomp to lie by Lenin's side. But here it stays, cold in the earth, amid our wild (or mild) Decembers, not translated to the sepulchral honours of the Workers' Republic that the prophet never lived to see.

Being small and undistinguished—what the cemetery attendant

calls ' a flat job,' meaning that there is no upright headstone—
the grave of Karl Marx is not easy to find. But inquiry will get
you to it. ' Look for the name of Scrimmage ' the warden
seemed to say, as he put me on the right path among the marble
forest. Scrimmage? Well, there is a solid family tomb of
Scrymgeours in front of Marx and to this he was alluding. There
are a great number of London Caledonians buried in Highgate;
at least so the names suggest: they leave me reflecting that here's
some corner of an English field that is for ever Scotland. After
all, Marx too was not entirely detached from Scotland! The
recumbent stone on the narrow grave (Registration Number
24748) grimly suggests a close fit. It registers, as well as Karl

JENNY VON WESTPHALEN (1814-1881)
BELOVED WIFE OF
KARL MARX (1818-1883)
HARRY LONGUET (1878-1883)
HELENA DEMUTH (1833-1890)

The name of Jenny was suitable: there had been some mixing
of Scottish blood, perhaps by a soldier of fortune, with the
von Westphalen family, people of birth and prosperity. Jenny
endured exile and danger and poverty with the joint author of
The Communist Manifesto, which is superb rhetoric, and of *Das
Kapital*, which is heavy going. Marx studied in the British
Museum and went daily past the Elgin Marbles and all the deposits
of strangeness and beauty fashioned by creative humanity to
plunge himself into the dry mysteries of economic man. Did
the studious Karl, as he ambled away of a morning to conduct
his reflections at the expense of the British taxpayer under the
museum roof in Bloomsbury, ever have Leigh Hunt's lines upon
his lips?

> *Say I'm weary, say I'm sad,*
> *Say that health and wealth have missed me,*
> *Say I'm growing old, but add*
> *Jenny kissed me.*

I presume that Miss Demuth housekept for Marx after Jenny had died. Little Harry Longuet was a grandson: the Marx daughters had interesting unions. One linked with the French Socialist Longuet, the other, Eleanor, with Dr. Aveling, well known (but not always to his credit) in English Socialist circles.

Hesketh Pearson in his life of Bernard Shaw says that he was attracted by Eleanor.

> 'He saw her constantly in the British Museum reading room, where she was working as a literary hack for eighteenpence an hour. When Shaw became a Marxist and took the platform for the Cause, they became acquainted as socialist comrades, and a fairly cordial friendship ensued. But before their relations had warmed into anything more intimate on her side, a rival snatched the prize from him. She announced to her friends that she was about to burn her boats and live with another comrade: Doctor (of Science) Edward Aveling.'

Aveling is generally supposed to have been one of the models for the glib Dubedat in *The Doctor's Dilemma*. Mr. Pearson records Shaw's opinion that Aveling had

> 'an incorruptible integrity as a militant atheist, a Shelleyan, a Darwinian and a Marxist, and would, Shaw believes, have gone to the stake rather than deny or surrender a jot of his convictions. But as a borrower of money and a swindler and seducer of women his record was unapproachable.'

Eleanor was abandoned by Aveling when he was at last free to marry her. She committed suicide, though possibly not for this reason. Hedda Gabler was setting a fashion and one of her kind may have taken the line that it was not worth while to grow old.

So there lies the man whose doctrine has torn our world in half, whose roll of verbal drums in *The Communist Manifesto*— 'Workers of the world unite! You have only your chains to lose and all the world to win' has echoed so effectively down the years. Concerning the voluminous and difficult *Das Kapital* one paradox abides. No book on the social order has been less read—and more potent. How many even of the most faithful comrades have actually waded all through it? When one thinks of the victories won in Europe and Asia by Marxist doctrine over the old rulers and, more remarkable, over the old, deep-set faiths and traditions, one can only agree that the Invincible has been struck down by the Unreadable.

Is that a victory for the art of writing? Perhaps not, but for the power of thinking, certainly. All around Marx in the deep, stiff clay of North London lie the representatives of mercantilism, men of means and power. Outside the cemetery sprawled the huge City that harboured him; a hostile city, to his way of thought. With nothing but the power of mind and print the German refugee has within a century brought upheaval to two continents: if there had been no Marx, there would have been no modern Moscow, no Lenin, no Stalin, no stretch of Communism from Prague to Pekin. And the young men of the eighties, in this country, though most of them rejected his theory of value and his dialectical materialism and turned to a milder, more humane form of ethical Socialism, were smitten in their day. Shaw has said that at the age of twenty-six he saw the Red Light that had been kindled by Karl.

'Marx was a revelation. His abstract economics, as I discovered later, were wrong, but he rent the veil. He opened my eyes to the facts of history and civilisation, gave me a fresh conception of the universe, provided me with a plan and a mission in life.'

Well, here were set the mortal remains of the man who managed to be the most fiery of the world's incendiaries and one of the dullest of the world's economists. Occasionally a comrade arrives and puts some red roses on this slender slab above the coffins. During my last visit there was nothing there but some completely withered chrysanthemums. I am surprised that the Communist Party does not make tending the grave a responsibility: it is now not only unflowered but sinking into an undignified slant. It may in some places be an essential tenet of Scientific Materialism that the dead be left to bury their dead and that sepulchral tributes be deemed bourgeois and unmanly.   In the case of Lenin, Moscow thinks otherwise, aware that martyrs are everywhere remembered by their graves.

It is strange that the ordinary, reasonably well-educated man knows so little about Marx. We are most of us vaguely aware that Marx believed in an inevitable warfare of the classes in which the united workers of the world would triumph over a collapsing ' boss-class ' since Capitalism ' carries within itself the seeds of its own decay,' i.e. the instability caused by recurrent over-production, slumps, and unemployment. He emphatically did not believe that Socialism could peaceably evolve out of Capitalism, which is the view of the British Labour Party, or at least of its largest and fairly moderate element. He further held that in the class struggle there could be no dilly-dallying with democratic methods; the Workers' Republic could be established only by a resolute, and even ruthless, dictatorship, determined to smash all Capitalist efforts to resist or to fight back.

So, in Russia, it has turned out in the event. But there, and in all the satellite Communist countries, the violence and vengeance of the Party Dictatorship have been directed quite as much at dissident or ' deviating ' Communists as at open opponents. Never in the history of religion at its worst have there been such narrow, bitter, and persecuting sectarians as the pioneers of the Marxian Revolution.

There is a deal more of Marxian dogma, about the ' surplus value ' of labour and about the capitalist exploitation thereof. But the class war and the following dictatorship, which it was said, might ease off into a tolerant and genial democracy—but nowhere seems to be doing so—are the root of the matter. Of the man who hammered this into the consciousness of working-class leaders, who in turn somehow hammered at least the head-lines of it all into the skulls of millions of workers and (with more difficulty) of peasants, most of us are ignorant. We can learn much of Stalin, the generalissimo of Marxian strategy—if the Trotskyites will permit me to call him that—from Mr. Deutscher's brilliant life of him. There ought to be a good, popular, picturesque English life of Marx, in addition to the many, often rather arid, treatises on Marxism. But where is it?

Such reflections are natural as one looks at the little family grave with its air of quiet domesticity. It is not easy to visualise Karl Marx as Papa, though Jenny's homely name makes her more imaginable as Mum. It is ridiculous to blame prophets for the excesses committed by their followers. Christ is not to be censured for the crimes that intemperate gospellers have committed. The doctrine of Marx was bellicose, but we cannot assume that he himself would have gloried in or permitted the mass arrests, fake trials, and prison camp atrocities which are everywhere the badge of the totalitarian state, whatever its colour.

There is a tradition, which a Labour veteran once recalled to me, that Karl Marx was fond of his glass and would take to it readily when his spirits wasted. On this news I can envisage the bearded sage, homeward bound after a long day in the British Museum, stopping for one or two at some North London ' local ' and being discouraged by his companion, possibly Engels, from staying overlong. ' One for the road,' says Karl stubbornly, while Engels elbows him out of licensed premises, insisting that at least another half-chapter of a major work or another section of a dialectical pamphlet must be finished to-night. So Karl, protesting, is bundled off to a sober supper with Jenny and a diligent evening at the desk. It may have been so; at any rate to think it so sheds a little warmth on a figure now so much associated with a cold kind of hate.

His underground company at Highgate include the Scrymgeours and one described as a ' Serbian Socialist Leader,' Douchan Popovitch (1884-1918), for whom a niche was found close to the grave of the German-Jewish prophet himself. Now the fellow-

countrymen of Popovitch have quarrelled bitterly with the High
Priest of Communism in Moscow and are 'deviating' cour-
ageously with Tito.   Marx himself, of course, may be approving
Tito from the shades and calling Stalin the betrayer of the true
faith. In that case Douchan Popovitch is well placed in death.

The Marx grave, this 'flat job,' is too slender a matter to be
called tomb, sepulchre, vault, or catacomb, the titles claimed by
loftier families with much larger and more imposing coverlets
of stone. It was curiously honoured during a recent Christmas
as I discovered when passing on New Year's Day. I have
previously mentioned Jenny and the possibility of a kiss. Now,
by a queer coincidence, someone had actually placed mistletoe
on Marx: but mistletoe is the Golden Bough as well as the
sanction for embracement. I suppose immortality of the man's
ideas, not of the soul, was implied by this action of a devotee.
A small but handsome circular wreath of red-berried holly and
of yellow-berried mistletoe lay on the stone: there was a label
inscribed in a most clear and beautiful hand-writing.

AD PRAECLARAM MEMORIAM CAROLI MARX
(*To the most illustrious memory of Karl Marx*)

and then followed some Latin verses. Surely, in England, this
was bourgeois obeisance. For how many of the Communist
Party can compose in or appreciate Latin?

The ground about here was—and still may be—unconsecrated.
That would not greatly worry some of its occupants. Hard by
lies a group of Victorian heretics and rebels. A dark monolith
records the grave of Mary Ann Cross (George Eliot), who was
buried here, aged 61, on December 29, 1880. It was a day of
violent wind and rain, but the flower of Victorian science and
philosophy came out to endure the climatic buffetings. John
Morley, Herbert Spencer, T. H. Huxley, Frederick Harrison,
Professor Tyndall and the painter Millais were among the large
company who attended a Unitarian service and the graveside

ceremony. Rarely can a burial assembly of ceremonial top hats have covered such a grave array of noble brains.

But now there are no flowers for the authoress of *Middlemarch*, which many good judges of to-day put very high in the mid-Victorian literary canon. She touched the mind more and the heart and fancy less than did the Brontës. That is not the way to widespread popularity. So the Cornish-Irish sisters, whose real name was Brunty or Prunty, have a museum in the Yorkshire rectory at Haworth and have thus made a Mecca of a grey mill-town, while George Eliot lies under her dark grey obelisk where nobody leaves laurels or indites Latin verses. But she is more solidly established in stone than are the Marx ménage and there were some verses graven for her.

> *Of those immortal dead who live again*
> *In minds made better by their presence.*

That is simple, true and apt to the subject of the epitaph.

Beside her is veneration indeed. For here lies Elma Stuart of Ladhope, Roxburghshire, ' whom for eight and a half blessed years George Eliot called by the sweet name of daughter. She was pioneer in England of the Salisbury System for the prevention and cure of diseases and author of "What Must I Do To Be Well and How Can I Keep So?"' To have one's works (or masterpiece) thus blazoned on one's tombstone is a novelty and perhaps not an example to be generally followed. Moreover to have a cure belauded on a grave is a little unpropitious. But I hold that the professions and callings of the dead should be modestly recorded in their epitaphic inscriptions, for the information of the passer-by.

Just behind George Eliot there is a grave topped by a noble head in stone. This is a sculpture of George Jacob Holyoake, Rationalist and Co-operator (1817-1906), erected by his comrades of the Co-operative movement. The finely carved face looks across the marbled hillside with the aristocratic air of a liberal Duke: I suddenly thought of Prospero, retired to Milan where

' every third thought shall be my grave.' Beside Holyoake are tributary stones to the Grand Old Man of Rationalism, Charles Watts, publisher and publicist, and to many of his family. This is Liberators' Corner. Herbert Spencer is also buried hereabouts, but I have not discovered his grave.

The Highgate Cemetery is closely packed as well as vast. Most people look for Tom Sayers the pugilist with his dog in effigy and Wombwell, the circus owner, with his horse. Herbert Spencer followed George Eliot. The folk of serious intention— and how very serious some of them were—lie among the artists, the drolls, the showmen and the failures. Dickens's father, with his Marshalsea memories, came to Highgate in the end, to share the stiff clay with Marx on the one hand and the solid merchants, stowed deep in family vaults, on the other. So Raleigh's invocation of ' eloquent, just, and mighty Death ' who has drawn together all ' the far-stretched greatness of man ' with his vices and his paltriness and covered all with two narrow words, *Hic jacet*, is whispered in the winds on Highgate Hill among the weeping willows, the yews, and the cedars.

Many famous people have been buried quite simply in Highgate Cemetery. Many of far less importance have had considerable sepulchres. Family pride, which soon is swollen to family vanity, prefers the mausoleum of a magnate to the ' flat job ' of a Marx. It is especially on the cemetery summit, at the northern end of precipitous Swain's Lane, that one meets the funerary habits of the English Victorians in their most imposing, even astonishing, form. There is nothing here to match the weird mixture of the vulgar and the sentimental that you will find in a French burial-ground. But there is a staunch upholding of the clan spirit in the substantial vaults maintained by the great families. Here lie folk resolved that they would be united only with their own in death, as in life, and would not share common clay with common people. The family pew in church led on to the family catacomb.

Half-way up the hill Dalziel of Wooler and Strathcona and Mount Royal have mortal mansions of their own. But it is at the topmost point that one meets the word catacomb with its ancient and macabre suggestion of the hunted in the tunnels and of Roman martyrs long ago. Family catacomb of the—Forsytes, shall we say? The term has an eerie ring and some of these sepulchral cells look eerie too. Mouldering with the years and possibly chipped and shaken during the bombing of London, when many a cemetery had explosive visitations in the night which gave to some once quiescent dead a violent and unexpected form of resurrection, the catacombs have a frightening as well as a depressing look.

Some are dropped well into the earth and there is a whole circle of them in a sunken pit with a vast cedar tree looming darkly handsome over the middle of the ring. Some benevolent person has had the fancy of founding a Columbarium or dovehouse as part of this circus of mortality. There is even a hand pointing to the Columbarium. But no doves were there when I looked timidly in. Why should there be? Such a spot is not for birds of love and spring. The fatal raven should inhabit Highgate's catacombs.

I am not much in *rapport* with spirit-rappings and other intimations of immortality. Some common superstitions seem to me so absurd as to make one despair of reason in a world where so many, seemingly sensible people, are genuinely affected by them. But nobody really likes intense darkness and I shall not hypocritically pretend to be unstirred by its power of fearful suggestion. On the whole, I have been out of luck when spooks were about, though I sometimes fancy that a Poltergeist (called Miching Mallecho?) must have been at work among the shelves and papers in my house. Books develop the strangest powers of evanescence, even without the presence of borrowing friends and strangers. Yet, decently proof as I deem myself against the spectral, I would certainly hate to be locked up accidentally in the catacomb area of the Highgate Cemetery after nightfall. Those thick-set ranks of mausolea, and, most of all, that sunken circle of cedar-crested vaults, would give me the shivers and shudders, if nothing worse, till dawn came and the sun peered over London's rim and brought back confidence of mind into this modern version of the ancient charnel-house.

Two final memories of the place where Marx lies and of the company which he keeps. I was once there on a day of looming clouds, sharp searchlights of sunshine, and brief, pelting rain. Then there came a rainbow of flashing brilliance which flooded the catacomb area with its sudden glory. A more apocalyptic vision of London I could not imagine. The graves would surely open and strange figures climb the sky. This was Blake's Universe.

> *The fields from Islington to Marybone,*
> *To Primrose Hill and Saint John's Wood,*
> *Were builded over with pillars of gold;*
> *And there Jerusalem's pillars stood.*
>
> *I give you the end of a golden string;*
> *Only wind it into a ball,*
> *It will lead you in at Heaven's gate,*
> *Built in Jerusalem's wall.*

My other thought is of those who lie alone. There is the mighty mausoleum marked Julius Beer who, presumably out-topping many others in wealth while he lived, was not to be o'er-topped by any man in death. The word catacomb is usually applied to group-burials. 'Catacomb of the —— family.' But here, close to Julius Beer, is another lonely one, the grey cell of a self-isolating singleton. It announces simply and frankly 'Private Catacomb of John W. Beetles.' He is remembered in his privacy, for there was a holly-wreath on his front door after Christmas.

I shudder a little as I walk away down the hill and as I pass such queer, disused, collapsing chambers of the dead. Here is the family catacomb of a K.C.B., but the door has come open and you can see decaying coffins. The proud and eminent families of London have not all sustained their dignity and their aloofness. If we are immortal, do our souls take cognisance of our sepulchres or of the cemetery company which the mortal clay now keeps? If they do, I fancy that many of the Highgate shades must be considerably perturbed to think of Marx and the 'flat job' just down the slope!

CHAPTER X
The Painted Field

———————✦———————

WE HAVE had a taste of what the Westcountryman calls 'Black Janiveer.' The sky curdles in a hard grey: there is a biting air, a present from Russia: there is black frost. As you turn the corner of the street, the wind comes at you like a beast with fangs. Outside London there is probably a glitter of brittle sunshine, scarcely warming to the flesh, but cheerful despite its unreality. I had happened to be in Stratford-upon-Avon, celebrating on January 25 the immortal memory of the other Bard, Robert Burns. Caledonians appear to abound in Stratford and their hospitality was lavish. But away from the whisky the cold there was keen enough to freeze the more placid edges and back-waters of the Avon: the swans, with the dingy look that such weather can bestow on them, stuck to midstream or found holes in the ice. It was a new view of Stratford for me and not unlikeable: but London, on return, was smokily grey, slightly foggy, and altogether repulsive. Nor was there any more invitation to be out of doors when some drizzle worked in from the south-west, combining the two cruelties of cold and damp; the moisture, freezing as it fell upon the frozen roads and pavements, made movement a speculation for walkers, and driving a torment for all upon wheels. Imagine having to take a lorry to the North to-night! Not always is it better to be a man of the open road than a man of the closed shop.

London has ample compensations and escapes at such a time for those who can make use of them and, being in Oxford Street, I remembered the late Walter Hutchinson's benefaction in Stratford Place, the cul-de-sac just north-west of Bond Street where once the house of Derby abode in its seigneurial state. Derby House became the National Gallery of British Sports and Pastimes, where, for eighteen pence, you may see a selection from three thousand paintings and coloured prints, relevant not only to hunting, racing, shooting, and fishing, but to most of the less lethal activities of playing-fields. The exhibition is vast in scope, certainly rather too inclusive, but, at its best, superb in quality. Had you realised that Zoffany painted the shooters of the field as well as the actors of the stage and the pensive milords of the Conversation Piece? I had not. ' As well ' has double truth in this case. ' A Sportsman with Dog and Dead Bird in a Landscape ' is a glorious piece of work. The man, a little moist with the autumnal heat and ' faint but pursuing,' looks pleased with himself, though he has but a single partridge for his bag. His dog surveys this pathetic product of the day's work with interested sympathy. It is one of the best dogs that ever I saw in paint.

So this latest of our National Galleries (admittedly the name National is here unofficial) offers every aspect of grace and colour for your comfort on a winter day. The cul-de-sac is a sweetly quiet deviation from the higher drapery and the seething promenade of the Women's Mile: it is as tranquil as central. Yet here, of old, was much halloing and absorbency of a very different kind. Before the site was developed and became Stratford Place in the eighteenth century the Lord Mayors of London, with their worshipful and convivial vice-gerents and followers, came here to inspect the conduits which supplied water to the city, presumably the Tyburn and other local rivulets. Their capacity for assessing the purity of water may not have been remarkable, but they had other sports and liquors in mind. They took the chance to cry ' So-ho ' and hunt what game might be lurking in the coverts of this rural district. And, of course, after that, the banquet. Where they chased, they dined: and perhaps, like Mr. Jorrocks later, where they dined, they slept.

But later Edward Stratford, Second Earl of Aldborough, found the place 'ripe for development' and so came the Big House which the Stanleys were later to occupy. It is good Georgian, with some gaily decorated ceilings, and, what is strange in that bustling part of the town, a back-garden with high, creeper-clad walls. As you look out over the grass through the windows northward, you may wonder what piece of Kensington is this.

The quality of painting on the walls is certainly mixed and the sniffier type of critic may therefore be disposed to underrate the whole. But this collection was made for the subject as well as for the handling of it: it is a tremendous piece of social history as well as a parade of master-craftsmanship by Stubbs, Sartorius, Ben Marshall, Ferneley, Dalby, and the Stable-Door School. If lesser men are allowed in, their theme is the excuse. For they are showing you the 'fun and games' of our people as well of our squires: they are reminding us of Tom and Jerry, of the sportive yokel as well as of the Corinthian play-boys: they are calling to mind how first we came to many an exercise, including the riding of a bicycle.

Consider in that connection Exhibit No. 203, 'Johnson's Pedestrian Hobby Horse Riding School, Published 1819. Artist Unknown.' Top-hatted gentlemen of the period are seated on saddles that are slung between two wheels. They apparently have no pedals, but they seem to walk or trot and then get a kick-off: after that they can put their legs up for a rest as the 'Celeripedes' circle round the smooth surface of Mr. Johnson's arena. The Prince Regent was said to engage in this exercise: presumably this was in his comparatively slender youth. By the time he reached the throne he would hardly have relished the meagre comforts of the Hobby Horse, Dandy Horse, or Celeripede, as it was called according to choice. The Gallery informs us—it provides extremely informative notes and labels in profusion—that the first bicycle was invented by a Scot, Kirkpatrick MacMillan, in 1840. The Velocipede, Penny Farthing, or Boneshaker, arrived, with its monstrous challenge to the rider perched upon its altitudes, in 1865. The celeripede of 1818 seems to offer mild joys: it has a nursery look. But it made wheelers' history and I am grateful to the Gallery for my introduction to it.

Should you be neither rider nor horse lover you may find the amount of equestrian portraiture oppressive. There is certainly a lavish opening of stable-doors, a non-stop visitation of heaths, paddocks, and hunting-fields. But there is no compulsion to look at all of these cavalry-canvases and the visitor who does not stop to draw breath in the Stubbs' room is missing a powerful form of exhilaration. For the very air of a Stubbs' background is tingling: the exquisite morning light seems to be working fruitfully across the miles of level and delicious turf where horses are trained and absorbing the dewy essence of it. The canvas appeals to the lungs and nostrils as well as to the eye and, on such a day of tenebrous cold as I have described, merely to have some vicarious fellowship with that gossamer radiance is to feel a great physical relief; you remember that chests were made for inhalations and not for wheezing and hoasting only. In all the great horse-painters' work, be it old Stubbs or new Munnings, the scene is integrated with the animal. You may not know, in your urban innocence, whether the beast is ' well-ribbed up ' or no, but you can, if you are not completely machine-minded, grasp the horse's place in a pattern, its corner of a trinity whose other members are sky and soil. Man, too, has his niche. There are some striking heads of grooms and jockeys, including a particularly vivid one by Stubbs.

To my non-equestrian eye horses seem to have changed shape quite a deal in a couple of centuries. That arched neck, so

extremely narrow at the summit of the arch, is surely not seen
to-day. The Stubbs' picture of 'Gimcrack,' who has named
Racing Stakes and a Club here and a Club in New York too,
especially emphasises this delicacy of structure. Men and women
have been growing larger for a long time and a ballet dancer
could hardly squeeze her way now into the armour of a Cœur-
de-Lion crusader. But there are some fine fellows on view in the
pugilistic section: Gentleman Jackson and John Gully did not
suffer from delicate arching of the neck. It is interesting to meet
Gully who by his fists and his endurance worked his way from
a debtor's cell in the King's Bench Prison to achieve great
prosperity, to win three Derbys, to beget twenty-four children,
and to represent Pontefract in Parliament. Gully was helped out
of gaol by Hen Pearce, the Game Chicken, who wanted a match,
got it at Hailsham almost on the eve of Trafalgar, and beat the
released Gully—but only in the 59th round!

A look round the Gallery presents a world which throve on
competition. 'Fair shares' into games will not go. Long ago
G. K. Chesterton sagely remarked that the British people are
little concerned about the equality of man, but very much concerned with the inequality of horses: or of whippets or of grey-
hounds, we may add, or of human runners or of boxers or of
football teams. A game of cricket in which every batsman had
to retire on scoring twenty would not draw large 'gates.' So
here is another stimulation which a view of the pictures affords
to us now, the glimpse of a tip-toe world, abounding in bets
and challenges, a world of noblemen continually pitting against
each other not only horse and hound but their own pedestrian
abilities.

I did not discover whether Captain Barclay, dear to me as a
fellow Aberdonian from the banks of Ury, the indomitable foot-
slogger who walked a thousand miles in a thousand hours on
Newmarket Heath, is on view: but, if he is not, his wagering,
hard-walking, hard-driving coevals certainly are. Their England

had plenty of faults we know: it was an Illfare State for millions and Dickens had to come along and paint, for reformation's sake, the kind of prison from which John Gully emerged. But Gully emerged and, once out, went up and up. I pity any shop steward who would have told him not to move so fast.

When we come to our own time the emphasis is still largely equestrian. There is plenty of Munnings on view, brilliant in craftsmanship, sometimes too facile, with those boot-and-saddle countesses rather too radiant to be true. But such pictures have to be taken, I said, as part of a pattern; neither lady nor horse nor silk is the content. Munnings is just as much attached to a shining sky and land in good heart as he is to the silk of the jockeys and a horse in good fettle. I would repeat for those who are not greatly interested in the various sports depicted that these exercises and pastimes are emanations of us and of our earth and that every good sporting print is a piece of landscape too. To me it is even more fascinating to watch an artist's response to country than it is to see his delineation of beast or bird, shot or stroke. The composition of his work is a much larger matter than its centre, a point which the critics of Munnings usually overlook.

In this matter of landscape the Victorian treatment of Scotland shows relics of the eighteenth-century conception of ' horrid peaks,' that is places so bristling as to be intolerable. The Victorians, inspired by their eagerly mountaineering Queen with her passion for Deeside, were ready to tolerate, even to enjoy, the banks, braes, and even the bens of this newly fashionable deer-park that Scotland had become. But they were determined to stress the bristles: they were resolved to have Nature ' with knobs on.' Clouds hung about the knobs, mystic and fearful. The peaks cut these clouds like daggers. In many of the places where the red deer can get a living and so provide a target the mountains are undulant, rhythmic, and comparatively smooth. The surge of most Highland landscape is not ' horrid.' (I admit there are astonishing exceptions in the West, but the stalker does not follow the rock-climber all the way to the bristles.) But for Landseer and his rivals Highland scenery had to play its part in their romantic scheme of values. It was not merely that this was what the public wanted: they painted their own dreams.

There are one or two stag-party scenes in the Gallery in which the peaks are positively Alpine. It was a shock, of course, to gentlemen chiefly accustomed to the Isle of Wight to find themselves in Deeside and they responded by turning every deer forest into a chasm among pinnacles. The painters of to-day are not so easily impressed: they can be content with the noble sweep of a moorland scene and need not split the sky with stilettos of rock. Nor do they follow the sportsman's victim into its final gory moments. If any corpses attract them now, it is those of fish, not of stags. The vast ' larder-scapes,' once so dear to the Dutch artists and sustained to some extent by Landseer's survey of the day's slaughter, have been replaced by modest essays in ' still life '—or more accurately of death. In these a single salmon does most of the work.

It is surprising that golf does not more attract the artist of to-day. The reason, I suppose, must be mainly economic. The golfer, rarely a rich man, is so beset by expenditure on club and clubs, travel, portage—if he can run to a caddy—and the minor outgoings of the game, that he is little likely to think in terms of oil-paintings. In the past the clubs themselves used to commission an occasional portrait of a worthy member or of a captain serviceable in committee and of widely approved popularity. But now the clubs economically collect cabinet photographs of their guides, pillars, and props. Somebody is bound to win the Derby and out of prize money, wagers, and subsequent stud fees he will be rich enough, even now, to commission a painting to suit the high occasion. But what golfing winner of the Amateur Open, this side of America, is in a mood to put down several hundred pounds after getting no monetary reward by his victory and incurring quite startling expenses for travel and lodging in the process?

Yet it is obvious that one or two of our golfers merit the palette and the brush. Leonard Crawley, with his challenging red moustaches, his defiant figure, his rich taste in tweeds and pull-overs, his azure haberdashery—Crawley, seen on the links at Rye, perhaps with that old harbour's modest acropolis in the background, is a subject that ought not to be missed. Golf links may provide rare loveliness of mingled sea-blues and grass-greens: lapped in a wave of spring sunshine they would be as exhilarating on canvas as are those Stubbsian horse-heaths which seem to be lit by the dawn of the world. They offer every species of back-cloth; there are Royal Wimbledon's heathery and triumphant pretence to be at least as far from London as Woking, mid-Surrey's sedate silvanity (thirteen minutes from Waterloo), Gleneagles with its sub-Grampian grandeur, the view of St. Andrews as one turns for home, or of the Bass Rock from North Berwick, the Archerfield woods, the Isle of Arran's leap into the sky seen from the historic links of the Ayrshire coast, and the majesty of Harlech under its castle. What temptations do such places offer to take the eye off the ball! On a hundred downs and dunes there are landscapes in which golf is crying out for pictorial honours. And may not the heroes of these fields be honoured as well as the turf itself?

The bloodless and non-equestrian sports are mostly on view downstairs. Cricket, of course, comes top-hatted down the decades, with the old masters, tiled and braced for action, standing contemplative before delivery of the ball. There are some nice youngsters of the eighteenth century, enjoying an ancestral park and defending a wicket which is really a croquet-hoop with a bat which is really a broomstick.

And why not croquet for the canvas? The slender life of that exquisite game (exquisite, that is, when seriously played) hovers on the lawns of Hurlingham and of the few well-established clubs outside London. Its mixture of chess and billiards on perfect lawns among spectator trees should have its painted chronicles before the sport has been finally condemned as bourgeois, a vermin vice, and the lawns all seized to make sites for Government offices, with a myriad files where once the mallets tapped. All pictures of human figures upon green lawns and fields evoke memories of the petty struggles of one's own and of the major spectacles of battling giants that one has watched in amazement, so indomitable was their spirit, so incalculable their skill.

If there is cricket being played on a village green or open town ground in England, the loiterers will be there; cars will stop and bicyclists dismount to give the entertainment ten minutes of their time. And so, in a public gallery, paintings of cricket always take the eye, with the delicate blue skies, the simple tents and pavilions, and the solemnity of the fielders. (How capable were these beaver-hatted warders? Sometimes one sees two rows on the off-side, each man requiring a reserve, like the long-stop behind the wicket-keeper: it does not suggest much certainty in getting down to the ball.)

Football has a picture or two for each code. Prince Obolensky's second amazing try for England against the All Black New Zealand team (1936) is on record, painted by Stanley Wilson in an action-picture of the most vigorous kind. Chelsea and Arsenal, of the great Association teams, are given place: and well might the former be honoured. Since the two main occupations of the riverside borough are painting and football surely the painters might pay some regard to their athletic colleagues who share the task of bringing glory to Chelsea. In that case Bloomsbury should be no less proud of Highbury where their nearest team, Arsenal, has won so many triumphs. But when did the Gordon Square School or the Camden Towner give a thought to Denis Compton or the flash of red upon their green field to the north?

The grace of games—it was among the primal discoveries of

that skin-clad *homo* who was struggling towards sapience. The first artists were the first hunters: defying all our notions of slow progress up and up and of capacity evolving amid experiment, they began with a blaze of pictorial genius in the caves and galleries of Spain and Central France. Their accomplishment is amazing: if to depict the chase well is, by aid of magic, to succeed in it, which is a common interpretation of the caveman artist's motive, then the hunting must have been very good indeed. After that the ancient civilisations celebrated, in poetry as in sculpture, the human exercise as well as the utilarian chase: the games, with their runners and wrestlers, their throwers of weights and javelins, were not only festivals of the Gods, as at Olympia: they were occasions for the artist. The sculptors gathered round the athlete-hero, since here was physical man at his finest: and the poets sang the spirit of the victor, the tenacity of will, the ardours, the endurances.

The Greeks put athletes into their Odes with the same honour that they paid to their heroes in war and even with the same tender affection that they gave to the flowers of the field or the beauties of a sunset city, ' violet-crowned.' In their world the track and the circus were fountains of verbal beauty as well as studios for sculptors. Games were in heaven too. The dead joined the living in this relish of the physical good. Their Valhalla was not a feasting-place of beef-witted lords proclaiming to all the sensual world that immortality was just a bonus issue of women and of wassail. The Elysian fields had a delicate air. Pindar imagined the dead in a pleasaunce ' cool beneath the shade of incense-bearing trees and rich with golden fruit.' There they took what strenuous delights they chose in the fragrance of untroubled skies, joying

> In chariot-race or young-limbed *exercise*
> In wrestling, at the game of tables *these*,
> And those with lute and harp.

This mixture of muscle and music the Elizabethans would have understood; our 'hearties' of the football field have become less eager for harmony. But, as the Gallery shows, far away from Olympus and on our wetter, greener fields, grace and games have gone together.

The Victorians had their own, quite different ideas about the advantages of athletics. Games for them were simply counsellors on the importance of being earnest. Austerely they would stress not the beauty, but the benefit of nimbleness with bat and ball. They emphasised the ethical and hygienic side of sport, especially the ethical. To Bowen, the Harrow schoolmaster, and his pedagogues of kindred temper, Games—they merit a capital letter in this case—were almost a manifestation of Godhead. Games sweated out the Satan of sex and, by their stimulation of healthy rivalries, sharpened the virtuous will while they blunted the unhealthy passions. Cricket was especially seized upon as the Great Improver: the few feet of turf around the wicket became, in this philosophy, the forge of human character.

In the Academies for Young Ladies, which began closely to imitate the Academies for Young Gentlemen, the same cleansing and uplifting quality was attributed to the games of hockey, a potentially savage exercise, and even of the milder net-ball. 'Run, girls, run' was the new slogan parallel to 'Play up and play the game.' There was no doubt in the mind of the school-ma'am that galloping did good, and no doubt too in the mind of the schoolmaster-cleric that athletics were a branch of ethics. I remember being in Nottingham once when a Cricket Test Match against Australia was being played at Trent Bridge. A large notice outside a chapel advised all of us bound for the Bridge, there to absorb the slow-moving pleasures of Test batsmanship, that we were attending an occasion of grave moral significance. The minister would address all-comers on Sunday on the necessity of 'Keeping a Straight Bat in Life.' This particular selection of Cricket as the great purge of vicious tendencies and uplifter of good, young lives is all the more odd since the milords who first led English cricket teams on to the fields of our southern Counties were hard-drinking rakes who betted heavily on the result and were not above curious practices to secure a win.

It used to be an accepted belief that if you scratch an English-men you find a Protestant and even a Puritan. It is hardly true now, but there is still a strong tendency to rationalise the love of games, which is natural, by solemnly endowing these antics with moral attributes. But while we are thus excusing our simple and inherent taste for physical fun, cannot we also claim that sport is justified by its appearances? To look at a wall of Stubbs beside a landscape of Constable is to appreciate the quality of a country-side: to move on to a Zoffany, with an emparked Palladian mansion behind its reflective owner and his cricketing boys, is to appreciate some of the queer, extravagant creatures who made our heritage and left us lawns and spaniels, colonnades and cricket-bats.

Stressing the beauty of games may lead to mawkishness: I certainly do not invite the reader to sit, like a whinnying Bunthorne, on the boundary or the touch-line, a mimminy-pimminy creature, exquisitely rapt. We can leave all that to the *balletomanes*. There is a middle path and the Greeks, with their genius for the golden mean, took it, steering between Bowenism and Bunthornery, between the ethical exultation of the schoolmaster when he watches a desperately contested match and the affected rejoicing of the very æsthetic spectator who pretends to ecstasies at Lord's Cricket Ground or any other arena of fashionable sport. A common-sensible enjoyment, assisted by the artist, of the coloured counties and of days in the sun is made pleasantly possible by the Gallery which Walter Hutchinson founded and housed.

So here is a chance of escape into calm, as well as into colour, when the press of Christmas shopping or of January sales turns Oxford Street into a place of torment. Turn up Stratford Place

and the clatter and the jostling cease. When he is behind the
doors that once were Lord Derby's the commoner of to-day has
the gaming grandees, with all their pride in hawk and horse and
hound, at his leisurely disposal. Also, if the town oppresses until
the senses ache, here is the other panorama wherein man and
horse and field are fused under the soft and lucent skies of
English mornings.

> *Inebriate of air am I*
> *And debauchee of dew,*
> *Reeling, through endless summer days,*
> *From inns of molten blue.*

Emily Dickinson's innocent alcoholism is not easily achieved in a
London day of frost and fog, on the overflowing pavements of
the haberdashers' headquarters and among the smart shoe shops
and the stores besieged. But slip aside into Stratford Place and
here is the next best thing. Some sort of inebriation awaits you.

CHAPTER XI

Among the Wells

———⋘⋙———

LONDON IS now such a monster that its working problems must be a continual fascination to the curious. How does such an enormity feed itself, water itself, and drain itself? To me it is a perpetual marvel not so much that sufficient food exists, but that it can be got round to those ten millions of the city, suburban, and Home County region. You do not very often see shops taking the stuff in. But there, somehow, it is. One reply is, of course, that I am not a sufficiently early riser to observe those distributive operations; but, even allowing for early morning market-work and cartage, the dispersal of all the bulky goods is a considerable achievement. Go, for example, to some vast area which is not handy for the Central Markets—these thoughts occurred to me in the huge, drab Acton region—and it is amazing that enough gets there every day. How many tons of bread and potatoes do the Actonians stow away in twenty-four hours? Yet, as you go by, you do not see much stopping and unloading.

Then there is the task of watering these hordes; and nowadays the hordes need much more water than of old. There was a time when to talk of the Great Unwashed was not just a sardonic jest. People, even if eager to be clean, had neither the baths nor the water to put in them. Water until Jacobean times was something to be fetched from a local well, by your own labour if

you were poor, or purchased from a water-carrier if you had the
money for such luxury. The laying-on of water-supply was a
seventeenth-century achievement. Those who like wandering in
Clerkenwell and Islington should lift their hats to the statue of
Sir Hugh Myddleton, who stands with his back to Collins's
Music Hall in Islington Green, facing the City which he so
hygienically served.

Lower down the hill lies Myddleton Square named after him.
He created the New River Water Company, obtaining a contract
in 1609 with the Corporation of London to make a river which
would carry the product of the Hertfordshire streams and springs
by way of Islington into London. This salutary enterprise nearly
ruined him and the Corporation was stingy when trouble came.
But Scottish James had a more provident, kingly, and canny
outlook. He bullied or cajoled the Treasury into advancing
£8600 to the New River Works, reasonably obtaining some
shares for the Crown, a good bargain both for king and commoners. By 1613 the New River was developed to the extent
of thirty-eight miles, Myddleton got one of the new-fangled
baronetcies, and London had a proper conduit of clean water
for its rapidly growing population. Between Myddleton Square
and Rosebery Avenue was the New River Head, whose old
reservoir was ultimately taken over by the Metropolitan Water
Board: the Board's big offices are still properly located there.
For the Board, London's life-giver and life-preserver, was, in
part, Myddleton's child.

London always had its separate springs and wells and we can
tell where the important ones were by the number and locality
of streets and districts which had 'well' for their termination.
But when thousands are turned into millions, rustic springs are
insufficient and village wells are but a fortuitous succour of the
multiplying need.

The vast city, with its rim of gentle hills, a rim chipped,
fortunately by the River Thames and the River Lea, and so not

continuous, is really a clay saucer. Cut through the clay and water could be reached; that was the old assumption. But in our time the lake beneath London has been much exhausted by the sinking of deep artesian wells. There was a strong economic motive for this. The water-rates levied on a vast hotel or block of offices were naturally heavy and new builders sought to circumvent the Water Board and its charges by scooping up water for themselves and utilising, by their own engineering skill, the resources of London's subterranean pools. But they have now, in many cases, been defeated; the water comes up insufficiently or muddily because the lake below the city's basement is giving out. Consequently it has frequently been found necessary to admit defeat, to turn to the Water Board, and to take, at a cost, the service of its mains. A case in point is that huge fortress of offices, Bush House, at the bottom of Aldwych. Its attempt at self-help petered out.

The explanation lies in the destruction, by building development, of water-holding land. It is obvious that streets and pavements, equipped with gutters and drains, rapidly decant the rainfall from their impenetrable surfaces; the water, which once was held for a while by the tenacious soil and then seeped slowly down into wells, springs, and the subterranean London Lake, is swilled clean away from slate, cement, and macadam and sent hurriedly into main drains and so into the river and the sea. It is a form of waste on the grand scale, but inevitable. That does not greatly matter so long as London can rely on its major rivers, which run through the clay saucer, and on the storage of their surplus in the huge new reservoirs built farther out in the Thames and Lea Valleys. But a few weeks of dry, hot weather soon cause alarm and the orders for economy are made. The suburban lawn must remain parched and the motor-car must stay unwashed. London seems to be living with a fairly small margin of aquatic safety. This is not a criticism of the Metropolitan Water Board and kindred regional authorities. It is the inescapable result of this mad massing of population in a comparatively small area.

The menace of drought works by double process. Every time we build a new suburb or a satellite town the water-gathering land is diminished because the soil which first holds and then filters the rainfall down to join the subterranean supply is replaced by roofs and roads which get rid of it as soon as possible. While less is retained, more is demanded. The many square miles of new urbanism cry out for water on an ever increasing scale, since the bathroom, which used to be a rarity, is becoming a commonplace and the washing of all manner of things, from the bodies of motor-cars to those of human beings, grows more and more lavish.

So the demand for piped water accelerates as the heaven-sent water is hurled away. All round London, the once water-storing rims of the saucer in the near Chilterns and on the North Downs, are being transformed by the makers of towns, suburbs, roads, roofs, and drains, into water-users. My own prophecy is that, if London is to go on growing, which it certainly should not do and almost certainly will do, pipes will have to be laid to the distant mountainous areas with their great natural cisterns, that is if London is to get through its summers without distress. It may be expensive to do our washing and rinsing by courtesy of Snowdon and Ben Nevis—the Pennines are amply engaged in watering the industrial North—but that may have to come if we work the Thames and Lee to excess. One may think this to be impossible when the February rains are beating on our heads with a merciless chill force and continuity, when the rivers are over their banks, and when reports and pictures of floods fill the papers and the news-reels. But the searing east winds of the spring, followed by a dry May and June, soon alter the balance and bring forcibly to mind the fact that London can drink and wash itself into scarcity and even into peril if it continues to war against Nature's own way of accumulating water underground, so that it may be drawn up again from the wells.

How important this business of the wells could be for those who did not share the benefits of the New River is shown by an occurrence in Muswell Hill, the hill of the Moss-well, or some say Mouse-well: the former sounds more hygienic. Only ninety years ago the public right to use this serviceable well was challenged by the owner of the estate on which it lay. His interference caused grave hardship. It was difficult to sink new wells thereabouts because of the depth of the clay and the less clayey spots were in rich men's grounds. There was a long quarrel and the matter went to the Law Courts. The public interest was upheld, but it is proof that little civic policy and development existed in 1860 if the water supply of a growing and prosperous suburb could depend on a few wells liable to be cut off from public usage.

Should I want to take a lunch-time walk in the Well Country, there is no problem of time or space. It is easy and it is also instructive, being water, water all the way. I actually start, south of Fleet Street, on top of one well, the Bride Well. Then, if I take a No. 44 bus from the Fleet Ditch to the Angel, Islington, I go by way of Goswell Road, which presumably was once the way to the Goose Well. And so to Clerkenwell, the Well of the Clerks or Clerics: here is (or was) a whole bubble of springs, including Sadler's Wells—and the now vanished Bagnigge Wells. John Burns aptly called the Thames liquid history: the compliment applies no less to this part of North London: Clerkenwell is a fountain chronicle.

The Clerks', or Clerics' Well, was the scene of scriptural play-acting in the Middle Ages: indeed, the records of this now unlovely, but still somehow fascinating, corner of London, are rich in two things, play-acting and radical politics. In Shakespeare's time the Red Bull Theatre, which survived to be mentioned by Pepys, was a house of the new professional theatre which had supplanted the well-side mumming of the Clerks. Leonard Digges, who wrote commendatory verses for Shakespeare's Poems in 1640, bade the needy Poetasters of this Age not attempt to rival his hero.

> But, if you needs must write, if poverty
> So pinch, that otherwise you starve and die,
> On God's name may the Bull or Cockpit have
> Your lame blancke Verse to keepe you from the grave.

Edward Alleyn, benefactor of Dulwich, was playing in Clerkenwell after the death of Shakespeare and of Burbage.

Clerkenwell has a direct link with Shakespeare which anyone may see by turning East out of Farringdon Street. That is St. John's Gate and the rooms over the arch; this was luckily spared in that air-raid which blasted the famous Clerkenwell Church of St. John, an eighteenth-century rebuilding of a medieval priory church which had once been roughly handled by Wat Tyler's insurgents in 1381. The Gate is the surviving relic of the wealthy priory of the Knights Hospitallers of the Order of St. John of Jerusalem, and is the headquarters now of the St. John's Ambulance Brigade. It is a handsome oddity, standing there close to the bustle of the Farringdon Street commerce of to-day.

Clerkenwell, as I said, brings theatre to mind: first because at the Gatehouse in the eighteenth century there was Cave's Printing Office, source of the *Gentleman's Magazine*, for which Dr. Johnson wrote: Cave's workers and acquaintances provided David Garrick with his first London audience in the Priory Council Chamber over the archway. This same Gatehouse had been the home of Edmund Tilney, Master of the Revels, whose license was necessary (and granted) for nearly all Shakespeare's plays. Tilney's task was a thorny one, for both Crown and City were nervous of irreverent allusions on the stage and he strove to keep the peace between the players and the Very Important People. Shakespeare may have been summoned to the Clerkenwell Gatehouse to discuss the possibility of this passage or of that giving offence. The sight of the old grey arch is a reminder of that Tudor London in whose suburbs, such as Clerkenwell and Shoreditch in the north, as well in Southwark across the river, it was safe to perform plays, masques, and interludes. The City would have none of this perilous nonsense as it deemed play-acting to be. Safe that is, if you were on the right side of Tilney of Clerkenwell.

Radical politics meet you when you turn into Clerkenwell Green, which is not a green now but a square, or more accurately an oblong, with the look of belonging to a country town. There is a whitish, pedimented building, low and solid and serene, which strongly proclaims its title and function. It is the Karl Marx Memorial Library. This is a Left Wing library and reading-room which lives on comradely subscriptions and arranges meetings and discussions. It was once the headquarters of the old Social Democratic Federation, led by the wealthy, bourgeois Marxian, H. M. Hyndman. Hyndman gave an office here to a refugee called Lenin at the beginning of the century. Lenin brought out in Clerkenwell a paper called *The Spark*, written and printed in Russian. Pushkin, the poet, had said of some previous revolutionary efforts that they were mere sparks. Lenin replied that sparks make conflagrations and here was one that would. In the end he was abundantly correct. Amid the Cockneydom of Edwardian Clerkenwell the dynamite was being prepared for 'Ten Days That Shook the World.' You can see the little office that was loaned to him and a copy of *The Spark* on the table.

Now British aristocracy decorates the rooms where the Russian aristocrat, Ulianoff or Lenin, rebel and refugee, had laboured in obscurity. The large mural painting of Labour surrounded by his paladins Marx, Morris, and many moderns, has been painted, and very well painted, by the present Earl of Huntingdon. The Earl studied painting under Rivera in Mexico: he has taken up Labour politics and has been a Junior Minister.

One has a feeling that he might, if he chose, be a senior artist. At any rate, like Lenin, who lived up at Holford Square near King's Cross while he worked in Clerkenwell Green, he has made his mark upon the region. Other active politicians of the area were those Fenians who tried to blow up, for purposes of rescue, the Clerkenwell House of Detention in 1867. They achieved a considerable bang, but their revolutionary detonation was on the parochial scale compared with Lenin's.

Part of the required reading for the enjoyment of Clerkenwell is Arnold Bennett's *Riceyman Steps*. Often London seemed to be a city which eluded the recording genius of the Five Towns. It has been said that, when Bennett left the Staffordshire of his birth and upbringing, he also left his mastery of craft behind him. *Riceyman Steps* disproves that completely. It is a London book, breathing and smelling Clerkenwell. It is also a superb essay in the macabre style. The miserly bookseller, Mr. Earlforward, and the widow whom he takes to wife, Mrs. Arb— the very names reveal a major inspiration—are intensely vivid creations; greater still is Elsie, their starving drudge, loyal, affectionate, and only rebellious when the emptiness of a skinflint larder has driven her to stealing scraps of bacon and eating them raw, or when her love for the forlorn and down-and-out Joe drives her to a noble defiance.

Bennett's *Riceyman Steps* led from the King's Cross Road to Riceyman Square. It has been generally supposed that he was describing Granville Square and the steps leading to it in the year 1919. The miser Earlforward's book-store stood at the base of the steps, opposite Mrs. Arb's fly-blown confectioner's shop. ' He dreamed that one day he would explain to her eager ear that once Clerkenwell was a murmuring green land of medicinal springs, wells, streams with mills on their banks, nunneries, aristocrats, and holy clerks who presented mystery plays.' (Bennett, perhaps, did not know about Lenin.) The Steps remain: but there are no houses beside them, except a few ' pre-fabs ' on the site of something bombed. Clerkenwell had its war-time 'packet' and Mr. Earlforward, had he lived to face and survive the bombs, would never have survived the shock of the war-time and post-war prices.

Granville Square has risen in the world and spruced itself up considerably since the days of Bennett's Riceyman Square, in which every house had a broken window: yet the frowst within was then so well established in time and so powerful in quality that mere currents of air from fractured panes could make no perceptible inroads on the atmosphere. The Square of those years had no electricity or telephones in its decaying houses of degenerate Regency style. It was a slum. But not so our Granville Square which now contains a golf goods depot—imagine Mr. Earlforward joining a golf club!—and has housed a well-known theatrical decorator. It is not quite a 'classy' Square, as Lloyd Square behind it has become. Lloyd Square, with its pairs of two-storey houses linked with triangular pediments, a charming essay in classical domesticity and Athenian villadom, is a piece of design that sets a smile upon the otherwise frowning slopes above the King's Cross Road. No walk up the hill to Islington should omit a glimpse at Granville Square and some dalliance in Lloyd.

After the hideous devastation of 1940-45, Clerkenwell's previous upheavals must look small. Yet, in their own day, they had seemed tremendous. The Victorian pioneers in 1861 drove the Underground railway beneath this difficult terrain, difficult because of the wells and springs and buried rivers. Tunnelling became a most challenging problem for the engineers, working among these ancient conduits. Bennett has described in a lively historical passage, how

'All Clerkenwell was mad for the line. But when the construction began all Clerkenwell trembled. The earth opened in the most unexpected and undesirable places. Streets had to be barred to horse traffic; pavements resembled switchbacks. Hundreds of houses had to be propped, and along the line of the tunnel itself scores of houses were suddenly vacated lest they should bury their occupants. The sacred workhouse came near to dissolution, and was only saved by inconceivable timberings. The still more sacred Cobham's Head public-house was first shaken and torn with cracks and then inundated by the bursting of the New River main, and the landlady died of shock.'

Yet worse was to come. The excavations at the mouth of the tunnel near Clerkenwell Green led to disaster. The pavements sagged and sank above the tunnel: the supports of it collapsed. Then the Fleet River, which had long been the Fleet Sewer, burst out in a hideous and septic flood, and created, for a while, confusion's masterpiece. But North London was not to be beaten: the clearing up of the hideous mess was achieved; the work was begun again. The railway came, dirty and stinking by our standards, the smoky, poky Underground of the pre-electric age. But it kept most of its dirt to its own subterranean self. While Clerkenwell carried on its commerce and its 'small business' crafts of jewellery and printing upon its familiar surface, City gentlemen were being transported by steam among the pipes and conduits of the Well Country from Kensington to the City, by way of Euston and that old Battlebridge which had later become King's Cross. And the tamed Fleet Sewer once more flowed obediently under Farringdon Street to disembogue in the Thames by Ludgate Circus.

Clerkenwell's place-names are rural in the Green and the Close (expect no verdure!) while postal Mount Pleasant proclaims amenities which it scarcely owns. The waters of Hertfordshire, harnessed to London's use by Myddleton, are remembered in the street names, Chadwell and Anwell, which are springs near Ware. There is a River Street. There is New River Head, with its imposing headquarters of the Metropolitan Water Board. There is great spaciousness too in some of the squares, notably that of Myddleton, which has been laid out on a scale of

Belgravian splendour. Hither came Elsie of *Riceyman Steps* to fetch the doctor for her pinched and perishing employers. Myddleton Square, centred on its church of St. Mark, a church large enough to be a minor cathedral, is testimony to the high civic ambitions of the new Clerkenwell that was climbing out up the hill to Islington and climbing also in pride of purse and power to build for an abounding and a prosperous middle class. You can imagine Mr. Podsnap surveying Myddleton Square with a confident assurance that no foreigner could do the like.

Beyond Myddleton Square the wanderer may find himself stopped by a flutter of fine robes. During my last walk at the top of Rosebery Avenue they were carrying in the wardrobe and décor for a new ballet at Sadler's Wells, and the street was in flower with silks. Clerkenwell was being true to itself, for Clerkenwell has been miming and clowning ever since Richard II, with a nicer taste than that of his beevish barons, watched the clerks devoutly performing *The Passion of Our Lord and the Creation of the World*, a drama which was spread over three days. His Majesty may not have stayed the course. Another play of this devotional kind took eight days. We do not hear of the King returning for that Marathonic mummery.

The Wells Country, which once had Nell Gwynne for an occupant at Bagnigge House, was a place of popular resort and therefore of play-acting. The King's Cross Road will scarcely seem impressive to anyone to-day in its old role of Gaiety Avenue, but it was once the Bagnigge Wells Road and Bagnigge Wells had its own life of revel as well as of salubrity. In this dip between the Gray's Inn Road and the slopes of Clerkenwell there was Bagnigge House, used after Nell Gwynne's time for general pleasuring: it had its long room for gaming folk, for tattle, and for refreshment; there was a well-watered garden with fish ponds and among its lawns a tributary of the still existing Fleet River. The tenant of Bagnigge Wells went bankrupt in 1813 and among the assets sold to pay his debts were two hundred drinking tables and four hundred dozen of bottled ale. So these Wells did not spout water only.

Far more important was Sadler's Wells, Georgian headquarters of Grimaldi the Clown, Victorian stage of Phelps the Shakespearean, and now the home of a Ballet company which has climbed from fairly humble beginnings to the highest peaks of international renown. Opera too is a Clerkenwell product, dear, especially on Verdi nights, to the little Italy of that area, associated with Saffron Hill, but also a magnet to the whole of London.

The name of Sadler goes back to the seventeenth century. A pamphlet of 1684 informs us that the new well at Islington is a spring in the middle of a garden belonging to the musick-house on the north side of the great cistern that receives the New River Water. Before the Reformation this spring had been deemed holy and a source of miraculous cures: it was exploited by the priests from Clerkenwell Priory, who cozened the people into believing that their prayers enabled the waters to do the trick. The Reformers would have none of this; to stop it they blocked up the well as being an object of superstitious regard: but Mr. Sadler opened up the freshet once again, showed some of the supposedly magic water to a doctor, and was told that he had better brew beer with it. He seems, however, to have saved himself the trouble and cost of starting a brewery by selling abundant wines and spirits with which to wash down the water.

Ned Ward leaves us in no doubt that holiness and hygiene had altogether left 'the Wells' by 1700. It had become as rough and raffish a resort as the Tudor Bankside. You might not then be able to see bears and bulls baited where now Miss Fonteyn dances, but you could watch a fellow, for a wager of five pounds, eat a live cock, feathers, entrails, and all, with a plate of oil and vinegar for sauce and half a pint of brandy for cordial. He rested for two hours and then renewed the feat. The same revolting ogre was said to have devoured a live cat on another occasion. The crowd who enjoyed such disgusting spectacles

were the riff-raff of the town, but the quality would come out
and sit in the organ loft of Miles's Musick Room, as it later
became, and watch their fellow-men having their fun (including
these feats of gluttony) or they would take part in the singing and
dancing. Though a newcomer—Miles gave his name to the
Musick Room—the Wells have remained Sadler's to this day.

The next tenant was a Mr. Forcer and after him came Mr.
Rosoman, whose name still survives in a street leading down
from Finsbury Town Hall towards Clerkenwell Green. He
substituted a new theatre for the old Musick Room, but saw to
it that the drinking facilities were more than adequate. A ticket
for the boxes cost 3s. and included a pint of port or punch. Pit
and gallery were 1s. 6d. and 1s. and included a pint of either
drink, if a surcharge of 6d. were paid. A good time was had by
all and Rosoman flourished for some years. Among subsequent
lessors were Mr. Siddons and Charles Dibdin.

To be a fountain in a dry land is to be a source of pleasure
and of profit. The existence of the Clerkenwell springs and the
coming of the New River, under Myddleton's diligent persuasion,
gave all sorts of chances to this area. Sadler's Wells Theatre
became famous later on for its lavish nautical effects and for
clowning. The actual waters made the fortune of the area, not
merely as offering a spa centre and green banks for alfresco fun
and games and for drinking and feeding, but also as a supplier
of theatrical effects. The Leicester Square Hippodrome, in my
boyhood, offered exciting aquatic spectacles by sacrificing some
of its stalls and drawing on the resources of the Water Board
to fill the hole thus made. At the old Sadler's Wells the manager
could turn on his natural tap. His water-nymphs were not just
young ladies fancifully pirouetting on his stage: they were most
precious servants, delivering the real thing in the basement. In
Ackermann's *Microcosm of London*, 1808, there is a plate by
Pugin showing an aquatic spectacle in the sumptuous four-tiered
theatre which Sadler's Wells had then become.

Later on London enjoyed the Wells of Sir Arthur Pinero's *Trelawny* and of the great Edmund Phelps. From 1844 to 1862 he restored to our stage the original texts of Shakespeare which had been replaced for three hundred years by actor-managerial garblings, by drastic revisions, and by wanton alterations. But perhaps the greatest figure and local genius of the Wells was Joseph Grimaldi. If anybody should haunt the once verdant and watery hill that runs up to the Angel Inn it is surely that famous clown who, though he died at Woolwich, was buried beside the Pentonville Road of his triumphs. His real name was Brooker; as Grimaldi he was linked with Clerkenwell and its pantomimes for thirty years; he survived in London's grateful memory for many decades after. Not to have seen Grimaldi was to be quite out of things in the London of the Napoleonic wars.

Joseph Grimaldi's striking achievement was to make the Clown, not Harlequin, the star attraction of the pieces in which he appeared. This he especially did in the *Mother Goose* pantomime of 1805. Like many great drolls he wore himself out before he reached old age; so much of his humour had been physical and exhausting. He was a daring tumbler and in the course of his career he put up with a great variety of kickings and drubbings; he united with this physical long-suffering and resource a great mental ingenuity in his ' constructions '; in these he turned ordinary articles of use and wont into the fantastic furniture of his game of let's-pretend.

It is foolish in these days to look at a text of his popular songs; great clownage is unscriptable, if such an adjective may be invented to meet the modern jargon of script and script-writer. ' Hot Coddlings ' in cold print now reads like the feeblest non-sense; yet that ditty was the undoubted delight of its hour. But it is always idle to describe what clownship actually did or said. Heaven forbid that we should hear Yorick's actual quips! Let nobody try to tell me in detail the patter and ' business ' of Dan Leno, whom I never saw. From his pictures and from the Leno legend I can imagine the man: I do not ask for his text. A great critical writer can give you the quiddity of a clown and paint in his own words the rich essence of the droll's absurdity. The recorder will prudently abstain from setting down the very words that were spoken. Grimaldi must remain a piece of that excellent and abounding London magic which from time to time bewitches the multitude; usually the magician is a rather frail and woebegone figure, beset with frustration, yet somehow emerging from under the legs of oppression to assault and outwit the pomp and power of authority. Charlie Chaplin, as most people know, came from Kennington on the other side of the river. It would have been seemly had he spent his boyhood in Clerkenwell; I associate his spirit with the Wells.

There used to be several taverns near Sadler's Wells with names and traditions that bound them in devotion to the craft of Harlequin and Clown. But the havoc created there during the war has been very great and some have gone. But the Harlequin and the Shakespeare Head are to be found just behind Sadler's Wells. I cannot find a Grimaldi Street or tavern: there should be both.

If new inns there are to be in Clerkenwell they should celebrate the new as well as the old conquerors of this region of the springs and slopes. The Sadler's Wells Ballet of our time began as a fairly humble appendage of the 'Old Vic' Shakespeare company, but it has risen, like its elder brother, to world-renown and its tour of 1949 in the U.S.A. spread its conquests on a colossal scale. To Ninette de Valois, who has built so high upon such difficult foundations—for there was no State Aid when she began—a proper salute should be made upon the spot. Here is a case for inspired statuary.

Surely we have some sculptor who could adequately catch the spirit of ballet and set the new genius of the Wells in stone beside the theatre. (I do not suggest Mr. Henry Moore for the job.) It is surely reasonable that the large premises of the Metropolitan

Water Board, at New River Head close to Sadler's Wells, should carry some testament in stone or bronze both to the water-nymphs of this Wells Country, who have given it such powers of serving London's thirsty need, and to the human sprites of the local stage who have bestowed such remarkable honour, here and abroad, upon the house first used by the pioneer of pleasure in North London, the original Mr. Sadler. The designing of fountains and of aquatic gardens with grouped statuary, as well as with trees and flowers, is an art in which the Scandinavians have greatly excelled, as any visitor to their cities, and most notably to Stockholm, discovers with gratitude. Stockholm is especially rich in fountains with animal figures, lightly, wittily moulded, as well as with nymphs and goddesses. What better patron to evoke and evolve a similar skill in this country than a Water Board? And what better place than the end of Myddleton's historic conduit and a high scene of London's pleasuring and play-acting ever since Thomas Sadler laid out his lawns and ornamental waters in 1684 and housed his first high jinks?

Strolling in this part of London I wonder about the part that hygiene plays in history. On the whole it is surely underrated by the historians, who used to think in terms of great men and their battles and now think in terms of great economic forces and great social pressures. Science, as a destroying force, is tragically the arbiter of world-events to day. Yet science, as a healer, has shaped the growth of nations more than the books allow; Hugh Myddleton was not a scientist; he was an Anglo-Welsh engineer whose father had been governor of Denbigh Castle; he was a goldsmith, and worked copper mines in Wales, especially in Cardigan; this gave him a considerable experience of mining, tunnelling, draining and embanking. He saw, as the men wise in other matters had not seen, the imperative need of clean water for London and, by bringing it from Hertfordshire to Clerkenwell, he gave a lead to sanitary engineering and made it possible for London to grow as it has done without continual water shortage and epidemics.

Perhaps the aquatic engineers have been too clever by this time. Might it not have been to the general advantage if the various Water Boards of the London and suburban areas had taken a firm line? They might have said, ' So far and no farther. We cannot guarantee supply if you keep squandering land with your everlasting building development. You must place your new towns—towns, not dormitory suburbs—farther out. You must space them strategically, with one eye on the water that you will need and can reasonably get and the other eye on the water you will lose by building and draining and generally dehydrating many square miles of water-yielding land.'

However that may be, there is no doubt that Sir Hugh Myddleton did far more . for London and its people than is generally acknowledged. Such private enterprise rarely gets public reward and Myddleton's case was the usual one. He got little but nominal compensation for his labours: he was given a title, which cost the country nothing, but there was no dividend paid for eighteen years on his substantial investment of cash and care in tunnels, cuttings, and aqueducts. It was said of him that his success was in reality his ruin: he had to put his New River shares on the market and live henceforward by his earnings as a mining engineer. So ' the wicked capitalist,' not for the first or last time in our history, enriched the public by his initiative far more than he ever enriched himself by any financial gain therefrom.

Myddleton brought London a chance of better health and he also gave it a chance of extinguishing the fires which continually ravaged the town. The New River Reservoir was formally ' opened ' with an inrush of Hertfordshire waters on September 29, 1613, after five years work. Shakespeare's Globe Theatre had been burned to the ground just three months before the arrival of the New River on the slopes where the Master of the Revels

(Edmund Tilney) kept house at what is now St. John's Gate. The contemporary notions of fire-fighting were slender and not all Myddleton's water was of any avail to save the old City from the devastation of 1666. But we may assume that both epidemics and fires would have been far worse without his pipeline to the north. So, as I previously urged, let us give a grateful thought to Sir Hugh as we pass him standing handsomely on his plinth in Islington Green; if man is to salute Prometheus, the discoverer of fire and flame, the giver of warmth and cookery, why no salaam to the water-bringers who carry fire's precious opposite to the teeming millions of our cities?

Clerkenwell, as described by Arnold Bennett and as known by many a medical officer in fact, has been a considerable recipient of unsatisfactory types with little regard for the health of themselves or other people. But it has also been the curer. There is the very old story of the doctor who recommended an evening with Grimaldi as a cure, only to discover that his patient was Grimaldi. No doubt this most beloved of our Joeys, blanched and raddled for the ring or the stage, did assist the good health of the town while he knocked himself to bits with his antics. Myddleton's salve for a pest-ridden City was of another and more obvious kind, but his 'long drink of cold water' was undoubtedly salubrious and much in social need.

But it is time to move north and follow the way of the waters to Islington. The New River runs mainly under Islington now, instead of through it, but Islington was always aquatic. Iseldon, corruptly called Islington, has given the scholars and antiquarians plenty of hard work.

Isendune, Isendone, Iseltone, Hisselton, Hyseldone, Yseldon and Eyseldon, are the various forms of the name which present themselves for Islington at various periods. Of these, Isendune, Isendon, and Iseltone occur in *Doomsday Book:* and Isendone in the most ancient records of the church of St. Paul's. Lysons, and others, think that this means the Hill of Iron, because various chalybeate springs are found in this neighbourhood. The name, however, of Iseldon occurring in *Doomsday Book*, induces Sharon Turner to derive it from Ysseldune, or the down of the Yssel, supposed to be the original name of the River of Wells, which fell into the Fleet River. Mr. Tomlins, in his *Antiquarian Perambulation of Islington*, thinks that Ysel, or Eysel, is the same as Ousel, the diminutive of Ouse or Eyse, the British for either a river or water, and, therefore, means the town of the river.

One thing certainly emerges from this. Islington, like Clerkenwell, has been a useful sponge; squeeze and it oozes.

Before the New River came through it Islington was famous for its duck and its dairies. Sir William Davenant, who claimed to be Shakespeare's natural son, rhymed the holiday pleasures of the Cockney sportsman of his day:

> Ho! Ho! To Islington, enough
> Fetch Job, my son, and our dog Ruffe;
> For there in pond, through mire and muck,
> We'll cry, ' Hey, duck—there Ruffe!—hey duck.'

Such was the popular fowling that flourished with its hurly-burly where now is the Balls Pond Road. Along with this sport went archery—between Islington and Finsbury were the training grounds for bowmen. There were also bowling, running, and jumping in plenty.

The fields and marshes of Islington were the north London playground of the seventeenth and eighteenth century. Pepys says that his father carried him there as a boy to eat cakes and ale at the King's Head, but that he was foxed on re-seeking the ducking-ponds in later life. He lost his way and did not know where he was: possibly the King's Head, revisited, helped him to his confusion. The old ' ducking-ponds ' were ponds for the sheltering (and subsequent shooting) of duck, not for ducking scolds and other human nuisances. But probably some of the latter discipline accompanied the spirit of the fowlers. At the dairies syllabubs and refreshments of all kinds were ready for the

spent archers or for the ' duckers ' to renew their vigour. Taverns
abounded in which to celebrate success or console the unskilful
or unfortunate.

Once you set foot in Upper Street, Islington, even in these
days, the broad thoroughfare leading from the Angel to the
Green gives you the image of a market-place. That comfortable
width of road, with broad pavements approached by steps leading
up from the streets, is pure country town. One might be in
Chipping Norton. There are still some red tiled roofs to be
seen and this is the most natural site for the Agricultural Hall,
which once used to be the scene of cattle shows and Crufts' dog
shows, of circuses too and animal business of all kinds. The road
past the hall is, of course, very urban and mechanical now in
its traffic, but the Green is still green and the local music-hall
still carries a personal name, that of Collins, instead of being one
of an Imperial or Hippodromic chain.

The taverns established long ago for the benefit of sportsmen
were developed to comfort the traveller. The northward coaches
tended to start there or at Snow Hill, closer to the City. It was
at the Saracen's Head, Snow Hill, that Nicholas Nickleby met
Mr. Squeers. Phiz's illustration suggests a galleried inn of
handsome quality and Dickens described a large array of Saracenic
heads for decoration. It was close to Newgate Prison and did a
roaring business, no doubt, after one of the public executions
so common there. It was also a much-frequented terminus
for coaches. It was at the Peacock in Islington that Tom Brown
waited for the coach to Rugby. A print of Islington Green in
1780 shows coaches abounding and sheep penned in the grass
plot where now is Myddleton's statue.

The Angel, one of the great galleried inns of London, was
another famous coaching base. It also had other claims to
renown: Thomas Paine wrote part of *The Rights of Man* while
staying there. It was a special resort of graziers and shepherds
bringing their flocks from the north to sell them at Smithfield.

The first rebuilding was in 1819: another followed in this century. It is now a Lyons café. There was a wonderful array of taverns in old Islington, whose names made music and history too. At The Rosemary Branch the archers had refreshed themselves: at The White Conduit House young Mr. Lord, subsequent founder of Lord's, looked after the cricket-pitch; at the Old Parr's Head, named after the Parr whose longevity was a legend, there was notable play-acting; and The Old Pied Bull was said to have been built out of Sir Walter Raleigh's residence.

Islington's attractions are not all matters of memory and imagination. Colebrooke Row is a nice piece of Georgian pattern and at the north end of it, in what is now called Duncan Terrace, is the little house to which Charles Lamb retired when free from his office work. It used to look out over the New River, which was directed that way southward on its course to Sadler's Wells —and George Dyer managed to walk into its waters. Lamb went there in 1825 and stayed till 1827, when he left for Enfield. It was a delectable spot then: or at least so Lamb saw it.

> When you come London-ward you will find me no longer in Covent Garden. I have a cottage in Colebrook Row, Islington; a cottage, for it is detached; a white house with six good rooms; the New River (rather elderly by this time) runs (if a moderate walking pace may be so termed) close to the foot of the house; and behind is a spacious garden with vines (I assure you), pears, strawberries, parsnips, leeks, carrots, cabbages, to delight the heart of old Alcinous. You enter without passage into a cheerful dining-room, all studded over and rough with old books: and above is a lightsome drawing-room, three windows, full of choice prints. I feel like a great lord, never having had a house before.

The house is now by no means white, but could be made so if the Elians would take it in hand. It is by no means rustic and the surroundings can hardly be altered. But the colour and covering of the house could be honourably improved. The New River has been put underground and is here invisible. But it is deplorable, considering the immense veneration justly paid to Lamb as a classic English essayist, letter-writer, critic, and as a cordial and most human man of letters, that this house of his, whence he toddled out to the Old Queen's Head for a pipe and the 'nut-brown,' should be left so shabby to the eye. If it is worth a memorial plaque it is worth a coat of paint.

The excuse may be made that the place has been a good deal changed: it seems to be rather smaller than Lamb describes and its detachment has ended. No strawberries will bring joy to it in June. But there it is and there, under this roof, was Lamb, free of the old routine, ' I have left the damned India House for ever!' he wrote to Crabb Robinson on March 29, 1825, ' Give me great joy.' And in April 6 he wrote to Wordsworth, ' Here I am then after 33 years of slavery. . . .'

> I came home for ever on Tuesday in last week. The incomprehensibleness of my condition overwhelm'd me. It was like passing from life into Eternity. Every year to be as long as three, i.e. to have three times as much real time, time that is my own, in it: I wandered about thinking I was happy, but feeling I was not. But that tumultuousness is passing off, and I begin to understand the nature of the gift. Holydays, even the annual month, were always uneasy joys: their conscious fugitiveness—the craving after making the most of them. Now, when all is holyday, there are no holydays. I can sit at home in rain or shine without a restless impulse for walkings. I am daily steadying, and shall soon find it as natural to me to be my own master, as it has been irksome to have had a master. Mary wakes every morning with an obscure feeling that some good has happened to us.

The house in which Charles Lamb was thus released and inspirited demands our respect.

If the New River has vanished, there is other water visible. That is the Regent's Canal which could not be coaxed up the Islington hill and so was driven through it. At Colebrooke Row it enters a tunnel more than half a mile long: its height is eighteen feet, including seven feet and six inches of water, and its width is seventeen feet. The New River, cutting across its track on its way south, must hereabouts run, encased, above the tunnel. The Wells Country has its tangle of subterranean curiosities and aquatic ingenuities.

An easy walk for Lamb was north-eastward to Canonbury Tower and it is a walk we still can make. Hazlitt has described how Lamb would watch the setting sun from the top of this ancient and considerable pile. ' He was intimate,' Hazlitt added, ' with Goodman Symes, the then attendant of this venerable tower and a brother antiquary in a small way: he took pleasure in entertaining him in the antique panelled chamber where Goldsmith wrote *The Traveller* and supped frugally on buttermilk.'

Canonbury Tower was recently the headquarters of the Baconian Society, whose members could there ponder on the injustice, as they see it, which has deprived a very great man of being acknowledged the greatest human miracle of all time. (For so Shakespeare-Bacon must have been, if he were one and the same person.)' Bacon was an occupant of Canonbury House, which included the Tower. Its list of residents names a tragic list of peers beheaded for conduct displeasing to their sovereigns as well as Speaker Onslow and the gentle Goldsmith. Canonbury is (or was—one never knows about ownership of land in these fast-changing times) the property of the Marquess of Northampton and the Tower was given over to be a social club for the benefit of the tenants round about. It is adjacent to the tranquil and elegant Canonbury Square and to several streets of early Victorian villas which run beside the now visible New River and make a very pleasant sight even in winter. In spring and summer, with the riparian gardens in their new greenery, Canonbury preserves that urbane rusticity which Lamb could discover in Colebrooke Row in 1828, but which has now been dispersed by the submersion of Islington in London.

This area north of Islington is pleasant to explore not only for its New River vistas, its contacts with history, and its Georgian squares: it has a rich kind of Victorian aroma in some of its terraces and churches. John Wesley lived in Highbury Place and Joseph Chamberlain spent some of his boyhood in the same house. Highbury is said to have been favoured by the Romans as a summer camp and this idea of æstivation on the Northern Heights was taken up by the priors of St. John of Jerusalem. At the Reformation Henry VIII sent the priors packing and reserved for himself, 'for his own disport and pastime,' and especially for the hunting of 'hare, partridge, pheasant, and heron,' all the country from Westminster to St. Giles in the Fields, to Islington, to Highgate, and to Hornsey Park. Penalties for poachers were to be imprisonment or what His Majesty willed. So, where now the Arsenal football team draws 60,000 spectators on a Saturday, King Henry's game-wardens would draw the coverts for the benefit of royal hawk and hound, and the commoners of Middlesex were left to wonder just how common were their lands.

But King Henry's pleasures are far away and long ago. Highbury was largely a Victorian creation and Highbury New Park, 'an imposing group of large villas,' measuring a mile across from east to west and a mile and a half from north to south, is typical development of the eighteen-sixties designed to meet the needs of the newly prosperous merchants and professional men. Nowadays the houses are too big for single families. The proper celebrant of that culture is John Betjeman, the poet who can make a little Helicon out of any suburban knoll, so dearly does he love the stucco, the drives, the evergreens, and the church with its 'Gothic enlacements' in the Butterfield style. That which has been ridiculed in English life he can relish. His poem to 'St. Saviour's, Aberdeen Park, Highgate, London, N.' expresses much that ought to be said about this region and about many another district of similar social quality and architectural development. With his permission I quote three stanzas from his tribute to what is now the victim of a frequent and facile denigration:

> These were the streets my parents knew when they loved and won—
> The broughham that crunched the gravel, the laurel-girt paths that wind,
> Geranium-beds for the lawn, Venetian blinds for the sun,
> A separate tradesman's entrance, straw in the mews behind,
> Just in the four-miles' radius where hackney carriages run,
> Solid Italianate houses for the solid commercial mind.
>
> These were the streets they knew; and I, by descent, belong
> To these tall neglected houses divided into flats.
> Only the church remains, where carriages used to throng
> And my mother stepped out in flounces, and my father stepped out in spats
> To shadowy stained-glass matins or gas-lit evensong
> And back in a country quiet with doffing of chimney hats.
>
> Great red church of my parents, cruciform crossing they knew—
> Over these same encaustics they and their parents trod
> Bound through a red-brick transept for a once familiar pew
> Where the organ set them singing and the sermon let them nod
> And up this coloured brickwork the same long shadows grew
> As these in the stencilled chancel where I kneel in the Presence of God.

After that there is no more to be said about Highbury. I can only wish that Mr. Betjeman will continue to be the Laureate of all our laurelled suburbs. To sing a song of rhododendrons is native to his gift. No one else has made such music of the tennis club dance and of the Austins parked outside the pavilion. There is so much in the Well Country to elicit his enthusiasm. The habit of laughing at Muswell Hill began when Hilaire Belloc wrote of the virtuous Master Fortescue.

> He thus became immensely rich
> And built the splendid mansion which
> Is called The Cedars, Muswell Hill,
> Where he resides in affluence still
> To show what everybody might
> Become, by Simply Doing Right.

In the same way Granville-Barker's picture of a prosperous draper's home on Denmark Hill in *The Madras House* inclined the young intellectuals of his day to regard that eminence and its Ruskin Park as a deplorable wilderness of bourgeois brick and ugliness. Well, go to Camberwell, climb thence, and see. Visit also the cliff-like eastern portion of the Mosswell suburb, looming over Hornsey and the New River. It is well-country, hill-country, and handsome country too.

CHAPTER XII

Some Games to See

———◆———

THOUGH I HAVE said kind things of the earliest part of an English winter, there do come days, and sometimes whole series of days, in which the urban sky is odious. It is damp and raw in the country: in London, the air, mixed with smoke and urban dirt, is discoloured as well as shiversome, not something to breathe but an ochreous affliction of the senses. The sensible person's immediate impulse is to dive as deep as may be into the comforts of what is commonly known as a 'fug.' Cinemas afford one kind of escape from an afternoon of this insinuating cold. But in cinemas, when they are not showing the main attraction, they are continually demonstrating, in travelogs—dreadful word!—documentaries, and other brief, colourful features, the glories of the great open spaces. Now great open spaces, especially in their winter garments, are just what I do not wish to see. I fly from the horrors of a January daylight and then am compelled to survey the movement of a glacier, the geology of the Rocky Mountains, the wonders of the ocean bed, or how medical relief is distributed in iciest Greenland. The picture-house itself may be snug and frowsty, a bolt-hole meet for the day, adorably remote from the rheumy, muscle-binding, lumbago-lavish weather outside. But these cinematic educators will suddenly plunge me into the domestic economy of the Faroe Islands. That is no relief.

One good resort, when you find Nature in the Raw (Central London style) intolerable, is a Billiards or Snooker Match. The big occasions of this kind take place deeply caverned and admirably free from fresh air. Once inside the building you feel that you really have dodged Nature at last. There is something wholeheartedly artificial about a billiard-table. I admit that in the Leicester Square temple of this cult there are some bosky and pastoral mural painting which invite you to fancy yourself in the lushest of our shires. But the room itself is decently dark with some tiers of seats round a brilliantly lit green table. The seats are in comparative darkness and full of sedentary figures, half somnolent, half vigilant. Most of the watchers are smoking and the place, already delectably warm, acquires a degree of frowst that is sweetly soothing to anyone arriving from a wind-whipped street or from the drift of sleet in a dirty sky. You may wholly disregard the summery suggestion of those misplaced murals, which ought to be replaced by some cordial, impressionist studies of barmaids, codgers about town, and modish loafers. Here, for a while, is total refuge, in alluring unreality.

For can they be real, these two dapper men who provide the entertainment? Not only is their skill too good to be true; they shine in sport while dressed for the Law Courts, the City, or the Legislature. Champions of the green cloth wear habitually the uniform of a financial magnate, a barrister or an administrator, that is to say, pin-stripe trousers and black waistcoats: the coat, presumably black, you do not see because they play in their shirt-sleeves, very neat, clean, smartly-striped shirt-sleeves, linked at the wrist and not rolled up. They vary in personality: here is Mr. Horace Lindrum from Australia who sometimes smiles as he is left in an awkward spot and has to plan self-extrication. Here is Mr. Walter Donaldson, who smiles very rarely indeed, even when he has performed the incredible. One would imagine that this grave, 'balding' fellow to be infallible as a chartered accountant or family lawyer. But here he is juggling, twice daily, at three and seven-thirty, for some two hours or so each afternoon and evening, with what used to be called the ivories and are now, I believe, the crystalates.

Or you may meet the one and only Mr. Joe Davis giving a handsome start and a beating to Mr. Peter Mans, champion of South Africa. Mr. Mans wears a brown suit and brown shoes and looks athletic, limber, an outdoor fellow, which is not quite right for a billiards game. But there is no doubt that he knows how to coax the ball into the pocket. He has a detached look when not actually concentrating on the shot; he might be musing on the eternal problems of mankind.

Mr. Davis, on the other hand, the world's undefeated snooker champion for twenty years, sticks to the pin-stripe below and the black above. He is chubby, pug-nosed, genial. He is this afternoon prepared to smile at the game, to wave an encouraging hand to a lagging ball—if a ball struck by him ever falls short of its duty, which is scarcely ever—and to make a quip or two, as the great Walter Hagen would toss a ' crack ' to the crowd during a needle match at golf. One is sorry for Mr. Mans, even with a handicap to help him; he is, while I watch, ' out-personalised ' as well as a little out-played. Joe Davis is something of a ' card ' as well as everything of a wizard in this world and so is everybody's darling. There will be no empty seats when he is on the players' list.

There they go, champions and challengers, gravely manœuvring so that the ball to be struck is either ' potted,' i.e. struck into the pocket or ' snookered,' i.e. hidden away behind a ball of another colour which must not be struck. What infinite practice and application have gone to the crouching over the table, the arching of the left hand's delicate fingers to make a bridge for the cue, the no less delicate play of the right hand as it rhythmically strikes the white ball; there is no jab but a graceful intimation to the ball that it should trickle exactly to a certain spot and there impel another ball into a pocket or itself lie 'snookered' in a certain nook. The intimation is obediently accepted. The ball, impelled with a gentle follow-through, as in a good putt at golf, does exactly what the professor ordered. It looks easy enough as you sit above the battle of touch and tactics. But try for a tenth part of that control yourself and you will seem the roughest and clumsiest lout. Messrs. Lindrum, Donaldson, Mans, and others (most notably Mr. Joe Davis) have given years of intense study, manual exercise, and maintenance of physical fitness to this crouching over a green cloth and passing of hints to the crystalate balls, hints which are so faithfully obeyed. Even the best of amateurs is not within measurable distance of their professional expertise. Here is the fruit of a life-work, the harvest of innumerable man-hours, as the economists say nowadays.

A life-work! Man-hours! Some indignant voice will assuredly protest that *Homo Sapiens* was meant for a finer form of sapience than this. These dexterous gentlemen, the voice will petulantly say, ought to be applying that astounding delicacy of touch to surgery or any other useful craft of high precision, not to the manipulation of a set of coloured balls in such a manner that A will 'pot' them all in the right order while so arranging matters that B never gets a good, clear chance to 'pot' anything at all. If they were just oafs, just common clay, the critic will continue, none would resent their self-dedication to a triviality. But such wise-looking men, so infinitely sensitive in the coaxing of a billiard-ball to curvet or to spin backwards as well as to behave normally and proceed straight forward, should have their eyes on far horizons, not on these few feet of flood-lit cloth upon a bed of slate.

I object to such reasoning. Driven home it would rule out so much of the world's fun and beauty. I would instead assert that any stroke in any game, if perfectly played, has beauty, its own true loveliness of certainty and rhythm. The player knows it by the feel of the thing: there is no jar, no sense of a harsh blow. Rather there is a sweet muscular thrill as the ball flies smoothly off the bat or club or racquet: correct hitting, based as a rule on timing of the impact, achieves the most speed with least effort. In billiards or snooker great force is scarcely ever needed: the triumph here is in the suavity, the subtlety of touch. But the result of perfect aim and perfect application of the touch is the same: it is, I insist, beauty. Mr. Davis, when he sits down to his supper, may not be an Adonis; but when he is in action on the cloth, he acquires grace beyond words: watching him makes life easier.

Moreover, we must stand up against the levelling claims of utility. If the artist of the billiard-table is contributing nothing to the food supply or the export drive—and possibly he may by exhibitions and by writing bring in large sums from dollar areas —he is making a living by delightfully entertaining his fellow-men. He harms nobody; he makes no mess; he creates no nuisance; he kills nothing; he interferes with none of us. Unlike musicians, he makes no noise.

So let us come in out of the cold blast that is whistling round that pensive figure of William Shakespeare given by Baron Grant to the honouring of drama and the adornment of Leicester Square. Grant's real name was Gottheimer; in high civic spirit he spent £28,000 (of a fortune questionably earned) on laying out Leicester Square; he removed an effigy of George I to replace it with Shakespeare. Gottheimer had a palace in Kensington, became a British M.P. and a Baron of the Kingdom of Italy: and, according to William Kent's valuable *Encyclopædia of London*, he died unknown in Bognor in 1899.

There was a time when Shakespeare on his plinth surveyed real theatres: there was a time when Daly's opposite had not yet been assigned with profit and with glory to Viennese waltzes of the lilting Lehar breed. Later the famous stage of Lily Elsie and José Collins was rebuilt for the pictures. Shakespeare's *Two Gentlemen of Verona* had sported there in the 'nineties at the instance of Augustine Daly and what Bernard Shaw, then critic of *The Saturday Review*, had to say about their capers (and Mr. Daly's) was lacerating without mercy. But the theatres of Leicester Square have all disappeared and the cinemas have replaced them with assorted and amazing styles of architectural bedizenment. Why leave poor Shakespeare here? Why not substitute effigies of Sam Goldwyn and of all the Brothers Warner in a row? As I write, Metro-Goldwin is reintroducing ballet in a mixed bill of pictures and varieties. But no authentic theatre is now in the Square.

Shakespeare knew something of billiards, it seems: at least his Cleopatra could have recorded in *Who's Who*, 'Recreations. Fishing and Billiards.' (This is reminiscent of the late Harry Tate.) She did some hopping and skipping too. Did old Nile produce good billiard-tables? How far had the Ptolemies anticipated Messrs. Burroughs and Watts? Had Tudor London truly circular and not elliptical billiard-balls? Certainly there is now a nice establishment of the fancy due west of the Shakespeare Statue in Leicester Square. So when the Square itself is emptied by the weather of those dozing elderly waiters, who come out after the luncheons are over and rest their aching feet on the benches, when the rain, or even snow, descends, when you feel that you can bear the films no longer, turn for alternative refuge into the Saloon where the dapper men so deftly show their cue-craft and have the billiard-balls on invisible strings, gliding, cannoning, pocketed. Yes, there is a beauty in this, the beauty of a pattern in the planning of a stroke, of rhythm in the sweet facility of its execution. Tap, tap, tap. Monotonous at times, but soothingly so. One nods; it is warm in here and the fellow in front has somewhere scrounged a real Havana cigar, and aromatic zephyrs proceed from his consumption of it.

You will not often see the royal and ancient game of billiards played publicly in these days. Its experts became too expert altogether; they invented so many and such tiresome means of non-stop scoring: potting the red or the in-off-the-red shot, with the red always accurately returning to let the striker use it again: the anchor-cannon, with the balls almost locked: the endless repetition of close (or nursery) cannons. These feats of cunning altered the arithmetic of the game and made record-smashing a routine. But it bored the spectators in an age of increasing hustle. The rules were altered to bar the repetition of these strokes, but billiards has scarcely recovered its magnetism or re-established its esteem.

Snooker, which used to be the jovial trifling of after-dinner parties, usurped billiards' place and also gained an entirely new role as a fine art, no longer a sporting knock-about, but a craft worthy of the finest cues.

Joe Davis in his book *How I Play Snooker* relates that he began to follow this ploy in 1924 and later began to take it seriously 'after I had won the first world's championship in 1927.' He adds, 'It was then that I saw that snooker was gaining rapidly in popularity and, moreover, that it was likely to have a very big following, chiefly because the very nature of the game, with the crispness and speed, was more in keeping with the times than was the scientific, elegant, and comparatively leisurely game of billiards.' At first professionals took their snooker casually: they expected to score a few ' pots ' and then give an awkward ' leave ': the idea of immediately clearing the table was not in their minds. But it soon was in that of Mr. Davis—after he had won the first laurels, not before. The Dickensian Captain's motto of ' when found, make a note of ' appealed to his restless and retentive intelligence.

' I started to study break-building, positional play, safety play, and the general strategy of the game. I became so interested that, when anything happened which surprised me, I immediately made a mental note and afterwards went away and tried the thing out to see what had happened and why. I have done that ever since.'

Twenty years of unbroken championship—and still, like any student, he makes notes and tries again! That is the discipline of the artist; that is the discipline of the golfer who goes out on a cold, drizzly day with a bag of old balls and hits them over and over again through wind and weather until he knows what is happening and why. Long, solitary practice of anything is tedium to most people: but artists can endure it.

The results, as I have said, have a beauty of their own. Cleopatra, moving, as we have moved, from billiards to snooker, would have beautified any table. One sees her, at play with her gentlewomen, while the scores

> Swell with the touches of those flower-soft hands
> That yarely frame the office.

(Or the hands might officiate at the 'frame,' since a frame of snooker is so named after the contraption in which the red balls are packed in position for the start.) It would not have paid Iras and Charmian to win more than an occasional frame, if any, from their mettlesome lady.

Mr. Davis is not a Cleopatra: but he is, in the highest degree, a decorator of life. 'Oh, luvely,' mutters my neighbour at the session, a northern devotee, 'Oh, luvely,' as a ball exquisitely glides to its appointed inch of space, just shifting another one and so bringing it into the field of play.

That proficiency in billiards is the sign of a mis-spent youth is a remark often attributed to Herbert Spencer. Actually it was quoted by Spencer as the observation of 'the late Mr. Charles Roupell.' Whether Mr. Roupell was right or not, watching the proficient at their billiards can certainly be part of a well-spent evening or afternoon. The game, which I play very ill and would adore to play well, has its own æsthetics; so have all games and, as a beauty-lover, I would much sooner dispatch a ball with genuine mastery to its appointed place, goal, boundary, hole, side-line, or pocket, than write or paint anything except the best.

' What a beauty ! ' is a phrase often on the lips of games-watching
men who do not closely consider their words, but do speak on
a true impulse. And here, in Leicester Square, in this assembly
of the average middle-brow man, here where no thoughts of
high art ever penetrate, where the names of Picasso and T. S.
Eliot are unknown, beauty is not only present, but acknowledged.
The salute to it is a round of grunts, unromantic, but utterly
sincere. What a beauty ! Luvely, yes, luvely, whispers my man
from the north.

In March, too, there may be a whipping wind that flays you
into taking cover: even if that month comes in lamb-wise, there
is still a good case for spending an afternoon or evening at the
All-England Badminton Championships. This occasion used to
be roughly true to its name: now it is as international as
Wimbledon and recent victories have been divided between
Denmark, Sweden, U.S.A. and Malaya as well as Great Britain.
The game has been regarded as worthy of championships for
40 years: but for long these events were not a great public
attraction. It is only a few years since the March tournament,
which marks the climax of the winter season, could be held in
the Horticultural Hall, Westminster, with temporary stands run
up round the courts. But now the public interest has so far
expanded that the Finals, usually happening on the second or
third Saturday in March, fill such gigantic arenas as those of
Harringay or the Empress Hall, Earl's Court. In 1950 the second
of these was the ' venue,' to use the sporting writers' favourite
term. Does anybody ever use the word venue in English except
a sporting writer ?

It is usually accepted that Badminton is named after the Duke
of Beaufort's estate and mansion well known to the hunting-folk
of England's Middle-West. His guests and friends, so the legend
goes, deprived by hard weather of their usual exercise in the
open, looked round for a suitable alternative to horsemanship
on winter days. They wished to work off their high living and

high spirits indoors and hit upon the idea that a safe missile, incapable of damaging ducal windows or furniture, could be made by driving goose-quills into champagne-corks. Hence the development of the shuttle-cock, once propelled by a battledore; this was originally a wooden bat used for beating dust out of carpets or wetness out of the washing. Now the shuttle is usually called the ' bird ' and the rough and ready battledore has become a light racquet, a subtler, gentler version of the one used in 'squash racquets.'

Subtlety too has enormously increased inside the game itself, which gives winter exercise to players of lawn-tennis and to many others as well. The demand for it and interest in it are now very great: the hampering feature is the necessity of a very high roof, as the game is spoilt if the shuttle hits the ceiling and so ends the rally with a ' let ': the ordinary school hall or parish hall unfortunately has a roof too low for a good game. Height is necessary, because one of the important shots is a lofty clearance. This is used to give the player time to get back into position after he has been brought right up to the net to deal with a ' drop ' shot, which just steals over the net-cord and falls almost straight downwards.

It is the existence of this shot which differentiates the game from lawn-tennis. The feathered shuttle can be struck, with an overhand stroke, so as just to pass the net and then to fall swiftly: because this can be done with an overhand stroke the player waiting for the shuttle cannot surely guess from his opponent's action, at least in its early stage, whether he means to strike high to the back of the court or just to coax the shuttle over the net with a last-second slackening of his force. In a good rally you will see a continual mixture of high, full shots intended to reach the back-line, of ' drops ' intended just to skim the net and then sink directly, and of smashes aimed to deliver a knock-out blow, like volleying in lawn-tennis.

It has been said that Badminton becomes monotonous: not

more so, I think, than any other game. It certainly has a beauty
of its own, especially when played by women of the first class.
In men's play the kill comes quicker and so may cut short a
delightful essay in tactics; the long-drawn rallies sustained by a
quartette of women champions owe their excitement and their
comeliness to the absence of shattering blows. They are more
varied and graceful than the parallel struggles on a lawn-tennis
court: there is a most delicate patterning of movement when a
couple in perfect *rapport* mingle high and ' drop ' play, now
seeking the side lines, now working patiently on the back line,
with one continually brought to the net to deal with drop and
the other patrolling behind her. In prose this may sound ordinary
enough, but in visual fact it takes on the quality of ballet. Badminton championships played on the flood-lit floor of a huge
arena create a picture like that of dancers on a stage; the trim
figures in white, tensely tip-toed for this game of lightning
movement, deserve a Dégas to paint them.

Such nursery names as battledore and shuttlecock probably
prejudiced the more austere opinion against Badminton for some
time: must not something played with a feathered cork be a
' cissy ' occupation? As a matter of fact the game is faster than
lawn-tennis, involving less strain on muscular strength, no doubt,
but more on agility: a Badminton single game is as strenuous
as anything to be seen in this line of sport, but is usually a less
good spectacle than a double. The last (Saturday) afternoon of
the championships, offering five finals (two singles and three
doubles) provides a fine blended spectacle, as it were of a winter
Wimbledon with a decorative touch of Sadler's Wells.

The chief magician in this ball-game without a ball appeared
in the March of 1949: he was David Freeman, the representative
of U.S.A. He had all the requisites: he always knew what his
opponents would do next and was on the spot to receive the shot
almost before it was on the way. (Query, is it absurd to believe
that a natural flair for a simple kind of telepathy has something

to do with exceptional success in games? Of course quickness
of eye, mind, foot, and hand are the essentials. But sometimes
I feel that the champions, having these essentials, owe their
further quality to their powers of anticipation. They not only
deduce from their experience of the game what the other player
is likely to do next and so are there to take it: they may also be
supreme because of an instinctive prevision. It is obvious that
a good deal of unconscious telepathy does exist in ordinary life.
We anticipate another person's remarks for no logical reason:
our thoughts are somehow and silently steered to the direction
of his. And if we thus anticipate remarks and emotions, why may
exceptional people not have some precognition of moves in a
game? That does not seem to me to be an impossible suggestion,
though it is obviously no more than a suggestion.)

At any rate Freeman, matched against the best of Denmark
and Malaya as well as of Britain, never lost a set in his singles and
was never extended in the least. He had, as I said, superb
anticipation of what was coming and a perfect technique for
flicking, dropping, or smashing when the shuttle arrived where
he knew it would arrive. In the following year Wong Peng Soon,
a sinewy Malayan, won easily: yet against Freeman he had been
powerless.

British Badminton is not in the winning class at the moment.
In 1950 a Malayan won the men's singles and the Danes swept
up all the rest of the trophies. Two English women, Mrs. Uber
and Miss Allen, reached the finals of the women's doubles and
took the first set by courageous perseverance after losing a good
lead. But they were seniors (Mrs. Uber first appeared in the lists
of championship winners in 1930) when one, perhaps both, of
her opponents was an infant in arms. The juniors inevitably
lasted the better.

Why has this falling off occurred in a game which we invented? We are obviously not finding the new talent. During
the long break in the war many halls were commandeered and

then retained for military or civil purposes at the end of it. So there was lack of premises, lack of equipment—shuttles were very scarce—and also a new lack of leisure. Young British players have less time and less money to give to games. To provide the special application and concentration which international championship standards now demand is outside the range of our middle-class youth. Badminton, it is true, is a truly amateur sport: there are no display games by professionals. But inside amateurism supremacy can only be won on the highest levels by constant practice, which means a total dedication of plentiful spare time. And how many can manage that now?

It is odd that the French, devoted and skilful lawn-tennis players, make no raid on our Badminton trophies. The countries interested appear to be Denmark (immensely), Sweden, and Malaya in addition to Great Britain. America looks in but rarely: and when Columbia did arrive in the person of Mr. Freeman he made all eyes open and stare in amazement. India, Canada, and New Zealand have also been represented with distinction, but Denmark, which first began to win in 1939, is now the most strongly represented and consistently victorious of the competitors.

Whether we find new first-rankers of our own or not, we shall not lack increasing numbers of those who play for fun and not for glory. The value of Badminton, as a provider of winter exercise, is paramount. We make a great fuss in our swollen, over-built London about the need for playing-fields—and rightly so. But playing-fields are only used in winter by the masses for a short time at the week-end and bad weather may curtail even that usage. Indoor exercise can be taken on any evening of the week in any weather and is a precious aid to getting through the dark months without loss of the fitness that we acquired in the sun. All appeals for more playing-fields should be accompanied by similar appeals for more playing-rooms. Badminton is difficult to house, whereas table-tennis is easy. But, where the

o

covered space is available and there is a decently high roof, it is well for this by-product of the Beaufort Hunt to continue to stretch the limbs of the townsman. The curious who seek it out when future championships are held will not spend a March afternoon to barren purpose. Few games are touched by more beauty of movement or a nicer blend of rhythm and of speed. The young Danes who come raiding our shores (more peaceably than their Viking ancestors) are Olympians to the eye; Pindar would gladly have sung then and Praxiteles have turned them into marble.

CHAPTER XIII

Going Underground

———————✧———————

I WRITE OF cellars, not of tubes. The ecclesiastical cellar is a crypt, which means a secret place. Crypt signified a tunnel to the Diarist Evelyn, who wrote of 'a crypt under the hill' as part of his landscape-gardening. Most of our graveyard English is lengthy, formidable stuff. Cerements, winding-cloths, sepulchres, catacombs, mausolea, and sarcophagi make up the polysyllabic music of our funeral march. The Scots still use the brief and sharply descriptive word lair for a grave. It goes well with crypt. 'A lair in the crypt.' There are many such in the cellarage of St. Paul's Cathedral.

Any person of intelligence who works daily in London must devise some lunch-hour resorts or exercises apart from recourse to the usual restaurant, café, or club. I have mentioned my own addiction to a Bankside walk to the Borough in search for some of its ghosts: but that demands at least a gleam of sun. On drab or 'dowly' days,' as they say in the North, one needs a roof and walls and it may be a pleasant escape from the buffeting visitations of January weather to go underground altogether. For those seeking an ostrich-like half-hour, with the head well tucked away from wind and rain, I recommend the Crypt of St. Paul's.

There is no need for alarm about the temperature. Cool in

summer, it is nicely warmed in winter. It is, in locality, 'perfect for a City gentleman,' as the house-agents would describe it, and the prisoners of Fleet Street, out on lunch-time leave, have it at their door. Publishers have been considerably smoked out of the area by Hitler's incendiarism. But I surmise that James Pope-Hennessy, author of that admirable book, *London Fabric*, was in a publisher's office when he made his escapes into the Crypt. Somebody had been giving him ethical promptings; from those he fled.

> There I would sit despondently wondering whether I should ever have a strong character. I don't know why it was such an immensely pacifying atmosphere. I would creep out of my near-by office (I worked then in Paternoster Row) and, paying my sixpence, slink down the sloping staircase to the crypt, and sit there for a few minutes in the cold stillness.

The charge is still sixpence. And, as I said, the stillness is not necessarily cold. St. Paul's stands firm with the anti-inflationary elements in London life, those steadfast friends of the people who will not raise their prices. The curators of Kew Gardens abide by their token-fee of one penny. Some newspaper proprietors and many weekly publications have stood firm at a penny and sixpence. There is the great firm of Lyons who, by substituting self-help trays for the attentions of the Nippy, have kept down the price of light refreshment to a most praiseworthy extent. When I first came to London as a boy before the first Great War, I paid fivepence for a pot of tea and a roll and butter in establishments of this kind. Now you get yourself a large cup instead of being brought a pot: this saves time and the charge is actually less, fourpence halfpenny in all.

So let us be thankful to St. Paul's which bestows on us most of its ground-floor glory for nothing and admits us to the shelter and spectacular memorials of its crypt for the same sixpence as before, the price now of three third-rate cigarettes. To see the monstrous Funeral Wagon which drew the Duke of Wellington's body in state to Ludgate Hill and to see it merely as one of a hundred tablets and urns which are Britain's history written in epitaph is surely bargain enough.

So much has been written about St. Paul's by devotees of Wren and specialists in architectural appreciation that I shall not attempt to add to so much love and learning. I simply salute the master-mind that built, with this grand simplicity, on this scale of grandeur. There are two kinds of temple: those which wrap the gods in glory and those which explain them in lucidity. Gothic soars upward to the misty heavens proclaiming the mystery of faith; classical design spreads outward, as broad-minded as it is broad-based and calmly proclaiming the logic of belief. In London it is St. Paul's that supplies to the observing eye the feast of reason; it is Westminster that provides the flow of soul.

In Gothic glooms there is always a lurking sense of fear: the very laughter of the gargoyles is macabre. The Middle Ages, at least for me, reveal their menaces quite as much as their enchantments in the gorgeous legacy of their master-builders. The classical and Renaissance styles establish confidence: they speak of a cosmic order at once rational and humane. There is always Hell round the corner of a Gothic heaven: but amid the architecture of Wren and his colleagues I feel assured that God has no need of fiery torments in order to affirm a wise dominion. This world of stone is too sane for Gehenna. The kind of wild rapture that might come to a man amid the soaring pillars and the heaven-aspiring arches of a medieval cathedral is not to be experienced in St. Paul's: here there is another and a cooler delight. One is entranced by the enormity of the design that covers 87,000 square feet and climbs the sky to the height of 355 feet; such size, such sweep, such dignity, and, with them all, such powerful persuasion that the Christian religion is based on Logos, the reasonable word, not on angels, demons and miracles which are the natural inhabitants of Gothic fanes.

And so, with a silent vote of thanks to Sir Christopher, one fumbles for the tanner and proceeds below stairs. Here, in the crypt, are the postscripts to a military or naval glory: the whole of our Victorian militarism—and that supposed age of peace had its steady flow of campaigns about the Empire's rim—are to be found in epitaph or effigy. The moustaches, bushy and drooping, proclaim a stodgy he-manliness rather than any flash of military genius. But it is not admirals and generals all the way: some quiet gentlemen are celebrated here with a charming lack of justification.

Almost at once the eye is caught by the tablet to John Wasdale, M.D., 'a native of the County of Cumberland,' who died in June, 1807, at the age of seventy-six. There are verses which take a very cheerful, hedonistic, even mundane view of what is to come. Cries Dr. Wasdale's confident spirit,

> *From Life's delusive, transient Joys I rise*
> *To seek eternal pleasure in the skies.*

Eternal pleasure! No talk of celestial bliss, which never sounds very promising, but good, solid pleasure, the earthy term beloved of the Epicureans, the Utilitarians, and all the encomiasts of the banquet of life. I presume that Wasdale was a capable leech and earned his place in such august surroundings by his craft. It is reassuring to meet him here at the top of Ludgate Hill, in the City's own high temple. For his name is wrapped in associations with the greatest corner of England, Wastwater and Wastdale Head with the Great Gable above them on the left, the bastion of the Scawfells to the right of them, and the grand canyon of the Sty Head Pass between these majesties. What happiness that little piece of Cumberland has given to the nation and what an honour to go through life with the name of Wasdale! I trust ' eternal pleasure ' has come the Doctor's way.

There is no Poet's Corner in the crypt. But here William Blake is remembered, which I think is wrong: Gothic is his spiritual home. The sculptors are in force, Thornycroft and Frampton, Lutyens and Gilbert, with a model of the Piccadilly 'Eros' to keep that sweet fancy with him in the grave. Landseer has a kindly dog with chin resting on the coffin and eyes that melt in mourning, an appropriate conceit. Journalism has its accolade in the person of Sir William Russell, first and greatest of war correspondents (1820-1907). This veteran is shown with a reporter's note-book, a just reminder that, while St. Bride's is the parish church of Fleet Street, St. Paul's is its cathedral.

Some men of might who were buried in Old St. Paul's and so underwent a belated cremation in the Great Fire of 1666 are listed by name in order to supply the continuity of sepulchral dedication. We begin with Sebba, A.D. 677, King of the East Saxons. The name carries us back to that land of Lud from which the Romans had withdrawn, leaving their pots and pavements for time to cover and for man to excavate. The Saxons are elusive folk to me. Were they as dull as they sound? Did they ever laugh or did they merely eat and drink themselves into a coma with their chines of beef and flagons of mead? Sebba! A name as heavy as 'sad' pastry. It is curious how he and his kind defeat the imagination. What were they up to during all those centuries before the Norman came? It is significant that in the most wise and musical of G. K. Chesterton's poems, 'The Secret People,' a brief history of the baffling English, he had to begin his analysis with 1066 and hurry to the collapse of feudalism and the coming of the Tudor despotism.

> The fine French kings came over with a flutter of flags and dames,
> We liked their smiles and battles, but we never could say their names.
> The blood ran red to Bosworth and the fine French lords went down;
> There was naught but a naked people under a naked crown.

Even G. K. C., though he could drive into the fog of history and make substantial ballads out of wisps of legend, was unable to make Saxon England attractive. On the stage, should anyone revive Tennyson's *Harold*, the thanes remain dummies, as it were 1066 in a tow wig and villainously cross-gartered. They inherited what massive works the Roman left and what the mighty engineers of Avebury and Stonehenge had left before that. They let things fade away and added so little. No, I cannot feel anything but boredom and distaste at the sight of Sebba's name.

Following Sebba on the list of Old St. Paulines, and following him at a considerable interval, is Sir William Dethick who was 'Garter' and much concerned with heraldic allotments in the time of William Shakespeare. It was Sir William Dethick and William Camden, officiating as Garter and Clarenceux, who 'assigned, granted and confirmed, and by these presents exemplified unto the said John Shakespeare and his posterity that shield and coat of arms heretofore assigned to him.' This included the Shakespeare spear and the *ermine fess checky* of the Park Hall Ardens. I think that Shakespeare enjoyed that kind of thing and could respond to the romantic appeal of *ermine fess checky* which he restored to his parents. Whether or no he was much concerned himself, I am certain that a young man who left Stratford 'without prospects' (quitting not only Stratford, but a wife and three children) and took a chance in London while his father's fortunes were sinking, had made a high resolve to justify his London adventure as soon as he could; so, when prosperity came quickly, he was instant to buy the Big House of Stratford (New Place) and to solicit Dethick and Camden for restoration of the gentlemanly and armigerent status which the Shakespeares claimed to have been theirs under Henry VII.

Coming across Dethick's name in the crypt I naturally thought of the College of Arms or Heralds' Office in Queen Victoria Street, close by St. Paul's. This has survived the almost complete devastation round about it. There remains the shell of St. Nicholas Cole Abbey, an exquisite church, Wren or School of Wren, in which I greatly enjoyed an occasional lunch-time session on hot days. It was cool, intimate, tiny, gracious, as it were something of Mozart's composed in stone. I hope it can be restored.

Heraldry is, to the rational mind, infuriating nonsense. But it has deep roots in human instinct and ambition and the courtly gentlemen who have surveillance over armorial claims in the handsome brick mansion, so fortunately spared, are beset with queries sent from all over the world by anxious claimants to a lion couchant or any other exhibit of the heraldic zoo. For my part, I can find no conceivable interest in coats of arms, but I am no spoil-sport and would hate to think that our frantic hunters of the Boar's Head Total Gules were being cheated of their rights and their fun. So I salute the name of the Dethick who greatly satisfied the greatest English writer of all time by allowing him to carry home to his parents the vibrant spear and the *ermine chess fecky*. And who will deny reverence to Sir Philip Sidney and Sir Anthony Van Dyck, also in that roll of Old Paulines which begins with King Sebba?

The most famous tombs in the crypt are those of Nelson and of Wellington. Nelson's sarcophagus of black and white marble, wherein was set a coffin made from the mainmast of the French ship *L'Orient*, was already a genuine antique when it was allotted, through an accident, to its new honorific purpose. The tomb itself has an extraordinary history. Pope-Hennessy quotes Dean Milman's story of Nelson's obsequies:

> . . . at the very moment of the arrival in this country of Nelson's corpse (preserved in brandy, the frequent, necessary changing of which had given a good deal of trouble on the voyage from Gibraltar), George III was busy with his scheme for converting St. George's Chapel at Windsor into a burial-place for his own family. Wolsey's empty sarcophagus, designed perhaps by Torregiano, was among the objects " thrown aside as useless lumber." What could be more suitable (and, one suspects, more economical), than to enshrine Nelson in this historic piece of porphyry? And so it was that the " fine work, marred in its bold simplicity by a few

tawdry coronets " became the last receptacle of that poor, bloated body.

The guide-books do not agree about Torregiano. Muirhead attributes the Wolsey kist to Benedetto da Rovezzano. To me that does not greatly matter. What touches my sense of irony is that Nelson should have displaced a Cardinal.

There is no need to investigate Wolsey's career and character in detail. He died, under shadow of a trial for high treason, at Leicester and was buried in the abbey there. The great tomb, which he had ordered in the days of his opulent dominion, was annexed by the King and remained royal property. So it happened that the mad monarch, when tidying up at Windsor, delivered the receptacle which is now the Admiral's and part of your sixpennyworth on Ludgate Hill. Wolsey in Shakespeare's (or Shakespeare's and Fletcher's) *Henry VIII*, ' left naked to his enemies' foresees the day

> *When I am forgotten: as I shall be,*
> *And sleep in dull, cold marble.*

He also foresaw a name not mentionable, because of his fall and his disgrace. But the marble he had planned was not to be of the dull order. The ambition which overthrew him had schemed more elegantly than that.

A very different type was his successor in that sarcophagus. When I was being educated at Cheltenham College, a new reredos was erected in the chapel with the great ones of our history erected in effigy. This was by way of inspiration for those setting out on their careers. Each calling had its representative. Franklin, not Nelson, was chosen for the Royal Navy. Nelson had erred and strayed. I cannot believe that much was gained for young virtue by this deed of well-intentioned piety. Boys, curious to know why Nelson was absent from the high parade, would surely do some private reading and discover that Emma was not only a heroine of Jane Austin's. Yet the lines spoken by Norfolk in *Henry VIII* about one 'not propp'd by ancestry' whose way is made by 'force of his own conceit' apply to Nelson: and both he and Wolsey were East Anglians.

Far more striking than any coffin or sarcophagus is the gigantic Funeral Car of the Duke of Wellington. This massive and bizarre hearse was made of the metal of cannon captured in his wars and was inscribed with the long roll-call of his victories. There is something proudly barbaric about such a relic of the old order in public funerals. Ebony horses, suitably draped and with nodding plumes and pom-poms of black upon their heads, escorted by top-hatted mourners with trailers of crêpe flowing down their necks, as it were the manes of more horses, dragged this iron six-wheeler to the Cathedral with every accompaniment of pomp and circumstance on that dark day in November, 1852. Much of the detail can be read on the chart set beside this chariot of lamentation.

Six battalions, eight squadrons, representatives of all branches of the Army, the Queen herself, all the civil magnates, the Duke's own riderless charger—it was a spectacle indeed. Nothing of ceremony was omitted. 'The service being ended, Garter will proclaim the Style and the Comptroller of the deceased, breaking his staff, will give the pieces to Garter who will deposit them in the grave.' Tennyson put forth his best in the way of epitaphic rhyme and struck out, among the inevitable common-places, lines worthy of a Laureate who took his public duties with a proper seriousness.

In

> *The shining table-lands*
> *To which our God Himself is moon and sun*

he presented a view of heaven more felicitous than most essays in celestial cartography. And

> *That sober freedom out of which there springs*
> *Our loyal passion for our temperate kings*

is a couplet which, while not inspired in phraseology, drives
justly into the quiet heart of British democracy.

> *Not once or twice in our rough island-story*
> *The path of the duty was the way to glory.*

is doubtless too gnomic for the modern taste, which is shy of
ethical simplicities. But the words ' rough island-story ' would
hardly have endured as they have done unless they had merit.
I do not know what exactly is meant by Garter ' proclaiming
the Style.' Tennyson proclaimed one of his own.

So there the great wagon stands, a notable exhibit from the
stables of Empire and the mews of Mars. There is nothing
mawkish about it, no hesitant second thoughts about the
glorification of war, no evasive effort to salute both Christ the
Peacemaker and the God of Battles. The Roman conquerors
drove in such chariots through the shouting myriads of the
capital with their lively parade of living captives and kings in
chains: it was Death's triumph when our veteran Duke was thus
conveyed, with an Empire's lamentation, ' under the Cross of
gold that shines across the river.' There is a lusty, unequivocal
paganism about the whole conception of the gun-wrought
chariot, so lethal in its material, so jubilant in its inscription.
One hears the drum-roll of so many battles, so vastly victorious,
far away and long ago. That myriads of ordinary and innocent
people had died for this seems easily forgotten.

Among the spectacles of the crypt it is far the most remarkable,
and I cannot pass it by without a sense of wonder. The early
Victorians had no doubts: an Iron Car for an Iron Duke.
Florence Nightingale, remembered nearby in unpleasing
alabaster, can almost be heard murmuring, ' So suitable.'

One wanders back into the avenues of peace and the tables
votive to the men of the arts. Here are the painters by whose
name nowadays the shrill derision, the facile sneer, or even the
crude guffaw are evoked. Here are the Academicians of the huge

canvases: some of their work is now, I suppose, amid the veering winds of fashion, scarcely saleable at so much a square yard. Are there any takers when Alma-Tadema is mentioned by the auctioneer? Yet vogue usually comes full circle in the arts and it seems almost inevitable that, within fifty years and possibly much less, the old contemptibles will be enjoying some return to honour and to sale-room value.

Sir Edwin Landseer has his Pauline tablet. Why not a Landseer boom? Why not renewed absorption in Scots' mist on soaring crags with a stag bleeding in the foreground? Our taste in plays, films, and books reveals a remarkable addiction to violent death and splashings of gore. Landseer is certainly well in the movement, if massacre be the whim. Not long I was privileged to picnic in the lodge beside superb Loch Affric, north-west of Inverness. Here Landseer not only stayed but left murals, presumably his bloodless pastime during one of the Highlands' usual series of wet days. There was in one room a whole set of Landseer engravings and in all of them appeared death in some form or another. Even the grisly business of gralloching a stag—i.e. evisceration—seemed to him a fitting subject for his art. True, he sentimentalised over dogs, as you are reminded by his memorial in the crypt. But he took a ruthless view of what man should do to beast and bird. An age which mocks at gentleness in the arts and holds starkness to be all should welcome blood-boltered Sir Edwin back on to its walls. Soon the upturned eyes of dying deer may vie with surrealist geometry for place of honour in the up-to-date galleries. So watch the market: I am ready to be a ' bull ' of stags.

We owe an obeisance to Sir Arthur Sullivan, another of the crypt's renowned, before we decide that we have had full value for the sixpence we have ' banged.' He, at any rate, if he could watch the box-office, need not complain of a fickle public. The operettas, which he sometimes wrote in order to get away to his beloved (and unlucky) tables at Monte Carlo, abide and will not wither. But he thought less of his profane than of his sacred music. What of his more spiritual compositions? We prefer the profanities. So irony persists, as always among tombs.

Let us go underground farther west. Another of London's famous crypts, handy for Baker Street's several stations and bus stops, is the Chamber of Horrors at Madame Tussaud's: there you may stroll, if not sup, with murder. In winter I find it worth occasional revisiting. Largely it is an assassins' assembly, with most of the homicides looking very pink and clean in their waxen effigies. The Chamber's reputation for being an unholy terror, the kind of place where nobody could be locked in at night without going crazy, is possibly not what it used to be. But you can see Charles Peace at the gallows-side, grey, dingy, and contemplating, unblindfolded, his destination. The melancholy of that scene is not for the immature or the easily scared. (During a recent visit to the Chamber a couple were carrying round their infant in a portable cradle: the enjoyment was certainly well over the head of that mite.) There are several specimens of torture bloodily on view and the Middle Ages are revealed without their last enchantments of Gothic architecture, but with considerable emphasis on their methods of mental persuasion in the matter of faith. Torture, in the eyes of the management, apparently ends with the lashed foot-slogger of the treadmill. Tussaud's have not pursued the subject into the political disciplines and persuasive technique of our up-to-date dictatorships.

Waxwork is used with abundance of artifice both in the cellarage and in the unhorrific Galleries upstairs. The difficulty is obviously to escape a kind of pink chubbiness and to reduce humanity to its normal pallor and bewrinklement. The murderers seem, on the whole, rather better than normal in respect of hygiene and general presentability. You could not here descry a special criminal or homicidal type. Prominent, bulging eyes? Crippen, as imaged, certainly has those and you may note an occasional fixed stare of narrowly set eyes which suggests the sinister intention and reckless courage for the horrid deed. But young Mr. Mahon, of the Crumbles case, could not look nicer and integrity is writ large on many a brow that harboured infamous plots and purposes of slaughter. The message of the Chamber is a simple one: never judge by appearances.

The late dictators and their lackeys are given a fair show. There is no cartooning of these bullies and they do not look as bad as they actually were. The Chamber is the right place for them, but some of their neighbours in this crypt, who only killed singletons, might reasonably be affronted by the adjacent presence of those who slaughtered by the million. Some, after all, of the Tussaud exhibits, were considerable sportsmen in their way. Take the example of Jack Sheppard, whom you may see in confinement at Newgate. His record as an escapist was of such a dazzling kind that he might well be a boys' own hero or even the darling of the sophisticates. Such, indeed, he was. ' If I could not have been Nelson,' wrote James Agate of Sheppard, ' I swear I would have chosen to be Jack.'

Sheppard related the details of his last escape from Newgate in order ' to satisfy the curious and do justice to the ignorant.' Knowledge of his greatness he conceived, with a most sweet vanity, to be part of our common rights and dues. How he slipped his handcuffs and made his way through one locked room after another for six hours on the afternoon of Thursday, October 15, 1724, is one of the finest stories in the Newgate Calendar, a volume which shared with the Bible the favourite corner in George Borrow's esteem. Having made his incredible getaway, by his rare mixture of force and cunning, Sheppard stole money and clothes, stupidly over-dressed, stupidly over-drank, and was recaptured. He was excuted three weeks later, 'with great difficulty and much pitied by the mob.'

A nasty scene, obviously, and one, I fancy, better meriting a full tableau in the Chamber than does the large portrayal of Peace at his end, faced by hangman, chaplain, and governor. But the world has forgotten Sheppard, 'the greatest slip-string' of his kind, and a fascinating character with his virtuosity in breaking bondage and his fatal love of a swagger. I have written elsewhere of the ghosts of the Tottenham Court Road. Sheppard has a claim to be in that company, since, after his last escape from Newgate, he worked his way down Gray's Inn Lane, still fettered, and came at two in the morning to Tottenham Court, in one of whose cowsheds he slept. He stayed there some time, explaining to the cowman that he had escaped from the Bridewell after incarceration for the getting of a bastard, an activity to which the cowman was sympathetic, having been thus troubled himself. After leaving the Tottenham Court area Jack got his fetters filed off and then proceeded to throw his hard-won life away by vanity, foppishness and drinking. Certainly he is one of the most likeable of the scoundrels now on view in the Tussaud basement.

The ascent from the Chamber to the milder halls above is a passage from the subterranean and the shiversome, not to the sublime, but at least to the solid and the statesmanlike. The Tussaud valuation of 'What the Public Wants' in the way of human effigy is very interesting. Some of it can be taken for granted. Royalty, sport, stage and screen one naturally assumes will be there; they are what is now so insistently called 'glamour.' But politicians, about whom the clever young men have down the centuries been peevish and pert, hold a very large part. It is the judgment of showmen, who may surely be deemed expert judges of public curiosity, that the figures and façades of Cabinet Ministers, past as well as present, do remain a matter of general concern. This is a consoling reflection for those who take the idea of representative government in earnest.

There was a somewhat curious choice among the Ministers of the day, when I last was at Tussaud's just before the General Election in February, 1950. In the group selected from among the Labour Ministers, Mr. Alexander sat on the right hand of Mr. Attlee and Mr. Aneurin Bevan was not to be seen at all. Nor was Mr. Shinwell. Mr. Dalton was given a background posting. It looked as though the selector was a Centre man in his predilections; but one of the Labour Left, Mr. Strachey, though not in the Cabinet, got a prominent position in the line-up. But he was then Minister of Food and food is always news.

In the Foreign Department Marshals Stalin and Tito were standing adjacent and apparently undismayed by this proximity. They were neither beaming amiably nor defying one another with a scowl. Friendly neutrality seemed to be implied, which was then very much against the run of the news. Does the Maison Tussaud retain a Foreign Editor to deal with the hurried revaluations which the helter-skelter of our European history makes advisable? Apparently not. Doubtless the average visitor is not alert to the fine points of protocol or diplomatic placing. But the exhibition would be more fun for the specialist if the assessment and grouping of the political and diplomatic big-wigs were more fluid and based on last-minute information and judgment. That, however, would involve much work for the staff, with frequent comings and goings of the models.

Our kings and queens, with some historical tableaux, have been retained in full panoply. This is Little Arthur's History of England in three dimensions; the early monarchs, all beards and baubles, and their velveted, sad-eyed queens gaze tranquilly out of their stances at the passers-by: not for these calm, immobile, lifeless magnates remains the wretched prowling and re-prowling of the gaoled lions and incarcerated tigers, infinitely bored, in the gloomy half-life of a menagerie or zoo. To-day's public may

be pardoned for regarding the Angevins and Plantagenets with
lack-lustre eye. History, as we know, is 'about chaps.' And here
are the chaps, robustly looking much of a muchness, and certainly
miles away from any kinship with us. We can gaze at the
monarchs and barons whose names we learned by heart; they
loom up before us like dates and battles in human form. We
can nod to some of Shakespeare's heroes and villains of the
chronicle plays, but they are not so lively in wax as in print.
One watches the strollers of to-day gazing at medievalism. Let
us move on, says Everyman, after coping with the first three
Edwards, and have a peep at the Eighth—and the Duchess of
Windsor.

She and her husband are in a recess near to the Royal Family,
but tactfully they do not impinge upon them. They are among
the most successful of the portraits and the passers-by do not
seem to walk so quickly on reaching this alcove of the royal
exile. Some of the Royal Family come out better than others.
Whether a waxwork 'comes off' must be partly a matter of
chance: the craftsmanship is the same, but any kind of drawing
or writing may or may not hit the target equally well on each
occasion, although the same hand is at work. I suppose, too,
that the artist, in this kind of modelling, is obviously handicapped
where the public are in advance expecting rare beauty or vitality.

For that reason the stage section seems to me the least effective
of the whole display. That is inevitable: actors and actresses
depend so much on their animation that only the best painting
can put their lively spirits upon canvas. In wax they can hardly
help looking inert; this is a weakness which does not matter so
much in the case of authors, thinkers and statesmen whose action
is chiefly of the brain. But Greer Garson and Sir Ralph Richard-
son, Vivien Leigh and Sir Laurence Olivier, Danny Kaye and
Gracie Fields, are nothing if not vivid persons: when silent
(and static) upon a plinth in Baker Street most of our familiar
bright-shiners seem only to be simulacra of somebody quite

different. Gentlemen of the 'mike' do not need to be so obviously alive and kicking. I was glad to meet Wilfred Pickles in the still tiny section allotted to the B.B.C.

The same holds to some extent of sport. Whether it be Denis Compton or Cecilia Colledge or Gordon Richards their life is speed and grace; a great sculptor might successfully capture their athletic essence and somehow symbolise their prowess on turf or ice. (The ancient Greeks managed to get the idea of movement into the still actuality of marble.) Wax is a baffling material for this kind of workmanship. The boxers get five places, the cricketers six, the jockeys and skaters two each. I was surprised that the Tussaud scheme of news-values makes such small allowance for football of any code or kind. Yet Association Football has far the biggest crowds of any sport in the country and I expected to find a whole group of the twinkling-footed goal-scorers to celebrate those who are responsible for the vast Saturday 'gates.' Stanley Matthews was the only exception when I was there. Of course there may have been new admissions since then.

How are the professions served? The Church does well with sixteen exhibits, from William of Wykeham onwards. The vestments are a selling-point. Here again there is belief in human toleration. Martin Luther puts up with Cardinal Newman by his side. John Knox and Calvin are the quiet and unprotesting neighbours of Pope Pius XII. Tussaud's administrators remain uninterested in academic life despite the allure of gowns and hoods which give gay colouring a chance; the extreme interest shown in the Law's victims down in the cellar, where 'the 'orrors' are massed, is not parallelled by much, or indeed by any, interest in the Law's executors upstairs. His Majesty's Judges and great Counsel have helped notably, by prosecution and sentence, to supply raw material for the raree-show of ruffians in the basement. But they get no award for it in their own superior quarters.

I am pleased to see that the exhibition directors, while chilly towards pictorial art (why no Munnings?) regard literature as worthy of their wax. Their taste is for the accepted masters of the immediate past. Shakespeare, benign and harmless, goes meekly to his corner. Hardy, Wells, Kipling, and Barrie are prominent. 'H. G.' I did not recognise and Barrie is suffering from swollen head. Shaw is there in fine fettle; this is not the vigorous Methuselist, snowy of beard, but a fiftyish, twinkling, diabolonian Shaw, the author of *The Anarchists' Handbook* not yet agonised by surtax, George the merry wrestler on the Fabian Socialists behalf. It was nice to meet that early G. B. S. once more.

Somerset Maugham does not yet ' make the grade.' Nor does J. B. Priestley. He would be a popular addition. Scott and Dickens are present, of course, but I was surprised to find Macaulay in this limited galaxy. Here are Burns and Byron, but no Shelley or Keats: and, surprisingly, no Tennyson, surely a wax-worthy Victorian, if ever there was one.

There is a children's section with the heroes and heroines of nursery rhymes. But the characters of adults' fiction do not qualify, save in a title, e.g. ' Sleeping Beauty, modelled from a Lady of the Court of Versailles.' I suggest that one of the duller historical tableaux be replaced by a set-piece of the local genius, honouring the detective maestro of Baker Street. Sherlock Holmes and Dr. John Watson could be shown, in their habit as they lived, at No. 221b. Mrs. Hudson would be seen removing dishes in the background, while Billy the page-boy introduces a trembling member of the distressful clientèle, seeking the favour of Holmesian intervention. She would be a late Victorian lady of title, distinguished but distraught, white, shaky, and oppressed by one of those menaces, snake, hound, or human, which Holmes could so lucidly explain and so effectively expose and destroy. Holmes would have a pistol in one hand—for he has just been practising his marksmanship on the wall—a drug-taker's syringe in the other, a violin handy, a pipe in mouth, and his dressing-gown for robe. Watson would be deeply perusing the *British Medical Journal.*

Here is a modeller's heaven and the adjacence of Mrs. Hudson's lodgings demands the addition. No room? Could we not spare 'When did you last see your father?'; a tableau of the Royal children of Charles I being mildly 'grilled' by the Round-heads?

For the first showing of the Holmes' group Mr. Christopher Morley might suitably be fetched from New York to draw the curtain and speak to the Immortal Memory. He is a mogul of the Baker Street Irregulars, whose sixty members—since there were sixty Holmes and Watson stories—meet convivially to celebrate the famous partnership of No. 221b. The fundamental doctrine of the B.S.I., Mr. Morley has explained, when they set aside for an evening the fundamental trivialities of their own lives, is that the Holmes-Watson saga, ' officially denominated by Mr. Elmer Davis, *The Sacred Writings*, is more actual and more timely than anything that happens to ourselves or happened to its mortal mouthpiece. The greatest art is the annihilation of art.' Mr. Morley would, of course, appear sporting the colours of the B.S.I., the three shades of Holmes's dressing-gown, which faded from royal purple to blemished blue and so to mouse.

The waxworkers, on the whole, do their job extremely well. Not every time, but reasonably often, they present the living image or, if you prefer the phrase, the ' dead spit.' (Why a ' dead spit ' should be a synonym for a living image I have never understood.) The legs they seem to find difficult and the feet and their coverings rarely seem altogether natural.

I hope that no whimsical director will arise in the firm eager to break with sober representation and to bring in New Art, proclaiming that in wax, as on canvas, not the man's lineaments and likeness but his soul and his subconscious must be expressed. This would soon mean transferring to Tussaud's the studied deformities of the modern art galleries. The public, which strikes me as simple and sincere in its pursuit of knowledge about men, women, and murderers, wants the actual, not the ingenious. Distortion, if you crave it, can easily be found on the ground-floor among the mirrors in the Amusement Hall, mirrors which make you swell like a prize vegetable marrow or taper like a gigantic and grotesque cigar. So far so good, with Madame Tussaud's. Let a decent conservatism prevent commissions from being given to modern sculptors who would only transfer to wax the tricks they play in stone and turn in a load of dropsical dancers, archbishops as goitred as gaitered, and film-stars with ankles as substantial and unlovely as a major drain-pipe. Such art may be all very well on the periphery of 'Torracorra' or the King's Road. But where the Marylebone Road, with its medical, clerical and general propriety, mingles with Holmesian Baker Street we shall neither expect nor endure anything of that order.

As a matter of fact revolutionary changes are very unlikely in this family business, whose chief artist is now Bernard Tussaud, great-great-grandson of Madame Tussaud. The original Madame began life as Marie Grosholtz, niece of Dr. Philippe Curtius of Berne who had used modelling in wax to assist his medical work and finally set up in Paris in 1762 as an exhibitor of waxworks on a commercial basis.

Marie began to help him in his work and the results proved extremely popular. Royal patronage was soon granted to the firm. Thus Marie became an intimate friend of the French King's sister Elizabeth, and went to live with her at Versailles, giving instruction there in this now fashionable 'Ceraceous art.' In 1791, when the crash of Revolution came, two Tussaud busts were carried in the rebels' van, although Marie was at the Court and so on the dangerous side of the social fence. The mob, carrying the Tussaud effigies of the popular Necker and the no less popular Duc D'Orleans, which they had seized from the exhibition, went storming through Paris. There was bloodshed and the busts were smashed. As images they were lost, but as symbols they were triumphant and the Bastille was stormed two days later.

Naturally, as the struggle grew more bitter, Marie's connection with the Court was a source of danger. After the September Massacres she was set to the hideous task of moulding impressions of the heads that tumbled at the guillotine, including even that of her patroness and very dear friend, Elizabeth. She was kept in a dungeon and was near to the knife herself, but the Reign of Terror was over before her turn came. On release she paid off large debts incurred by her uncle, Dr. Curtius, and set the business going again. But Napoleonic Paris became a difficult market and Marie, who had now married a Burgundian engineer called Francois Tussaud, and had cleared up all her uncle's liabilities, packed up after the Treaty of Amiens in 1802 and came to London with seventy exhibits and her abundant skill at adding to them. 'Tussauds'' began its London life in 1803 at the Old Lyceum Theatre.

The show later went on tour, traversing Scotland and Ireland and having many vicissitudes. Madame was ready for a caravan life in hard and uncertain times; she nearly lost all her stock in the Reform Bill Riots at Bristol, and finally set up at the Portman Rooms in Baker Street. She was then seventy-five and still a vigorous worker and manager. She died in 1850 at the age of ninety. Her sons carried on and their successors, still Tussauds, moved to the present address in 1882. The disastrous fire of 1925 and severe war damage in 1940 have meant much renewal of effort and the renewal has constantly been made. Waxworks, it might be thought, would suffer from the charge of being antiquated and utterly out of date in an age of television. But their appeal abides, especially with the country visitors to London, and there is no sign of languishing favour.

The Chamber of Horrors was a name invented by *Punch* and shrewdly adopted from that source. The Chamber began in Paris as ' La Caverne des Grands Voleurs ' and in England was called ' The Separate Room ' since the famous might reasonably resent sharing a plinth with the infamous. For the pleasure of entering this segregated rogues' gallery the charge was sixpence. No reward has ever been offered to those who would dare to sleep all night in the ghoulish atmosphere of the Chamber; the legend about a Tussaud challenge to would-be ' all-nighters ' has attracted myriads of acceptances, but the whole thing is a myth. There is no challenge and at closing-time all visitors must quit. The cleaners come in and intending stowaways stand no chance of achieving their gruesome nocturne.

Down in the cellar you do, in fact, touch grim history. Since the fire damage was least in the underground section many of the Chamber's originals remain; some are actually the surviving work of the foundress, Madame Tussaud herself, the same Madame who had to wait upon the guillotine for her subjects and was so nearly a victim of it in person. The French Revolution Death Masks are hers; Robespierre's model was fashioned by the woman he purposed to destroy. Those who have enjoyed James Bridie's play *The Anatomist*, which introduces the Edinburgh body snatchers and criminal suppliers of the medical dissecting-room, will not only find those scoundrels on view: here are the original images made by Madame in Edinburgh, where, flinching from nothing, she modelled Hare after a visit to the prison and Burke from a death mask taken three hours after his execution.

Bernard Shaw called the Jacobean dramatist Webster a ' Tussaud Laureate ' and certainly to sup with horrors was very much to Webster's fancy. He knew about waxworks, which were then one of the pleasures of the town. His Duchess of Malfi refers to the old witchcraft, which would kill a person by stabbing his image, when she refers to:

My picture, fashion'd out of wax,
Stuck with a magical needle and then buried
In some foul dunghill.

This occurs after she has been presented with a dead man's hand, presumably in wax for stage purposes, and shown, also presumably in wax, ' the artificial figures of Antonio and his children, appearing as if they were dead.'

Madame Tussaud would not have lacked employment in Webster's London. Her profession is as old as Babylon. The word mummy comes from the Arabic for wax and that turns up again in Webster. 'Who am I?' says the tortured duchess. ' Thou art a box of worm-seed, at best but a salvatory of green mummy' is her tormentor's reply. Morbidity and waxworks have long been companions and Tussaud's firm itself relates the case of a Mrs. Salmon who kept a waxwork show in Fleet Street during the eighteenth century.

> She married an undertaker named Death, dressed in white crêpe, and wore a bonnet bordered with coffin trimmings. Every night she slept in a winding sheet, laid on a mattress under a canopy of state. A shroud served her for a night-dress while a pall was her coverlet. Her favourite occupation? Watching public executions!

A lady much to John Webster's fancy!

Those destined for a niche, criminals apart, are invited to give an interview, to be measured carefully, and to be photographed from a number of angles. Rarely does the modeller have to rely on the photographs only. Those portrayed can go and see their images, raise objections, and ask for alterations. None has ever demanded a complete cancellation. It is easy for critics to advise the management on policy and to tell them whom to remove and with whom to replace the exiles. But in these days the cost of materials plus purchase tax (plaster of Paris, artificial eyes, bees-wax and vegetable wax, and hair) runs high: so does the cost of the time and labour involved. Without reckoning on the bill for uniform or clothes, a new figure will now involve, merely as a figure, an expenditure of one hundred and fifty pounds.

I do not often quarrel with an essay of Sir Max Beerbohm's, but his piece on Madame Tussaud's in the volume called *More* is an attack based on a misapprehension of this peep-show's purpose. 'Life, save only through conventions, is inimitable. The more closely it is aped, the more futile and unreal the copy.' That is a half-truth, but it is a half-truth which only applies if you visit Tussaud's in search of profound artistic valuations of character and personality. Nobody, surely, imagines that modelling in wax, applied in a spirit of surface-realism to plaster of Paris foundation, is going to rival the interpretative power of the great sculptor or the great painter. No craftsman of a wax-work exhibition makes that sort of claim: he is entertaining the public by showing his own dexterity working on the superficial likenesses of others. He has no ambition to be a Rodin or a John.

So Max's lamentations about ' barren effigies,' ' cadaverous and ignoble dolls,' ' fatuous puppets,' are beside the point. He thinks of people haunted by the knowledge that ' a ghastly double ' of themselves is standing all day, catalogued and stared at by the blinking passers-by. I do not believe that it ever worried anybody to be thus docketed—after all they are catalogued at the Royal Academy—and set on public view. They can easily have their image removed if it does not please them. And when Max adds,

Is the condemned murderer ever appalled by the thought of his sure survival under Madame's roof ?

I reply that most murderers are obviously immensely vain— often vanity has been their overthrow—and would be furious at the idea of being left out.

No, when we descend to the cellar, we need not shed tears for the tender sensibilities of outraged homicides, whose shrinking nature would absent them from publicity awhile. Nor, in the Upper Halls, need we worry over 'this hateful craft' and 'obscene images.' This is a Peep Show for the People, dealing in a craftsmanlike way with certain human appearances. If, like Max, you want profound artistic realities, you have only to slip down Baker Street, turn left, and enter the Wallace Collection.

CHAPTER XIV
Fresh Air

—————————⟨∿∾⟩—————————

LONDON'S NEAREST seaside town is Southend. You may call it riverside if you like. To be exact, it is estuarial. It lies to the east and since London is sharply divided into east and west, it is little visited by Kensington, Hampstead and the like. Their Marine Parade is at Brighton and Brighton certainly has more to offer in the way of history and elegance. But Southend, with Thorpe and Westcliff and Leigh, has swollen so rapidly and so vastly during our own time, that its population has risen to rival Brighton's. Many City workers, who use the City termini, find it a handy as well as healthy home throughout the year; and in summer it is the chief resort of East London, with a beach packed to its last inch of sand—or low-tide mud. The very mud can be publicised. It is said to have its high, hygienic merits and to yield a nice, clean aroma of iodine. Moreover the 'tripping' Londoner can go there by water, which is difficult in the case of places beyond Margate and wellnigh impossible in the case of Brighton. To go down the river is a form of travel that employs the eye and quickens the imagination.

But I am writing of London in winter and Southend has nothing to match the winter season that Brighton celebrates. But it is there and the air blows keen and the approach by land is swift enough whether you go by rail or by car. The great arterial road which runs from Ilford to the sea is straight and broad and the distance from much of London is under forty miles, in many cases far less. North Londoners can get there by taking the North Circular Road to join the Southend Arterial, but the sign-posting of the former is extremely bad and you may disastrously wander south into Walthamstow, Wanstead, and utter perplexity. But if you manage to skirt securely round the south side of Epping Forest, there is quick, easy going, at least in mid-week, once the Arterial is safely achieved.

The drive, on a winter day, across the flats of southern Essex, is certainly unromantic. London is devouring that terrain with unremitting greed, but all that it consumes it does not necessarily destroy. The new factories of light industry that keep appearing where once our kings were wont to hunt are chiefly dependent on electricity. They raise no chimneys, belch no smoke. They show traces of good, functional architecture and they often spawn housing that is no disgrace. The myriads of little villas and bungalows appear to be decently kept, are cleanly curtained, and suggest a fairly high degree of happiness and well-being.

I do not know why the superior so often sneer at ' bungaloid growth.' The one-story house does not affront the sky or smirch the sky-line and it is a precious friend of the harassed housewife. Behind all these frontages there is a woman slogging away to get the man to work, the children to school, and the house in order for their return. If she is spared the drudgery of stairs—or has no more than one upper story to tend—she feels the benefit, as they say. Building low may eat up more land than building high and it is true that we need, and shall increasingly need, every acre of ground for our food. It is a miracle to me how all this over-spill of London is fed and watered and given its fresh milk, as the farms vanish and the grass yields to brick and cement. But so far we have coped: and, as I said, there is an air of satisfaction about these new and multitudinous habitations. I refuse to sigh for the Dickensian London because the poor could then have oysters: they did not live long to enjoy them. And their children had rickets: and many other bad things too.

You are whisked along past signs of a fairly wide prosperity. The kind of home which you would not expect to have any spare pounds for the more sumptuous pleasures now frequently sprouts the horns of a television set. That means a widening access to all kinds of spectacle: the inhabitants of Oakdene and Elmhurst are thus given the best possible view of State processions and of the principal athletic panoramas, for the viewer in his parlour gets the front seat all along the ceremonial route or round the sporting arena.

I shall at this point be told that I am taking a mechanical, a materialistic view of life, but I am not abashed. The man or woman working at a routine job in a factory beside the Southend Arterial will not easily find 'joy in labour.' If he or she has joy outside of it, laid on by this device or that, we are inhuman prigs to be sniffy about the release and the escape that these things offer. Half our lives are spent in winter, when the pleasures of the open—if they are at all pleasant in February— are denied to the factory worker for five days at least in the week and to the housewife nearly all the time.

Some smile sadly at the alleged snobbery which will not be numbered in its dwellings, but stands out for Elmhurst and Oakdene. That habit, no doubt, increases the perplexity of postmen and of others seeking to find addresses. But surely it is a demonstration of independence, a snatch at some distinction, made by the members of massed populations, who feel their personality menaced. In logic it may be absurd to see a bungalow in southern Essex carrying a name from Snowdonia or the Grampians: but in principle it is a healthy reaction to environment. To refuse to be No. 228 and to insist on being a Cumbrian lake or sylvan glade instead is an assertion of human pride that I find far more likeable than ludicrous. 'Over the hills and far away' is a line of folk-poetry as splendid as it is simple and it is deeply rooted in English sentiment. If the tenant of a mountain-clamorous villa never gets to the mountains at least he has had the glimpse in his mind's eye. He transcends the factory: he soars above Essex.

After Romford the countryside, seen, perhaps, on a grey March morning, is admittedly, a thin, semi-rural thing. But the side-road labelling is attractive. That way to Childerditch! Some comfortable, square church towers suggest the old solidities of a settled countryside. The main road, as always, evokes the architectural worst, imposing new houses of call—they cannot be called plain inn or tavern—with mock-Tudor frontages, assorted outbuildings, vile lettering, and no structural soul of their own. But we are past them—and here is Southend. A prominent advertisement proclaims Somebody's Meat Pies and another adds, in sinister proximity, Prepare to Meet your God.

The West End of London is not only sniffy about Southend. It is extremely ignorant. Southend has had both history and clientèle of the highest distinction. It was evidently a notable resort in the Stone Age. The Romans regarded the estuary as excellent for oysters. Canute the Dane won a battle nearby. The Normans built Prittlewell Priory—and what was the first Southend but Prittlewell Parva? The Plantagenets used it for the chase, the Tudors found some of their stoutest sea captains and chivviers of the Spaniard in the harbour town of Leigh, and when the Dutch sailed up the Thames Southend had a nice view of the proceedings. True, it was a very small Southend, still Prittlewell Parva, but glory was coming.

The enthusiastic historian on whom I am drawing, Miss Kate O'Brien, renowned novelist but indulging in no fiction, I trust, in her Essex Estuary contribution to a volume called *Beside The Seaside*, admits that Southend had only fifty-one houses in 1768. But the age of sea-bathing had arrived and what Martha Gunn did for Brighton by dipping the nobility and their ladies, a Mrs. Glasscock did for Southend. Bathing machines were trundled

down the shore. Mrs. Glasscock set folk bobbing and ducking.
And Royalty arrived.

The Regent himself did not come: his Brighton loyalties were
strong. But his Princess spent two seasons there; hence Royal
Terrace. Emma, Lady Hamilton, with Nelson away, attempted
to banish her tedium in the newly fashionable little town, which
soon had the usual apparatus of pleasure, Assembly Rooms,
Theatre and pleasing opportunities for social encounter. Jane
Austen heard of it and sent some of her characters there. Then
came the new-fangled steamboats, rivalling the Margate Hoy.
Dickens had strong Kentish loyalties, we know, and knew
Thanet's marine pleasures from cliff to cove. Did he never seek
Southend? It seems absurd that a shore so lavishly Cockneyfied,
so richly relished by the London millions, should draw its literary
réclame from the genteel Miss Austen of Hampshire rather than
from the exuberant Londoner that was Boz.

Round about, as Miss O'Brien reminds us

> There are churches at Prittlewell and Ashingdon and Rayleigh
> and Paglesham and Rochford and Hockley and Great and Little
> Wakering, which provide enough worries in the way of Norm.
> and Perp. and Early Dec. to satisfy the most madly masochistic.
> And at Prittlewell there is one lovely fifteenth-century window.
> If you do not instantly pick it out from among its nineteenth-
> century sisters, do accept the test in humility, abandon the pursuit
> of difficult æsthetics and come back and be natural on the pier,
> where beauty is not very hard to coax.

Very well then, I return to the pier, for that, not the ecclesiastical
architecture of South Essex, is what have we set out to behold.
But the pier we look upon in winter is not the pier that she
describes, with lovers and intending seafarers and amateur anglers
all massed in their various felicities. The pier is a mile and a
third long, a record, and not a bit of Southend fun only, but
extremely serviceable to the Navy in wartime. Southend may
have had an amusing view of nautical manœuvres in the seven-

teenth century: in the twentieth, its site was unenviable. After all, here are London's gates, as the fortifiers of Shoebury and Sheerness well understood. A similar comprehension was shared by the Germans.

This pier, which covers nearly the distance of the Derby horse-race and suitably provides mechanical transport to roll you to and from the sea, may, from June onwards, be as tight-jammed as Leicester Square on a Cup Final night. But on a cold Monday in March it is a desert peninsula on which you are monarch of all you survey. There is a charm about this great empty proboscis. Indeed, there is a charm about all piers, a form of construction in which the English have notably excelled. The utilitarian Scots have landing-stages: the notion of invading the sea with a Moorish pleasure-dome, a bulbous Oriental palace, a dancing-hall with minarets, and a raree-show of automatic fun, games, fortune-telling and tentative improprieties, never drew capital investment from the Clydeside men of affairs: not for Rothesay, Largs, and Dunoon such maritime frippery as this. The Southend pier is by no means as Kubla-Khanish as many others, but, as well as serving the ships which cannot get near Southend itself in most tides, it offers abundant recreation. But not on a cold Monday in March.

The sea-front, too, is all but empty: ozone is plentiful, the iodised ozone that should send us back into the town with an appetite craving more than the shell-fish for which Southend is famous. The place caters on the grand scale. One feels that, though the world's larder may shrivel yet again to a brace of baked beans, you will always find satisfaction here. You walk westward under the shrub-covered cliffs. The Palace Hotel towers above you; so does the statue of Queen Victoria: so does the old Terrace which is Southend's claim to style. The shrubberies provide shelter for snoozing and flirtation (but not in March) and the beach-side road invites to brisk exercise.

Westcliff immediately begins. It is trim, orderly, well-to-do.

(What a captivating word is this well-to-do: 'possessed of a competency,' says the *Oxford English Dictionary* and then, somewhat sombrely, it cites this example of usage: 'it is only idle and well-to-do people who kill themselves: 1850.' But Westcliff was hardly there in 1850 and I am sure that the suicide-rate has never run high amid this serene spread of villadom.) There is no pretence about Westcliff: it is a home, not a home from home: it is lived in by sedate people who surely listen at nights to the Home Programme with only occasional meanderings into the Light and no truck at all, I fancy, with the ambitious austerities of the Third. Back it stretches to the high ground—high, that is, by the modest standards of altitude existing in South Essex—and it never loses character. Well-to-do, possessed of a competency; taxes may press, but the standard is not lowered. Decorum prevails. Church services and devotional facilities are as strongly publicised in Westcliff as are more worldly activities in Southend. You work your way towards Leigh, which, at a cursory glance, is disappointing. It may have been the sea-dogs' kennel in the old days of sail. But it has no such character to-day. Doubtless had you time to dig yourself into Leigh you would strike what is left of maritime life. But the wind is a little too bracing: and, after all, you came to see Southend.

A seaside resort in winter has a dormouse quality. In March the long sleep is beginning to end. The verge of the seaside promenade is covered with boats which have been hauled up for their months of repose. But their owners are tinkering and painting against the coming times of prosperous hire. The sails of the model of an Elizabethan vessel that lies in dry dock beside the pier-head are being gently exercised. The roundabouts and children's railways are being surveyed by their proprietors with oil-cans and tins of varnish handy. There is a month to go till Easter, when the great Fun-Machine will be cranked up for summer's action.

The shelters are always a conspicuous feature of the English seaside. For the seaside, which is the playground of the active, is also the refuge of the old. They come with their overcoats and their limping, rheumatic walk to take the health-giving air: but not too much of it. There are limits to salubrity. With a rug and a newspaper and a municipal shelter the best may be made of both worlds. Just enough ozone, just enough protection. Here one can look out across the misty estuary and speculate, without excess of exposure, on the nature and purpose of the ships that are going up to the Port of London or going out again to the real, the uncomfortable sea.

It is time for tea. You enter a vast hotel, how vast is only discovered when you tread the furlongs of the enormous corridors. (Might there not be mechanical transport in here as well as on the pier, with separate trams conveying you to the right room for the repast or the lounge specially appointed for teas or merely to the lavatories?) You encounter huge deserts of space with but a singleton customer surveying a plate of cakes. In a month or two the Palm court, the Chinese room, the Oriental lounge, the whole Taj-Mahalish palace will be packed with tea-consumers. At present life seems to be centred, at the end of another furlong of corridor, in the Billiard room: at any rate there are voices there and the click-clack of the game. But tea arrives and you take it gladly. It is beautifully warm: prodigies of central-heating are going on somewhere, seemingly for the sole benefit of you, the singleton, and the staff. You are served quickly and well. Then two substantial ladies arrive, tea-craving, and occupy a distant cranny. It is almost a crowd.

You like Southend on a chill Monday in March. Up in the town there is bustle enough and the chain stores, glaring at each other in colourful rivalry across the High Street, have their press of local customers. But here, in a vast Hotel, is the paradise of solitudinarians; here is the Nirvana of those who would nod above a toasted tea-cake. Outside is the ozone; but not here.

The war may have smashed a lot of windows, but the glaziers have done their work well: you are safe from the superfluities of tonic air. This is a super-shelter. You can hardly stir yourself to face the Arterial again. But you have seen the sea. You have cried ' Thalassa, Thalassa.' You have ' felt the benefit.'

On the way to Southend by road one skirts the southern verge of Epping Forest. It is another instance of the East-West partition of London that few Kensingtonians, even the most active, take the woodland way on foot from Chingford to Epping Village; nor do the inactive drive their cars from their own High Street to the eminence of High Beech in order to bask on this summit and look out over Hertfordshire. The Forest is fairly quickly reached by the North Circular Road, but Kensington is a long way from that and involves a tedious drive to it. Hampstead, however, is not; yet how many Hampsteadians have any knowledge whatever of the best bit of real country (apart from parkland and garden) within ten miles of the City?

I cannot remember ever being taken to Epping during my boyhood. The place, one gathered, was East Endy: you went from Liverpool Street, which was pestilent: it was more Epping than Forest: and so on. Certainly it is N.E. London, but now you can go by Tube to its edge or you can take a bus straight to the Royal Forest Hotel, Chingford, right among the oak-glades, from a number of places including Victoria and Golder's Green. As for the last indictment, ' more Epping than Forest,' it is absurd, because the Forest is large, genuine, and easily provides solitude if solitude is what you seek, while the broad main street of Epping, a townlet set high at the north end of the wooded ridge, is a charming piece of rural England and might be a hundred miles from Liverpool Street. Indeed, it is just here, so close to Ilford and Walthamstow and the like, that you encounter, with a shock of delight, a still unbroken rusticity: the feeling of country comes much quicker in this part of Essex than it does in Surrey.

Take for example, Waltham Abbey, which lies in the Lea Valley to the west of the Forest heights. (Heights? Well, one has to use words comparatively. In the kingdom of the blind the one-eyed man is king. In southern Essex High Beech's altitude of 388 feet is something of a mountain.) The little town beside the Abbey, despite the presence of permanent munition factories, remains, obstinately, an Essex market, where farmers have bought, sold, and worshipped for centuries. There was a big church there in Saxon times and after the Conquest the Normans put some of their best work into what became an Augustinian Abbey of considerable wealth and rare beauty.

Here is one of the cosiest of our famous ecclesiastical buildings. It is not so large as to dwarf the individual worshipper: the Burne-Jones' windows radiate a mellow glory and the roof painted by Poynter adds to the air of a domestic holiness. Restoration and renewal have here been at their happiest. The massive columns, oddly marked with chevrons as though they were to be given non-commissioned rank in the Building Corps, suggest enormous endurance, but there is nothing overbearing about them. If you consider New Year's Eve to be a family festival, then the association with that date of this comfortable Abbey is particularly apt. Here was ' the single church below the hill ' from which Tennyson called the wild bells to tintinnabulate to the wild sky. The sky, on December 31, might well be wild. But is this also the right adjective for metal instruments strictly and harmoniously controlled by the human hand? Well, we need not argue the point.

Ring out the thousand wars of old
Ring in the thousand years of peace.

Waltham Abbey is still ringed round with factories of death: as I came out of its placid medievalism, there sounded the tic-tac of machine-gun fire. Ring out, wild bells! Your summons dismally abides.

The Reformation proved advantageous hereabouts to the Denny family: Sir Edward of that house lies in comfortable sleep upon his tomb, like one who had done well for himself, which indeed he had done as a good Protestant subject of Henry VIII. The only disturbing feature in this congenial fane of the Epping country is the museum in the Lady Chapel which makes a special feature of the machinery of punishment. Here are pillory and whipping-post: the latter is a piece of rare craftsmanship and far too handsome for the grisly office which it served. It can hardly have compensated the wretched victim of the lash to know that he was fettered to a work of art. A reassuring feature is the set of nice little pews set aside for the boys and girls of the Sunday school. Seeing them, we realise that this is a family Abbey and not a great cold pile, fuller of embattled history than of workaday humanity.

But we must get back to the woods. Waltham was mentioned to remind Londoners that you need not go to Tewkesbury or the Yorkshire dales in order to find English Abbey architecture at its best. Travel but a dozen miles north of the Bank of England and there is the testament of Norman faith set in stone, let us hope for many a century to come. It is only a short journey eastward to High Beech and to the Forest famous for its oaks and hornbeams. On a week-day in winter you will find almost nobody about and the ten-mile ridge—rather narrow, it is true, with a breadth of one or two miles—seems to be deep country, leaving the eye vexed by no interruption to the exquisite umber tints of woodland in winter.

In spring there will be infinite green and far more people. But now there is the russet carpet of dead bracken and dead leaves and the curious smoky colour that hangs over naked branches in the pale sunshine of cold weather. There are birches in plenty to break the pattern of brown and grey and to streak the sombre tapestry with silver. But when all the praise of proud-pied April has been sung, I shall not yield in my admiration of

the leafless branch and tracery of twigs which the dark season
brings. Our copses at this time have a variety of tint which
summer never equals. Among these hues they yield a purplish
fume in certain lights which is strangely beautiful. The flush of
May delights us by its youth, its promise, its flood of new vitality.
But, after all, the winter woods are not dead, but sleeping, and
out of that life delayed there come various emanations of the
most delicate kind. Grey tree-tops wave like ostrich plumes
before the winds of March above the orange waste of undergrowth in ruin. Those Londoners who like that sort of landscape
have only to take bus or tube to have the possession of it and to
enjoy the legacy ' of all the woods that autumn bereaves in all
the world.'

This piece of goodness was saved from the land-grabbers and
the destroyers by unselfish mid-Victorians, as was Hampstead
Heath on the other side of North London. One of the chief
rescuers was the City of London. The Forest had dwindled to
nearly 3000 acres by 1851, but it was restored to 5500 by the
time that Queen Victoria, coming from Windsor by train via
Acton, Hampstead, Victoria Park, and the N.E. Line to Chingford,
opened this enlarged domain for public recreation in 1882. It
was further increased in 1930 by the addition of Knighton Wood.
The City has also turned a swamp into a lake. Few people
realise what far-seeing and beneficent Foresters have been the
Lord Mayor of London and the Common Council. Far to the
west, north of Slough, they own and administer Burnham
Beeches for the general good, just as they are the guardians of
Epping on the east.

I have said that this would not be a book of grumbles: but
one complaint must be made about our open spaces. It seems
impossible to make our local authorities realise that summer
restaurants in places of this kind, with music added, can be
desirable additions to the public enjoyment of a summer evening.
There are inns and hotels round the Forest and I am not denying

the service they may render in their own way. But, when one thinks of what other nations do in order to give parkland catering a standard well above the sort of thing that we endure, it is really humiliating to meet the entertainment usually offered in English ' beauty-spots.' It is sadly characteristic of our country that ' beauty-spot ' has now become a word of derision, suggesting careless crowds and their litter of broken bottles and cigarette cartons, newspapers, and sandwich packing. People who come out in that mood do not care about what they eat or the conditions of the meal. Yet other democracies manage to cater for the myriads with taste and cleanliness, presumably because the myriads have some discrimination.

When I go to a place like Epping Forest, I always remember the enchanting hours I have spent in the Royal Deer Forest at Klampenborg, which stands to Copenhagen as Chingford does to the City. There, open to all, is a rolling demesne of open grass land and huge beeches, with tinkling and horse-driven droshkys (no motor traffic allowed). It was once reserved for the regal chase, but is now the free rambling-ground of Danish Social Democracy. At the end of the park nearest the railway station is a summer fair-ground. That, by our practice, should be dirty, dusty, and dishevelled. But in Denmark it is gay without being rough and noisy. Moreover it has a score of the most excellent restaurants to which people of all incomes come out from town, not only for a special celebration but as a routine of civilised pleasure. The standard of cooking and service is as high in some of these *al fresco* restaurants as it is in the august establishments in the city—and the Danish standard is very high indeed.

There is none of the lamentable English belief that, once on an outing, anything does or that a beauty-spot must inevitably become a bear-garden. Denmark is not alone in such nicety of management. In other countries people of discretion would decide, on a radiant evening of June, that nothing could be so

agreeable as to slip out and dine in their Forest. But that sort of
resolve is not made in London. I am not singling out Epping
alone for censure: in my own Hampstead, the facilities for
refreshment on the heath are on the tea-and-bun level—and
there is not much even of that. But I am becoming peevish,
which was none of my intention.

Working westwards round North London it would be folly
not to pause at Ken Wood, which is entered either from Hampstead Heath or from the summit road which unites Hampstead
with Highgate, passing the old Spaniards Inn. The Spaniards
has Turpin legends and a more substantial ghost in Mr. Pickwick's
Mrs. Bardell. It was the landlord of this inn who chiefly saved
Ken Wood House from the fury of the Gordon rioters: having
sacked and burned the hated Lord Chancellor Mansfield's house
in Bloomsbury Square, they surged out to do the same for his
country seat at Ken Wood. But the innkeeper served them
liberally with liquor and Lord Mansfield's steward then bettered
the instruction: so the marauders became as reeling drunk as
Caliban when plotting in the company of Trinculo and Stephano.
Accordingly they dallied over their plans for destruction and
there was time to fetch out protective troops from London. Thus
the Adam mansion was spared to stand upon its terrace; and
still it looks out across the paddock dipping to the ponds with a
majestic fragment of the old Middlesex forest climbing the hillside behind them.

Since I have lived in this district most of my life, and Ken
Wood has been open to the public since 1926, I have had the
opportunity to walk on the terrace in every month of the year
and every phase of the weather. Here is, for me, the most
beautiful sylvan view of any within the London district, including
even Richmond. Behind one, to the north, is the Adam façade:
in front of this lies a magnificent surge of giant timber with the
little, lily-covered meres in front and behind them the old
artificial bridge, completely unreal, just a piece of stage-scenery

serving no purpose, which it was one of the pleasant whims of the Age of Reason to construct. On an autumn or spring day, with the cream-and-blue Constable sky, with the old foliage in its tatters or the young in the bud, here is a piece of landscape which is a superb possession for London people and is absurdly ignored by them. Even on a fine Sunday you will not meet crowds there, though the gates be passed by a frequent bus service and the whole distance from Charing Cross cannot be much above five miles. On week-days it is a case of desolate splendour: you would probably pass more people on the way up Scawfell Pike than you would meet in Ken Wood on a Monday afternoon.

William Murray, Lord Mansfield, the famous but not the first owner of Ken Wood, was a Scot who rode up to London as a boy of fifteen because he could not pay the coach-fare: he had the traditional sack of meal to keep him in calories and his great brain and relentless determination to provide him with a career. His meal-sack he transformed in time to the Woolsack. He was not a likeable man, but, as a landscape gardener and a planter of trees, he had taste to match his wealth: the Londoner who now relishes the layout of the timber and avenues round the Adam house owes much to Mansfield, but still more to another peer, Edward Guinness, Earl of Iveagh, who gave the mansion to the nation together with its notable collection of eighteenth century paintings and furniture and a handsome endowment.

Damaged during the war, the house remained closed for several years, but it has now been reopened as a specimen of eighteenth-century elegance and comfort with capital examples of the portraiture of the time by Gainsborough, Raeburn, Reynolds, and others. Whether you stroll inside or take what winter sun may be trapped on the southward-facing terrace you are enjoying the best thing in London of its particular kind, the milord's retreat as the milord knew it, the Palladian house in all its trim, and the completely pastoral and sylvan view with which he had defended himself against the pressure of the growing city.

The gardens are now economically kept and might be much richer to the eye, but the great colonnade of giant limes beside them is a matchless aisle of timber and the beeches on the hill are some of London's best. The guide-books assure you that foxes and badgers still lurk hereabouts; but, as you can never be there at night, the only time when such beasts may be visible, there is no need to be concerned about the quadrupeds. Bird life is ample and visible in day time. Jays and magpies you may easily glimpse amid the naked trees of winter and there is usually a rich flighting of tits: the waterfowl on the ponds vary according to season: I have been told of kingfishers seen here, but have never had the luck to share that cerulean flash.

The Ken Wood ponds are the top of a chain of informal reservoirs developed by another of North London's thoughtful careerists from Scotland. This was William Paterson; he originated the Darien Scheme. This ought to have opened up the isthmus of Panama long before the canal was cut, but it was killed by jealousy and suspicion: Paterson succeeded, however, in assisting the creation of the Bank of England of which he was a director. He planned, by damming the rivulets emerging from Ken Wood, to store enough water to give Hampstead and Kentish Town (presumably Ken Wood and Kentish Town refer to a common origin or owner) an adequate and hygienic series of cisterns. But the New River Company, not strong when Myddleton, its founder, died, was now vigorous enough to defeat competition such as Paterson planned. So the ponds remain untapped, but serving the nesting swan, mallard, and moor-hen, the human bather, the swimmers and high divers, the owner of model yachts and of the fussy, noisy mechanical boats, and, also, of the patient fishermen who sit out in all weathers, escaping the wife's tongue, perhaps, but catching little save a cold.

There is at present no statuary in the grounds of Ken Wood. Were any funds to be available I suggest that Paterson, Mansfield and Iveagh might be suitable subjects; their figures should stand above the waters which the first collected, among the plantations which we owe to the second, and beside the mansion so generously given by the third.

London has gained enormously in lung-power by such acquisitions as that of Ken Wood. I remember gazing from behind bars at much of its parkland when it was the private golf course of the mansion. Delectable acres were firmly fenced off. Now the people have all that, as well as the wood itself. The presence of this extra space for peaceful wandering makes it fair enough that much more of the old heath should be used by the allotment gardeners and by the players of games. There were no Sunday games in such places when I came to London and not many on Saturdays. Now the young people really can strip for action on their limited occasions of leisure instead of loafing about and waiting for sexual encounter as the only unforbidden sport of the Lord's Day. Hampstead Heath, with Ken Wood, is far better employed for the public advantage than ever before and I fancy that the same is true of all such open spaces, where the balance between the growing of food, the playing of organised games, and the gentle exercise of strolling is now sensibly maintained.

If I may have one more grumble, it is about the complete refusal of the users of our commons to tidy up their mess. After a sunny week-end the litter of papers is always appalling: even worse is the scattering of broken glass. Picnic parties, bringing their bottles of milk, usually deem it essential to the day's fun to rob the dairy company of its bottle and to use the same as a target. After it has been duly smashed the jagged fragments are left under trees and in the grass to the very great peril of children playing and tumbling about and to the peril of the dogs' feet too. This is a vicious form of stupidity which you would think that anybody would be ashamed to practise, but it goes on wherever the public flock for recreation in the open: you will even see these broken bottles on sea-beaches where children are naturally running with bare feet.

Most of our open spaces are, following a fine Sunday, repulsive to look at. I would like to see by-laws which allowed flagrant offenders to be sentenced to a punishment fitting the crime. They would be ordered to spend a whole day (or more) in special and easily recognisable overalls, marked Mucky Pup, scavenging around the places in defiling which they had been caught. When that mess was cleared, they could help the park-keepers and gardeners with their duller tasks. But of course nothing so sensible will happen; the ratepayers will continue to pay for clearing up the filth scattered by the unpunished barbarian.

But even when the litterer has done his most in order to leave the world a worse place than he found it, you can lift up your heart unto the beeches in these London woods and forests. There is, in deep forest, always the source of fear. (Panic is named after the terror caused by the rustic god-sprite Pan.)

> *The trees in whose dim shadow*
> *The ghastly priest doth reign,*
> *The priest who slew the slayer*
> *And shall himself be slain.*

The English forests are old enough to have housed Druidical rites and I know of nothing more sinister than a really dense forest of fir-trees: they cluster so thick, and create so airless, so intense a gloom. One meets them especially on Scottish hill-sides, forming coverts almost impregnable by the ordinary walker and blacker than pitch within. But what is left of London Forest is never of that breath-snatching, suffocating density; Epping lies high and is beautifully broken up with open spaces so that the wanderer draws in some true East Anglian air and not just the residue of London's fume. In such minor glades as Ken Wood the land is high and the plantation not too thick. The timber colonnades are as cool as a cathedral: for secular retreat I know no better sanctuary.

CHAPTER XV
Storied Keep

———————⟨◦⟩———————

THE NORMAL ruined castles of the English country-side can
add considerably to the local appearances, but, if they are
to be carefully inspected and tramped through with guide-book
explanations laid on, I prefer to be ' included out ' of the perambu-
lating party. There is a singular monotony about turrets, a
damnable iteration of keeps, dungeons, and moats. Some dead
buildings have a pulse of life in them: the Parthenon is forever
Athens. But I find no animation in these baronial skeletons.
With trees about and a door-mat of buttercups your rustic castle
can be the gracious centre-piece of a May morning: in the dusk,
with the light behind it, the ancient pile may pass for rather more
than picturesque. But get to grips with the sightseer's job, and
most bastions are bores.

Perhaps the dullness is in myself: the fool sees not the same
castle that the wise man sees. Is it a gap in my chronicles? I was
never taught well about the Middle Ages and I am now totally
incapable of feeling my way, by imagination's light, into the
medieval and baronial way of life. I can read that Leofranc
Fitzurse or some such gentleman of France acquired the land
hereabouts and coaxed, bribed, or terrorised the locals into putting
up this monstrous fort in order to keep themselves down. Such
erection of walls is a job in which the British have patiently
excelled; consider all those miles of solid stone-work set round

the park-lands of noblemen's seats—especially note the vast and imposing walls in lairdly Scotland—set up while the later Fitzurses and McWhustles made wassail and battle. If Balbus be the head of the wall-building clan, as my Latin grammar used to suggest, then we are a nation of Balbics without doubt. China had its Great Wall: we have a myriad park and castle walls, erected by the humbler natives with heavy labour and with small reward, for the express purpose of keeping themselves out of their own land.

I never could feel at home with the Leofranc Fitzurses. Our Norman conquerors had evidently a nice taste in ecclesiastical as well as defensive architecture: they had the means to indulge it and this they triumphantly did with the aid of the masons and hewers and carriers who gave their anonymous services to create the magnificent cathedrals and less exciting castles of our land. What did they do, these Fitzurses, in their keeps while they were waiting for their neighbours, the Fitzgodrics, to come and smoke them out? Wine and women? No doubt, and much of the chase. Perhaps some commissioning of tapestry lest they be deemed no more civilised than the Saxons. But compared with their Tudor successors, so multifarious in creation, so quick in fancy, who came to the hurly-burly of life with a sword in one hand and a sonnet in the other, with the pleasing of a lute as well as with the grasping of a sinecure, the Normans seem as dull as their own castles. Those great grey testaments of theirs, all bone and no heart, are symbolic of the unproductive centuries till Chaucer came and the new English language broke into flower.

In London we have the Tower, or rather that series of linked Towers, which stands on the side of Tower Hill beside the Tower Bridge. Nearly everybody is marched round it in childhood. The Beefeater, who explains that his name is really Buffeteer, the server of the snacks, carries on with his oratorical routine. (The *Oxford English Dictionary* denies this interpretation: but I shall take the good man at his word: he looks so eminently

sound in all things.)   Onward he goes. Bloody Tower . . . Little
Princes . . . and nowadays he comes right up to date with Herr
Hess, among the latest to be incarcerated herein. The Buffeteer
does well by his school parties and eager, culture-conscious
foreigners. At least such was my last experience. He speaks
clear and loud, ' plods on and keeps the passion fresh.' If you
are going to revisit the Tower, I suggest a bright day in winter
as the best. Under a strong sun the cobbles can bully the feet:
on a stuffy day it is hard slogging to go puffing up the White
Tower and gazing at all those acres of armour, those forests of
swords and spears. Let February sunshine speed you: it may well
be warm enough, if the wind can be dodged, to sit out on the
terrace overlooking the river and to watch some seemingly un-
substantial vessel compel the sundering and up-lifting of the
mighty Tower Bridge. There is no need to enter the Tower
itself in order to sit and stare. The outer terrace is common
ground: and there is always considerable delight in watching a
river that is also a port with ships stirring, flags flying, and the
barges and tugs in full and fussy operation.

It is worth while going back to the Tower. Few western
Londoners realise how easy a journey it is. Tower Bridge
Station, the new and more explanatory name for Mark Lane
Station, is on the Inner Circle as well as on the District Railway
running east and west. Trains pass by almost every minute. At
lunch-time Tower Hill is a rhetoricians' and mountebanks'
jamboree. The state of the nation is canvassed here: brands of
haberdashery are being sold there. You jostle through this circus
of salesmanship and statesmanship; it is friendly and gay. No
need to hurry. The clowning of the salesmen is often very
good. So down to the riverside and the entrance of the Tower
itself. If you are already feeling weary, there is a bright, clean
restaurant outside the pay-gate. (Licensed, if that concerns you.)
I would not call this resort Gourmets' Gate, to match the famous
Traitors' Gate, a couple of hundred yards down river. But it

suffices. Tower-plodders get their fish and chips and their nice cup of tea.

To go inside costs sixpence, with official guide-pamphlet for another threepence. If you join a conducted party you will be expected modestly to swell the collection for your escort which is taken up after you have been shown the dainty, midget Chapel of St. Peter Ad Vincula, a title which belies daintiness and severely rattles the punitive chains. The Buffeteer will have earned his small silver by then, but there is no need to join his rubber-neck squad. You can stay apart and absorb in seclusion the melancholy of this blood-boltered keep.

The Tower is odd because it looks so like a toy. This is not merely caused by the peaceful transmutation of the broad moat into chicken-run, vegetable garden, and sports pitches for the garrison: it is due to the formal patterning of a group of little towers. To one standing apart on Tower Hill the view is like that of a children's fort: you expect toy soldiers, not real ones, to be on parade. But it was certainly not meant as a toy, this Norman corner-piece imposed upon the old Roman defences, bits of which can still be seen. Nor has it functioned as a toy in its long, grim history of dungeon and gallows.

Looking at armour in the huge and central White Tower soon becomes monotonous unless there is in you some deep spiritual sympathy with breastplate and morion. I have no such feelings myself and, however brilliant the craftsmanship once engaged on this cautious canning of the human frame, I cannot gaze at very much of it without fatigue. Nor do the Crown Jewels in the Wakefield Tower (bang goes another saxpence) do more than dazzle me; they are colossal, they are Oriental and Babylonian. But they are rarely, I think, beautiful.

Yet history sparkles in them and may set poetry on your lips. That ruby in the King's Imperial State Crown was worn, we are told, by Henry V in his coronet surrounding the helm he wore at Agincourt: Shakespeare gave that battlefield all he had,

as the phrase now goes, and the great rubies of blood-red speech
were brilliantly qualified by the pearls of discreet prose spoken
by the King in the colloquy with Bates and Williams.

Jewels began their glamorous career as charms. They were savers:
they were life-givers. One may use the adjective glamorous,
now worked to death by being applied to any trollop who has
flapped a leg in a chorus or been an ' extra ' in a film, because it
does really mean magical. The early Egyptians valued gold
because they thought it was chips of the sun, particles of light
and warmth that had fallen from heaven. The sun gave life:
therefore gold, being a sun-flake, gave life. Therefore you buried
your dead with gold in their tombs to help them to immortality.
Therefore gold was very precious indeed. Because of that ancient
faith the not very attractive mineral has become the financial bully
of the modern world: gold is tenacious stuff and warm and
mellow to the eye, but that it has any unique, distinctive loveliness I cannot see. I would sooner see silver plate on the table
than golden, but, because of the old Egyptian fancy, gold has
remained the sovereign metal, the standard of value, and the basic
material of all regalia. No king or queen could be crowned
without it. (Nor could a money-lender's tooth.) And regalia,
golden at the base and monotonously ablaze with diamonds, are
not for me greatly fascinating. It is certainly very strange that
the vaults of American forts should now be stuffed with countless
ingots of this malleable metal—and that the economic destinies
of a whole Dominion, that of South Africa, should depend on
keeping up its value. All this because some Egyptian priest
started a yarn about sun-chips and caught his king's ear with
his fantasy.

Gazing at the Regalia, I am turned to curiosity by that seemingly absurd implement, the Mace. Whence and why maces?
What do you do with maces? Cromwell had a brusque answer,
but the matter deserves more polite attention. Neither Mayors
nor Kings nor Justices can get on without maces. Kings have

orbs and sceptres too. The orb symbolises the globe, but, since no king has ever had world-suzerainty, it is rather a foolish form of flattery to insist on the constitutional monarch of a democracy carrying such a token of omnipotence. The sceptre was an ornamental wand and symbol of authority: the Romans had their fasces, bundles of rods, whence came the name Fascists for authoritarians. The sceptre is less bulky, spectacular, and domineering. It fits in with democracy well enough, as it were the baton of him who conducts a disciplined social orchestra.

The mace began as a knobbed stick useful in various types of combat: it might be called a metal shillelagh. The mace is laid on worshipful tables, when worshipful people are dispensing wisdom or justice, because with it an outraged dignitary might, in the old days, have rapped the opposition as well as the table. It could have a stunning effect and was used metaphorically so. Says Brutus in *Julius Caesar* over the drowsy form of Lucius,

> *O murderous slumber!*
> *Layest thou thy leaden mace upon my boy*
> *That plays thee music?*

But this symbol of weighty power, of which vintage specimens are on view in the Wakefield Tower, has also a playful significance. One of my dictionaries, Chambers', gives this further definition of the mace and its various functions. ' A light flat-headed stick in use at billiards before the introduction of the bridge or cue-rest,' while the *Oxford English Dictionary* says that the mace was used for propelling the ball in bagatelle and in early times in billiards. As an afore-time bagatellier I have frequently held the wooden mace in miniature without realising that it was first cousin to so august an Emblem of Authority. Had Cromwell this old usage in mind when he asked for the offending bauble to be withdrawn from a Parliament which frowned upon the sins of ritual?

One of the oddities of the Tower is the lonely plaque, with

head-portrait, erected in honour of a Scottish minister of religion.
This celebrates the strange achievement of the Rev. Alexander
John Forsyth (1768-1843), Minister of Belhelvie near Aberdeen.
Mr. Forsyth's mind did not dwell in green pastures and heavenly
gates alone; piety of that order does not lead to a niche in what
has been so largely a penal settlement. His ministry was of
munitions as well as of souls. In 1805 he made experiments in
the Tower under the Master of Ordnance: while Nelson sailed
to Trafalgar there was the reverend gentleman from Aberdeen-
shire working away in London's fortress on a new system of
percussion for the discharge of explosives. It is stated that the
Forsyth System was adopted—twenty-four years later. The
Admiralty and the War Office were not hustlers; so it was not,
apparently, in the pulpit of Belhelvie that the Battle of Waterloo
was won; but it might have happened so, if Whitehall could
have reached a decision in less than a quarter of a century.
Presumably the Belhelvie recipe was put through 'the usual
channels' and got stuck, like so many other good ideas, in the
usual tunnels. However, justice comes at last and there are the
image and superscription of the Rev. Forsyth, in glorious isolation
by the side of Tower Green.

I have said that the tower seen from a certain distance, has
the look of a toy, so natty and regular does it seem. At a close
view it is strangely lacking in ferocity. Considering that its
floors and grass have been soaked in blood, much of it innocent
enough, and considering that the vilest crimes against the defence-
less have occurred in the various turrets, one might expect the
most bodeful of buildings, merely to look at which is to shudder.
But there is a kind of placidity about the place. The atmosphere
is almost genial. Some of this, no doubt, is due to the kindly,
avuncular Buffeteers, loquaciously shepherding the teachers and
their charges; they spread benignity abroad. Then there is the
fact that the Tower contains residences of mellow brick, serene
and reassuring. Also there is the inclusion of a military hospital

I cannot feel frightened in the Tower of London, as I can almost anywhere in the Old Town of Edinburgh. A dark canyon among the soaring warehouses of the river's bank is more sinister than the Bloody Tower itself. There you might meet at any moment the most macabre of the human ogres that Dickens drew with as much relish as power. But here, in the Tower, you cannot fancy an encounter with anything more formidable than a request to keep off the grass and not to throw your orange-peel and sandwich papers on the sward.

The visitor, as he or she scans the list of the Tower's inmates or the Tower's burials, will shudder at the print. On Tower Green, now so tranquil outside the Chapel, all these lost their head to the axe or sword, and many of them in public, before ' good houses,' as theatre people say.

1. Lord Hastings, by order of the Duke of Gloucester, in 1483.
2. Queen Anne Boleyn, second wife of Henry VIII, May 19, 1536.
3. Margaret, Countess of Salisbury, May 27, 1541.
4. Queen Katharine Howard, fifth wife of Henry VIII, February 13, 1542.
5. Jane, Viscountess Rochford, February 13, 1542.
6. Lady Jane Grey, wife of Lord Guildford Dudley, February 12, 1554.
7. Robert Devereux, Earl of Essex, February 25, 1601.

Sir Walter Raleigh does not occur in that list. For each Tower tourist, who has any historical sense, there will be one or more names which have a power to haunt. Whose spirit—of all these sufferers—and those named were but a fraction of the whole host of the captives and the condemned—whose spirit walks for you? The wild Essex, who thought to tumble even Queen Elizabeth from her throne, Essex who led Shakespeare's patron, Southampton, to melancholy years behind these walls? Or Raleigh, the bitter enemy of Essex, who had two spells of confinement in the Tower and here wrote his *History of the World*. The terms of imprisonment were not too harsh. Raleigh could erect a shed in which to carry on his experiments in chemistry.

Here is my Tower ghost, this dark, brilliant, frustrated figure. ' He was the first that brought tobacco into England, and into fashion, They first had silver pipes: the ordinary sort made use of a walnut shell and a straw. It was sold then for its wayte in silver. I have heard some of our old yeomen neighbours say that when they went to Malmesbury or Chippenham Market they culled out their biggest shillings to lay in the scale against tobacco.' Thus John Aubrey in his longish ' brief life ' of Raleigh, ' tall, handsome, and bold ' but ' damnable proud.' In an age of universal smoking and of vastly rich tobacco combines we owe a vote of thanks to Sir Walter, who pioneered with the weed and cherished it even to the grave. ' He tooke a pipe of tobacco a little before he went to the scaffold, which some formall persons were scandalized at, but I thinke t'was well and properly donne: to settle his spirits.' Aubrey again. ' To settle his spirits '—with the headsman waiting! Was ever such advertising copy in the world? Have W. D. and H. O. Wills raised statues to Raleigh? Bristol should have a masterpiece in this kind.

He had all the talents, save the most important, at least in the slippery Court of ' Eliza and our James ': he could not make himself liked: in fact, he seemed to make himself comprehensively hated. It was that ' damnable pride.' He had ' that awfulness and ascendancy in his aspects over other mortalls.' Other mortals rarely care for that.

Yes, Raleigh is my Tower ghost. He went there for the first time in 1592 because of his affair with Miss Throckmorton of whom he later made an honest woman. Queen Elizabeth's jealous regard for virtue in her ladies at Court was not to be appeased by cloaks in the mud—if that incident ever occurred. King James was his next persecutor. There was a scandalous trial for High Treason and for conspiring with the Spaniards, preposterous charges followed by a death sentence, a last-minute reprieve, and then twelve years in the Tower. Twelve years of it, from the age of fifty-one to sixty-three, for a leader of his adventuring kind, an explorer of the Indies, a sailor and a man of science!

True, he could live there in some state. His wife was with him for a time and his son too. They had their servants. They were in the Garden Tower, now called the Bloody Tower. Gosse in his biography of Raleigh says that his windows looked westward and that he had access to a garden: therein was that laboratory of his. He could potter about. But what was pottering to such a spirit? When at last released he was sent to rob the Spanish while commanded to keep peace with Spain. It was an impossible commission and he came back to be executed on the old charge.

He faced the axe with his finest haberdashery and even finer courage: his wit was ironic and unquenchable (feeling the blade, he said, ' 'Tis a sharp medicine, but one that will cure me of all diseases.') He had put on a ' black embroidered velvet night-gown over a hare-coloured satin doublet and a black embroidered waistcoat: he wore a ruff-band, black cut taffeta breeches, and ash-coloured silk stockings,' so mingling magnificence with a sense of the mortal occasion. He had the nerve to speak on the scaffold for twenty-five minutes in self-defence and said, adjusting himself for the blow, ' So the heart be right, it matters not which way the head lies.' The severed head was shown to the spectators and dropped into a red bag. Lady Raleigh had the head embalmed and kept it with her all her life, allowing favoured friends to see it and even kiss it.

How are we to understand the Elizabethans and Jacobeans, with their cruelty and morbidity as well as their dedication to beauty and the graces of life? Lady Raleigh's relic is beyond our comprehension. A severed head, at the end of a Shakespearean tragedy, cannot be shown to-day: the audience has to laugh to hide its disgust. But it was a common-place of Shakespeare's

London: Raleigh's head, it is true, did not fall on Tower Green, but 'up West.' The Tower, however, had similar spectacles as a regular attraction, and the whole episode drives into the black heart of Tower history.

Raleigh touched nothing that he did not kindle: yet the flames of his achievement did not endure. He had no party: he had few friends; his schemes had no permanence: his poetry was brilliant, but most of it was unpreserved and so the remainder seems scrappy. He had the versatility, the unquenchable and superb amateurishness of his age in which a gentleman was soldier, sailor, courtier, squire, poet, historian, philosopher and scientist all at once and possibly good at all. I have mentioned him at some length because he is the one person who most poignantly walks by my side when I take a lunch-time stroll beside the Tower. Aubrey wrote of Raleigh's love of jewels, especially pearls, of his extravagance, and of his 'exceeding high forehead.' He was 'long-faced, and sour eie-lidded.' Perhaps he did not laugh warmly: his wit was sardonic. A few of his poems are often quoted. This, to his son, not so often. (A wag was a youth then and the word did not imply playfulness or facetiousness.)

> Three things there be that prosper up apace
> And flourish, while they grow asunder far,
> But on a day, they meet all in one place
> And when they meet, they one another mar;
> And they be these, the wood, the weed, the wag.
> The wood is that which makes the gallow tree,
> The weed is that which strings the hangman's bag,
> The wag, my pretty knave, betokeneth thee.
> Mark well, dear boy, while these assemble not,
> Green springs the tree, hemp grows, the wag is wild,
> But when they meet, it makes the timber rot,
> It frets the halter, and it chokes the child.
>> Then bless thee, and beware, and let us pray
>> We part not with these at this meeting day.

There is much of Tower history in those sixteen savage lines. Should you be more susceptible to the tenderer victims of the rage of power, Lady Jane Grey or the Little Princes or rash Anne Boleyn will be names of grief for you as you stand by Traitors' Gate, where the barges drew in with the victims aboard and ready for consignment to the scaffold. But Raleigh, the genius ' damnable proud ' and thereby damned, the owner of all the talents, the loser of all affections, the Elizabethan *manqué* is my choice among the local shades.

The stone material of the Tower is now a sooty grey and neither attractive nor menacing. Some of it came from Caen, at Conqueror William's command; he knew the value of the Calvados quarries. Some more of it was from Kent. A little from Ketton in Rutland. One easily forgets that London is a composite city, an amalgam of English and French rocks. Lying in a clay saucer, it has no building stone of its own. It shows the strategical value of the Thames and of its potential bridges and fords that the Romans should have bothered to drag stones to it from considerable distances in order to have the stuff to make a castle and a wall. Since their day Londoners have been drawing on Reigate and Rutland, on Bath in Somerset and Beer in Devon, above all on Portland in Dorset. From the Tower you look out, even despite Hitlerian blastings, on the bright magic of Wren's spires, whose creamy radiance is due to the Portland stone on which he insisted with such wisdom. The weather washes the face of this stone: where it is sheltered it darkens: aloft, exposed to the wind and the rain, it is its gleaming self. No poets, as James Bone has pointed out in *The London Perambulator*, have sung the praise of this stone, though they have paid tribute to everything from mice to sofas and marine engines.

Yet it is a great and magical stone, more beautiful, I think, even than the Roman travertine, with its marmoreal quality that responds so exquisitely to wear. Portland stone seemed ordained to form the face of London, its surface so finely mirroring the fitful lights that break through her river-mists, blanching in her towers and spires to a finer whiteness as the darker grow the coats of grime at the bases and sides. How those towers and spires come and go through the mists as you watch from Waterloo Bridge over the grey-blue Thames on a spring morning! Who can ever forget his first vision of it all as he beheld, round the bend of the river, the apparition of the mighty fleet of Wren, with their top-gallants and mainsails of stone?

Beside St. Paul's the Tower, compact of Caen and Kentish raw material, has a dullish look: a gaol cannot, of course, be expected to smile; on the other hand this one fails to be really sinister. There is no comparison between this and Edinburgh Castle, if fearsomeness be the standard. Yet there it is, the handiest of roaming grounds for City workers who can spend a sunlit hour on the terrace watching the bargees' mastery of the waterman's craft or wondering what shelf or counter of the grocers' store will be restocked thanks to that vessel just coming to the wharves of Bermondsey. Or turning to the keep they can see the clipped-wing ravens hopping in a raucous frustration upon the lawns whose ancestral worms once dieted upon the blood of queens. The raven does not say, 'Never more.' Like little Oliver, he is positive and brief. 'More, more, more' he grunts and possibly is happy none the less. But I think that his impulse to soar—for the raven is a natural swimmer on high oceans of cloud—tugs at him all the time. In that case, though it be hard on the bird, the symbol of his presence is well justified. Hundreds of human beings have lingered within the Tower and striven for liberty, like these great black cripples, in convulsive and un-rewarding fidgets. Captive lions, too, were long among the inmates. While Raleigh was writing his famous invocation to 'eloquent, just, and mighty death,' the wretched beasts in the Lion Tower were being baited with the King's mastiffs to make sport for that Scottish James whose treatment of Sir Walter Raleigh was nothing else than a murder.

How many people know that there is in London a bastion called Bruce Castle and that it is named, with fair enough reason, after the Royal Bruces of Scotland? Very few, I fancy, outside the Borough of Tottenham. Yet there it is, not far from Bruce Grove Tube Station, a Tudor building on the site of a more ancient keep. A Scottish marriage is supposed to have carried the manor into the family of King Robert Bruce, but England's Edwards, hammers of the Scots, made an end of all that and gave Tottenham its own again. But the name remains, though I am not informed that any local Burnsians insist on eating a haggis therein with musical honours, pipes, and reels and in toasting the Immortal Memory on the birthday of their Bard.

There is a nice solid, old church and a good house beside it called the Priory. Bruce Castle, now owned by Tottenham, has large grounds which are a public park and playing-field. During my visit (March 1950) the latter looked grey and arid because no new grass had had a chance to cover its nakedness. The youth of Tottenham must use this open space vigorously to have scalped it so effectively. My works of information tell me that the River Mosel or Moselle flows round about it and may once have assisted it to own a moat. I have always found that stream as elusive in fact as it is alluring in name. A London Moselle! What vineyards might have clothed its banks when England grew its own wine! In The Historic Map of Hornsey, based on Rocque's Map of Middlesex, 1757, and reproduced in an excellent booklet on Hornsey called *Beauty and the Borough* by Councillor F. Cleary (they take the public arts and amenities very seriously in Hornsey) the River Moselle debouches from the neighbourhood of Lordship Lane and enters the New River close to Hornsey Parish Church and under the heights of Muswell. Hence, presumably, its name of Mosel or Moselle. Whenever I look for this runnel, it seems to have dried up or been deflected or gone underground. But it delights me none the less to know that London has a river so named and that it ought to be discoverable amid the purlieus of Tottenham's Antique Exhibit No. 1, Bruce Castle.

One of the Castle's functions, during its later, less Scottish, and more pacific history was to house a school conducted by Sir Rowland Hill, who gave us our long lost penny post. Consequently and appropriately part of the Castle is now a Postal Museum. But it is also a Tottenham Museum and a cleverly chosen series of exhibits makes one fully aware that the home of the Hotspurs (football) has a lengthy and illustrious history going back to Lake Dwellings and stone axes. The urbanisation of this Bruce Country was quite recent: when I was a boy I could, had I known it, have bicycled through pleasant water-meadows hereabouts and even seen the River Moselle plain. As ' developed ' much of it is seemly as well as serviceable.

The new North London is enormously populous and so, since Londoners usually prefer the small house, which, in its myriads, is undeniably wasteful of space, to a niche in a large tenement, miles of country have been overrun. I am not blaming this preference: people should live as they choose and this is probably the better way for family life. But it is noticeable in a huge city like Glasgow, which used to build upwards instead of outwards, that the country is reached far more quickly than it would be in an English ' conurbation ' of similar size. Tottenham is now submerged in the overflow of North London, but much of this new building looks attractively planned on garden suburb lines and the keep of the Bruces, complete with Tudor Castle, explanatory museum, and parkland is, in its present state, no reproach to the City Fathers or the Welfare State.

It is a long journey from Tottenham to Eltham in Kent, where another of London's castles or moated palaces is to be found. Anyone who is in the neighbourhood of Blackheath or Greenwich, for exploring which there is ample cause, should, if possible,

drive on to Eltham. On the waterside at Greenwich you encounter the world of King William the Third and of Queen Anne
and a masterpiece by Wren, not to mention a park with a superb
view north over the river and much pleasant hillside villa-
building of the later centuries; but at Eltham you pass straight
from City Gentleman's Tudor-style (all mod con., thirty minutes
City, golf links adjacent) into the authentic heart of the Middle
Ages.

My curiosity about Eltham Palace should have been aroused
long ago. As a very small boy I lived in neighbouring Blackheath
and so I should be fired with a local loyalty. But at the time I
was too small to care about palaces except those in story-books.
All I can remember of that region is a fiercely cold winter, with
everything frozen and water fetched from stand-pipes in the
street, a great deal of fog, and a horse-bus, with straw on the
floor to keep one's feet from frost-bite, which rumbled across
the dark waste where the hungry Kentish rebels, Tyler and Cade,
marshalled their men for raiding the sleek, oppressive capital
below them; where later, too, King James imported the Scottish
game of golf to the heathland. Presumably, when revolt and
riot were afoot, the royal palace at Eltham, moated and defended,
was by-passed by the invaders. But it was an awkward establishment for the despoilers of London to have on their lines of
communication.

The palace of Eltham, I learn from Mr. William Kent's
Encyclopædia of London, was possibly Saxon in origin and
was a favourite house of hospitality and revel for many
English kings. Henry II kept Christmas at Eltham in 1270 and
Parliaments were summoned hither in 1329 and 1375. King John
of France was splendidly entertained here in 1365. Richard II
was particularly fond of Eltham and he was deemed a man of
taste as well as of luxury. One of the scenes in *Richard of Bordeaux*,
Gordon Daviot's play about Richard II which had such a success
with John Gielgud in the title-role, was laid at Eltham. The

Palace was continually visited by our monarchs down to the time of James I. Queen Elizabeth, born at Greenwich, was there as a girl. It was known as King John's Palace by a mistake, in the opinion of Mr. Kent. The eponymous John was a Prince, son of Edward III, not the King of that name.

So this quiet spot had some centuries of glory and the falconers made sport with their tassel-gentles where now the Eltham golfers drive. What is left is the great Banqueting Hall with hammer-beam roof, and the moat crossed by a fifteenth-century bridge. And here a warning must be issued. The Palace, which has much new building in addition to the old Hall, is occupied by the Army for some purposes of education, and may presumably remain so. At the time of my wandering this way public entrance was limited to one day of the week and, if you wish to do more than walk round it and dream yourself back into the days of Angevin, Plantagenet, and Tudor, with jousting, tourney, and banqueting afoot, it is well to make inquiry in advance about your rights of approach. But, even without entry, the Palace deserves a deviation from the main road. It is surrounded by fine trees and beautiful houses, including a sixteenth-century manor. With only an outsider's status you can here indulge your eye as well as your backward-ranging fancy. It is a rewarding escape from the surrounding miles of increasingly built-up area where London marches into Kent down the old roads to Canterbury and the eastern sea. Secluded in its nook this fragment of old pomp is atmospheric still.

CHAPTER XVI

East End

———————◦≈◦———————

A<small>T ONE</small> time many motor-coaches used to assemble near Trafalgar Square in the evening in order to carry sightseers to Limehouse. Thomas Burke had aroused a legitimate interest in London's China Town which was thus rather wantonly exploited. I see less of such journeying now. For Limehouse, as they say, has 'had it.' You will find abundant ruins, going east from the City, a Sahara of rubble. As usual there is the East-West partition of London, and the West, though it has its own copious and calamitous gaps, knows almost nothing of the appalling desert that begins at Stepney and runs on through Limehouse and Poplar to the extremes of the dockland. After five and a half years there is still a vast limbo of dust and rubbish. New flats gradually, very gradually, arise and the pathetic colonies of 'pre-fabs' are scattered among the wreckage. Perhaps those motor-coaches should be more numerous, though there are no opium dens and fewer Chinese faces to show to the rubbernecks. It would give the tourist a salutary jerk to realise what miles of domesticity, drab but beloved, the East Ender lost, and what the Port of London endured while brave men, with their tiny homes shattered and families intermittently dispersed and then returning to the ruins, carried on with the job of keeping the river open and at work. I would also like to pack some of the eastward-bound motor-coaches with those who talk smoothly about rearming Germany as a safeguard against Russia. Safeguard? I wonder.

It can, of course, be argued that we now have a good chance to begin again and properly to rebuild where our ancestors made so vile a mess. The desert that is Stepney is scheduled to flower as a model riverside region for our visitors of 1951 to look upon. I am writing just a year before the Great Exhibition is to open and there will have to be some hustle if the new Stepney is to be decently in bud. But the chance exists. There is not the least reason why this area should not be made as pleasant to the eye as its docks are serviceable to the physical needs of London. Shadwell had already provided its example of a riverside park; and Southwark Park, which is a sizable lung and playground for Bermondsey on the south bank, may well be repeated, with improvements, on the north.

There are still some inns with river-balconies and I trust that we shall build more of them. You can drink and feed in West End style at the Prospect of Whitby, which now stands in some isolation, overlooking the waters of Wapping, whose working humanity W. W. Jacobs and Will Owen made humorous and moving to my boyhood. The Prospect has a wondrous collection of nautical bric-à-brac and expensive-looking cars are parked outside it of an evening. But sipping a gin-and-it at the Prospect is about as far as the West goes in its eastward exploration.

It is preferable, if you really want to move normally about this area, to feed, should you get the chance, in a more ordinary kind of East End tavern, where locals come in for a pint and sit, with their women-folk, quietly easing tired limbs. The East End, thus encountered, seems far more tranquil and pacific than the West. Crimes may occur, but the criminally intended young have obviously far more reason to make the prosperous areas their hunting-ground. It is the slums of the Harrow Road not of the Commercial Road that make the attractive lair for the marauding columns of gangster youth. The plunder lies handier.

I spent a fascinating evening in what might be called a luxury pub-crawl round the balconied inns of the riverside. (Luxury applies only to the transport which had been kindly laid on for me by a friend who knows the routes and the ropes hereabouts.) We met chiefly river-workers, not sea-going sailors, and, if anybody romantically expects to hear shanties sung or talk of distant oceans, he is unlikely to be satisfied. At one house of call there was a tavern sing-song in progress: it was a Friday night and there should have been money for beer. But the drinking was moderate (all the publicans were sad about trade) and the singing was of the cosmopolitan, croonery-moonery kind.

Although the room was small, there was a microphone provided, an utterly unnecessary piece of furniture, but evidently much favoured. Young men in turn approached the ' mike ' and poured into it the latest doleful melody from Tin Pan Alley or the Charing Cross Road. Inevitably the din which the machine made was terrific, but the row seemed to give general satisfaction. Outside there was the plashing of the greatest English river; the moonlit water was seeping up with the tide into the creeks and beating gently on the moored barges and some veteran craft laid up for their old age and perhaps waiting to be scrapped for firewood. Inside there was the swamp-music of another continent, too raucous, because of the absurd, irrelevant microphone, to be decently plaintive, but enormously enjoyed. Never an idle moment! When Cliff had done his piece, Ray or Stan hurried forward to contribute. There are few of the Alfs and Berts of the W. W. Jacobs days now. Nomenclature has risen in the world and we are all noblemen of the middle ages to-day, Stanleys, Cliffords, and Raymonds, nothing less. The girls, of whom a few were dancing in the sad, shuffling way of these years, take their names from the films. Maureen seems to be an especial favourite; whenever I sit in public parks of the plebeian kind I hear the mothers summoning the errant daughters, with ' 'Ow, come 'ere, Maureen.'

The Grapes, Limehouse

It happened to be a calm, clear night and not too cold. I had the privilege of a voyage with the River Police: we ranged the great Port from Greenwich to Westminster, moving at speed with a proud sense of mechanical power and governing authority, watching vessels coming up with the tide, the tide which really is London's fortune. There are some people eager to abolish the London tides by defence works lower downstream which would lessen or stop the great ebb and flow. But it has been pointed out to me that this great lift and fall of water brings up the ships and takes them back again with far less use of power and effort than would be needed on an unchanging river. The tides save a deal of steam. The squalid mud-banks of low water may offend the sensitive landsman's eye, but they are the price we pay for a great natural utility, a labour-saving benefaction, provided by the sovereign moon.

The moon was certainly doing its best for beauty as well as for use on that evening. It showed up the fine sharp ridge of Greenwich Park and silvered the incomparable work of Inigo Jones, Wren, and Vanbrugh in the Queen's House and the Old Hospital, which is far better described as a Palace. It is a major scandal that London's public transport by water, scarcely enough in the summer, should stop altogether in the winter. A covered launch, no doubt, can be hired at some cost to make the journey that I was given on that lucent, just frosty, January night. But it should not need preparation and expense to enjoy the superb spectacle of the Port of London's nocturnes at any time of year. The giant cranes rise up with curious, ghostly gestures from the light-studded banks: the warehouses are turned to mountain-sides. For a moment you might be entering one of the darker, narrower lochs of the hill-girt Clyde: then you are past this great black pile of storage and out surveying the curves and sinews of London lit-up. I was lucky, as I said, with my illumination; that beautiful word, moon-glade, which means the path of light thrown by the moon on water, was never more apposite to the scene. By lunar favour a radiant roadway carried us through the bricky forest of the shores. We shot, thus be-glamoured, past St. Paul's, whose dome was more than ever the emblem of endurance, as if it were a serene, celestial guardian over the jumble of the fretful City beneath it and around.

The River Police patrol incessantly from Teddington to Gravesend. They must put up with some chill and squally as well as menacingly foggy occasions, but I would far sooner be on their waters than directing the roaring, reiterating traffic in an icy or a scorching London street. Their functions are varied. They have many types of thief to watch. There may be pilfering from the moored barges, for these have valuable cargoes. Coal is precious, but not easily removable. Tobacco, which is unloaded lower down and often comes up by water in small craft, is nice to snatch. Smuggling from ships in dock is the care of the Port of London's own force of watchmen and what incoming seamen may do in the streets of dockland in their leisure is for the ordinary police to investigate. The River Police are limited to river troubles. A barge may break loose and cause considerable nuisance and danger. News of that must be flashed and precautions taken.

Then there are the human bodies, of which far more than you would expect are part of the flotsam of the Thames. If they floated, the collection would be easy. But bodies usually sink and suicides, I was told, are often determined to make a thorough job of their unhappy end. So they load their pockets with heavy stuff, just to make sure of a rapid disappearance. (Also they tend to destroy all evidence of identity, so puzzling the police the more.) Gradually they drift down under water: as the gases multiply within, the corpses may come up again, but before that they may be tangled in moorings. The recovery is neither easy nor pleasant and what is at length found is not for the squeamish to see.

This grisly kind of harvesting is one of the old waterside

occupations, as Dickens well knew. The first chapter of *Our Mutual Friend* describes the privateers at work for profit on what is now the public office of the River Police. Hexam was ' in luck again.' Said Gaffer Hexam's rival, surveying ' the find ' in tow,

> Been a knocking about with a pretty many tides, ain't he, pardner? Such is my out-of-luck ways, you see! He must have passed me when he went up last time, for I was on the look-out below bridge here. I a'most think you're like the wulturs, pardner, and scent 'em out.

Hexam told his daughter Lizzie, who rowed on these expeditions, that she need not be queasy about the river and its offerings. By it and its gifts, animal, mineral, or vegetable, they lived. He had no qualms.

> What he had in tow, lunged itself at him sometimes in an awful manner when the boat was checked, and sometimes seemed to try to wrench itself away, though for the most part it followed submissively. A neophyte might have fancied that the ripples passing over it were dreadfully like faint changes of expression on a sightless face; but Gaffer was no neophyte and had no fancies.

I suppose, that a recruit to the River Police may have, for a while, his fancies. But he would not meet such an array of bodies as Dickens provided for Mortimer Lightwood to inspect at the beginning of his story. We had, fortunately, no ' tow ' that evening.

I had a meal later in the night in Limehouse at The Bunch of Grapes, which is accepted as the original of The Six Jolly Fellowship Porters, where Miss Abigail Potterson, christened sixty years before in Limehouse Church, was ' the supreme.' Dickens realised that barmaids or feminine innkeepers are not all of the gay and easy kind. I have known them to be disciplinarians who packed off the too liberal and dallying drinkers to catch their trains home to wife and weans and who had the air of

Victorian schoolma'ams, which, indeed, is exactly the description given of Miss Potterson. There is no such dragon in charge at The Grapes now, but the cheerful little establishment with a quiet, kindly landlord, can still be called ' all but afloat at high water.'

> . . . indeed the whole house, inclusive of the complaining flagstaff on the roof, impended over the water, but seemed to have got into the condition of a faint-hearted diver who has paused so long on the brink that he will never go in at all.

Dickens had obviously made a close study of one particular, river-balconied house, for he describes in utmost detail the curious effect of light on the old panels as well as the equipment of the bar and its tin utensils for mulling ale and so providing ' those delectable drinks, Purl, Flip, and Dog's Nose.' Purl was the specialty of Miss Potterson's service. Purl, with plain advice for nuisance-drinkers and scamps of all kinds. It is no longer the habit of the English to drink their beer mulled. How many houses are there where this would be served if you asked for it on a winter day?

The chief room upstairs looking over the river is now a kitchen. Dickens is said to have stayed here to write. It would be a good crow's nest for that far-ranging eye of his. He was so precise in *Our Mutual Friend* about everything in The Six Jolly Fellowship Porters that he may well have made more than a casual visit to the tiny bar. Incidentally, he could make mistakes of detail. In describing the cab journey to the East End taken by Mortimer Lightwood after Mr. Veneering's dinner party, the route is described as including the Monument, the Tower, the Docks, Ratcliffe, and Rotherhithe. This is a north-bank journey. But surely Rotherhithe was always in the south bank. Or was there another place of the same name in the Stepney area?

The conspicuous figure of the river for those who can sit on riparian verandas and watch the day's work is the waterman.

This is a generic term which includes bargees who are barge-occupants as well as barge-mariners and lightermen, who have a shore address and are daily workers of the stream. It is astounding that one individual can control with his 'sweep' the movement of a big and heavy-laden barge, working it through bridges despite the vagaries of currents and bringing it round into the nooks and creeks. He is using his brains, his local knowledge, the tide, and his strong arms all at once; in a highly mechanised world, equipped with every subtlety of applied science, he still stands, an industrial innocent, in the watery kingdom of the trireme and the galley, the gondola and the pleasure punt.

One by one the original crafts, even the most obstinately simple, suffer their various forms of 'progress' and acceleration. For centuries the ploughman was doing what the Greek and Roman had done with a ploughshare scarcely different. Robert Burns had no tractor, But now the tractor has come to save labour on the land (and, as some sharply remind us, to diminish its natural manure). Speeding the plough is an accuracy of to-day and a most precious fact in war-time or in any economy short of rural labour. But the single waterman with the 'sweep' is still there, the handyman invincible, captain, crew, and master of his craft, edging up and down the tide-way, with results for the warming and feeding and comforting of London which few of us stop to consider.

Amidst the rubble Sahara of East London, 1950, the old churches make happy and most handsome oases. They were sorely battered by bombs: some vanished. But there is St. Dunstan's of Stepney, now in splints, there St. Anne's of Lime-house, there St. Matthias of Poplar, which dates back to 1650; it has four acres of surrounding green space, now largely used for recreation. The East End was architecturally in luck when in 1711 Parliament approved of a scheme for the better 'Advancement of Religion': London was spreading rapidly and the new myriads were not conspicuous for their morality; so fifty new churches were to be built, financed by an increased duty on coal and equipped—on this Parliament was imperative—with towers or steeples to each of them. There was to be no excuse for those who said that they could not find their place of worship. Bells would ring for the ear and eyes would be guided by the spires. Four new parishes, St. George's-in-the-East, Bethnal Green, Limehouse, and Spitalfields were created and a superb architect was commissioned for three of them. This was Nicholas Hawksmoor, Wren's pupil and lieutenant. So it came about that Limehouse, St. George's, and Spitalfields had buildings of the highest distinction. St. Mary's, Rotherhithe, on the south shore, is another notable church of that period. The East End churches can hold their own in looks with any of the West.

And in spirit, too, one may conjecture. With playgrounds about them for the children of the streets and with no sort of aloofness in their relation to ordinary man, the gracious buildings are in sharp contrast to the shabby housing which the Age of Anyhow scattered on their flanks. Now that housing, cracked and paintless, looks worse than ever, where the explosives and incendiaries have allowed them to remain at all. Pass by at a week-end and you will see the wedding confetti flying on Saturday and the small, serious parties of young parents and friends coming in for christenings on Sunday. Unaffected clergy give them domestic welcome. Religion is made to seem a natural solace and the church a friendly neighbour.

The East End is largely Jewish and Roman Catholic in faith, but ' C. of E.' is traditional. Is not every Englishman born at sea supposed to be a parishioner of Stepney? St. Dunstan's, the oldest building in East London with Saxon stone-carving still in its ancient heart, proclaims the length of days and spiritual suzerainty of this ' Mother of the East,' begun, so the legend tells, by St. Dunstan himself, when he was Bishop of London and Lord of the Manor of Stebenhithe, whose imposing name

Stepney carries on in somewhat decadent form. St. Dunstan has been a great name-giver to churches, schools and hospitals. He is nowhere more honoured than in Stepney.

One feature of this remarkable church is the new East Window, designed by Hugh Easton, who did the Battle of Britain window in the Abbey. His work for Stepney shows Christ crucified and there is nothing new in that. But Jesus hangs in a conqueror's cloak, in the act of blessing, while he suffers, the modern Stepney below him. And here is no legendary Palestinian, certainly not the pale Galilean with whose breath, cried the angry Swinburne, the world has grown grey. The Christ is a vigorous, golden-haired man in the flush of youth, such an one as any healthy lad in the parish would yearn to become. He seems the very spirit of life's spring, the eternal source of rejuvenation; the emphasis is on the exultation of the Saviour, not on the agony of the Martyr: and also upon a victory of the spirit. There is a challenge in this light, conspicuous window which has none of the cosy quality of old stained glass. Stepney, too, it proclaims, will rise again.

Naturally the East End churches have been constant burial-grounds of the mariner: also of his employer. I especially liked one plaque on the wall of St. Dunstan's. It celebrates the energies of Mr. Joseph Somes who ' by the sedulous application of a powerful mind raised himself to the position of the most extensive ship owner in this commercial country.' Dickens would have liked to meet him and to set him dining with Veneering or with Gradgrind. The friction of powerful minds, thus sedulously applied to one another, would surely have produced some notable sparks.

With Limehouse Steeple, so curiously blunted, yet always taking the eye, Hawksmoor gave something to the world or at least to the seaman's share of it, since it has often been cited as London's most beloved landmark for the approaching vessel and the sailor home from the sea. It may not have the surprise and cliff-like splendours of New York arising from Manhattan to scrape the skies and astonish the westward traveller: it is small, homely, bright, and friendly; it suggests nice things about London. Its like appeared again in Hawksmoor's work for St. George's-in-the-East and for All Souls College, Oxford. Hitler could not dislodge it and there it stands in welcome, as it did when Dickens was discovering Miss Potterson and Rogue Riderhood in the neighbourhood of Limehouse Hole.

Further east lie Poplar and Bow, which has its Roman Road and a higher standard of building and housing. Southward lies the Isle of Dogs from the corner of which you descend into the Blackwall Tunnel for an under-river passage to the levels of East Greenwich. This vast and skilful burrowing of 1897 is a mile and a quarter long and would make an extremely boring walk: with its glazed walls it looks like an endless ingress to a lavatory, but it is difficult to see how tunnels can be turned into beauty spots.

The name of the Isle of Dogs has been explained by the presence of the Royal Kennels whence hounds were ferried to Greenwick Park and its region heaths or loosed upon the marshes of Essex. (Charles I is said to have killed a stag in Nightingale Lane which is now Thomas More Street, close to the Tower of London.) But the Isle's title has also been attributed to a corruption of Ducks or of Docks. St. Peter's Church in the Isle had a religious revival in the middle of the nineteenth century when a ritualistic priest of singular character and courage, Charles Lowder, fought physical epidemics, including cholera, as well as general apathy and lack of morals. He organised the public and processional side of religion with success, although the East End had known anti-ritualist riots of a long and bitter kind. If the Isle of Doggers would not come to hear his faith, he would take it to them. This he did, with much acceptance.

The Isle has seen other heroes. It is exciting to realise, when you are in Blackwall, that hence sailed three ships on December

19, 1606, on a voyage of as much success as audacity. The vessels were *Sarah Constant*, *Godspeed*, and *Discovery*, of 100, 40, and 20 tons respectively. The 105 adventurers on board them managed to set up in Virginia under Captain John Smith of Jamestown, the first enduring English settlement in America. It is amazing to think of a 20-ton boat setting out on that journey and in December of all months, with the Atlantic gales of the New Year and early spring to come. Not all the valiant pilgrims sailed from Plymouth Hoe and Americans who salute the coast of Devon have just as much cause to make obeisance to the Isle of Dogs. Incidentally, the adventurers missed, by a week, the first night of *King Lear* which—odd choice!—was the Christmas play at Whitehall a week after their departure. But King James and his taste in play-acting were doubtless of no interest whatever to them. Furthermore, the storm scene, with its colossal eloquence of hurricanes and cataracts, would not have been an encouraging send-off.

The Isle, however, has had its place in poetry. But the allusion made by John Davidson was not complimentary. He contrasted the beauty of the ships with the meanness of the houses on land.

> *Mirrored in shadowy windows draped*
> *With ragged net or half-drawn blind,*
> *Bowsprits, masts, exactly shaped*
> *To woo or fight the wind,*
> *Like monitors of guilt*
> *By strength and beauty sent,*
> *Disgraced the shameful houses built*
> *To furnish rent.*

Will even the most patriotic East Ender deny this grievance? Still, it could be reasonably replied that the housing of sailors aboard ship by the Victorian shipowners, who made monstrous fortunes out of sea-traffic, was just as vile as the housing of their families and of the shipwrights and dockers on land. A vessel can be both a beauty and a slum.

St. Dunstan's Church, Stepney

Early in the sixteenth century Sir Thomas More wrote, ' If the discommodities of the City offend you, yet may the country, round your Parish of Stepney, afford delights.' Now Stepney is to have the first chance of London's blitzed boroughs to show the world how the new East End will look. It is appropriate that all this should be taking shape during the second Premiership of Clement Attlee, who has devoted so much of his life to the East End and to the representation of Stepney in particular. It was the East End that brought him, as a young barrister, to his way of thinking, for which many people will not thank the East End. But all must acknowledge his continuing and abounding eagerness to end the ' discommodities ' of existence east of the Tower.

The area which begins with Cable Street, a dingy, melancholy thoroughfare with its own problem of homeless coloured men, and works east into Commercial Road and so down the docksides of the curving river, can hardly be recommended for pleasure travel. The stranger must be an addict of observation, though he need be nothing so formidable as a sociologist, if he is to enjoy a spectator's progress to Canning Town or West Ham. But, after all, there are people who care for observation and there are many London buses, as well as the District Railway, to take them to their East End termini; one bus, as I said, goes under the river and will thus provide a return journey by way of comely Greenwich. But I do not suggest midwinter for such an excursion: a bright day in October or March, a day whose twilight will be gradual and make temperate way for

> *The moons and lamps in the lapping Thames*
> *When dusk sails wavering down the Pool.*

That second line of Wilfred Owen's, in a poem on Shadwell Stair, is accurate reporting as well as poetry. There is a quivering light above the water as the evening wings its way over Wapping, like the slow heron over Richmond's Thames.

CHAPTER XVII

Pleasaunces and Pleasures

WORKING OUR way round London in search of breathing-space we come, inevitably and delightfully, to Richmond. Richmond has the material advantage of the best communications of any of the more pleasant London suburbs. Apart from its many bus services it can be reached by non-stop trains from Waterloo, of which there are two every hour, in thirteen minutes. (I know of no other such instantaneous change from mid-London to near-pastoral.) There are also numerous slow trains which take about twenty-five minutes. Then there is the approach by the District Railway; this brings you straight there from the City, South Kensington, and Hammersmith areas with a train every twenty minutes. Furthermore there is the old North London service, circling round from Broad Street, Canonbury, Camden Town, Hampstead, Willesden, and Acton, with a half-hourly supply of transport. (At rush hours most of these services are increased even above this high level of convenience.) I have not in this book said much about travel facilities, because I did not wish to compose an epilogue to Bradshaw and the A B C railway guide. But in the case of Richmond the communications are indeed exceptional and deserve a special note.

Richmond offers both town and country of the best. It has the bouquet of history: it has the bustle of the present. And by bustle I do not refer only to the massed traffic of its medievally narrow High Street; there is the happy congregation of its athletes, especially at week-ends. Nowhere do I get a stronger sense of tip-toe expectation than at Richmond on a Saturday noon. This applies to winter as well as to summer. In the long, sunny days there is, of course, the allure of the river, since here under the grey sweep of Richmond Bridge and among the leafy eyots, is the first place on the journey upstream where punting, as well as rowing, becomes general. The Thames is still tidal, but it has ceased to be industrial. One may love to watch the traffic of the Port of London with all its range from stateliness to little tug-boat fuss. The Port reaches in administrative authority beyond Richmond to Teddington: but it becomes possible after Kew to meet that other less commercial river of holiday basking, of flannelled leisure and of dalliance under the willows, the pleasure-stream which meanders from Richmond past all the regatta towns with their summer *panache*, past Oxford and the serene solitudes of its Upper River, past William Morris's Kelmscott, to those superb tributaries, the Windrush and the Evenlode, and so to the Cotswolds, mother of many waters.

At Richmond one knows that this is the same unsullied (or at least little sullied) water that has come down from Seven Springs and Lechlade and ' Yarnton's tiny docks of stone.' For my part, I find the curious solitudes of the Upper River more attractive than the well-known glories of the Home County Thames. There is a special magic about the ' stripling Thames at Bablock Hythe ' and its still earlier reaches of which Hilaire Belloc wrote, absorbing the mellow genius of the middle-western hills and of the Thames Valley below them,

> The quiet evening kept her tryst:
> Beneath an open sky we rode,
> And passed into a wandering mist
> Along the perfect Evenlode.
>
> The tender Evenlode that makes
> Her meadows hush to hear the sound

Of waters mingling in the brakes,
And binds my heart to English ground.

A lovely river, all alone,
She lingers in the hills and holds
A hundred little towns of stones,
Forgotten in the western wolds.

In connection with these exquisite lines I may add that, when I cited Belloc in an argument about some of our up-to-date (and to me cacophonous and obscure) poetry, I was informed by one of the latter's defenders that Belloc's rhythms were no better than ' brass-band ' stuff. One cannot argue with such opinion. I leave it and pass on, merely remarking that, when I stand beside the river at Richmond, it pleases me to think that there goes a runnel of Windrush, an eddy of Evenlode.

Since my subject is wintry London I cannot fairly linger over the pagan, pleasure-seeking quality of Richmond on a summer evening, when there is an abounding spirit of release. How many courtships and couplings, which came to holy wedlock or evaded it—one cannot be censorious on these banks—have originated and matured around the plashing shores of the old, royal borough where Queen Elizabeth once lay dying and young love is continually born again! Even in the short, cold days, which are my theme, there is a rich stirring of week-end life. The place is teeming with young people going to ride in the Park: they do not look like expert equestrians and nowadays they are dressed and booted for the exercise in anything they can find. But, whether or not they waddle in the hired saddle, whether or not they would pass the standards of sporting haberdashery expected of old in the Row or in the Shires, these desk-free cavaliers have a light in their eyes. They are London let loose. In short, they are Richmond, the headquarters of liberation.

Then there are all the scampering young men and women who dash out of the Saturday trains with bags containing their hockey-apparatus, their golf-clubs, or their football kit. Rugby football is a major occupation, not merely for the Grade A performers of Richmond, London Scottish, and Rosslyn Park, but for second and third teams too, who find pitches on and around the Old Deer Park. Now more than ever, now in these years of harassing doubts and fears, do I, as a senior, who had my youth when life was free, calm, hopeful, and happy, welcome the snatching at these recreations and escapes by those who have endured the drudgeries of the conscript and dare hardly think of what may be. Any suburb of London which brings balm to them is blessed and Richmond is pre-eminent in its provision of such salves and benefactions. Indoors, too, it offers a much sought skating rink and you may see as many bringing their skates to risk a tumble in their violent glissades as come with equipment for games in the open.

Games have a doubled value when played in places of beauty and football matches conducted with the background of Kew Gardens have certainly an added grace. The horizon of trees seen on a winter afternoon from the athletic ground makes as handsome a backcloth as can be imagined for the dark blue vests and scarlet stockings of the London Scottish fifteen. There is the absurd, irrelevant, delightful pagoda striking up into the sky. Why Sir William Chambers decided, in 1760 or thereabouts, to put a little of Burma into the lawns and copses of Surrey, who shall say? The English have always had their follies, as such architectural clownings were called, and the Kew Pagoda is a minor anticipant of Sezincote in the Cotswolds and the Pavilion at Brighton. It ought to clash abominably with the sylvan façade of Kew—and yet, in a mysterious way, it only sets one smiling.

The long line of timber where Kew Gardens march with the Mid-Surrey Golf Course has its own nobility: you can watch a football match and lift your eyes across greens and fairways to giant beeches that will shade a bluebell carpet in May, but are as striking in their nakedness and grey winter severity as ever they will be in their green renewal after Easter. It is proper that James Thomson, the author of *The Seasons*, should have been for twelve years a Richmond man. The transforming months work their changes most suavely in these riverside woods, where careful clearances give ample avenues of vision.

The scene may be enjoyed the other way by walking along the tow-path from Kew, past Sion House and Isleworth, with the Gardens on your left. Gainsborough and Zoffany were buried at Kew and London has not yet let them down by turning old Kew to modern chaos. Sion is an Adam mansion of 1760 and has not yet been wrested from ducal ownership to become an institution. It survives rock-like among the seas of social change, rock-like too among the water-meadows which undergo fairly regular flooding. The great house stands up to be looked at from the river; it leaves one not only gratified by its solid fascination, but wondering sympathetically what coal bill is needed, when coal is available, to keep it dry amid such watery demesnes. Its great kitchen gardens should be of service and of profit. But, while we admire the view, we cannot envy the Duke of Northumberland his responsibilities.

The herons stand pensive on its shore or rise to go flapping off, with their great rounded wings, slowest and most stately and, after wild geese and swans, the largest of our English birds, to their haunts in Richmond Park. It is always a happy surprise to see a heron rise before you in London and go plodding off on his deliberate course. Ducks are plentiful and, when they have the feel of spring in their pinions, go flighting high and swift across the gardens: there is the low, whirring flight of partridges, the harsh trumpeting of an occasional and regal pheasant. Kew Gardens are Hanoverian in spirit and in origin and the dædal-tinted pheasant suits their majesty. Swans too will take the air and move processional across the lower sky. The brief river-front of Isleworth, seen before the tow-path swings round towards Richmond, together with the Sion meadows is the proper setting for a Zoffany conversation piece: you can almost envisage milord, milady, their carefully posed progeny, and a brace of spaniels, beside a garden-temple in the classical style. There might be a gamekeeper in the offing and cricket-bats in the foreground. It was a constant and pleasing affectation of the eighteenth century to mix the architecture of Apollo with the discharge of fowling-pieces, playing of the newfangled cricket, and the enjoyment of a life as essentially English as an elm park.

Richmond Town itself has such ample chronicles and such a quantity of literature that one hesitates to say more. Far better than most pieces of London or the London fringe does it marry old and new. Here 'the centuries kiss and commingle'; they do not, as elsewhere, harshly clash. What is left of the old Palace of Sheen, rebuilt by Henry VII, who gave Richmond its name after his Yorkshire earldom of that name, has no stony chill, but a warm domestic air about its dark, long-mellowed brick. It does not clash with the trim, Georgian perfection of Maids of Honour Row, where George the Second's Queen Caroline so neatly housed her ladies-in-waiting. The Palace's great ghost is that of Queen Elizabeth, who died there, 'a haggard husk,' in Lytton Strachey's phrase, on the morning of March 24, 1603. At her extremity, she had gone there for curative air, but too late. She lingered speechless in a chair for four days and nights. Cecil had said, 'Your Majesty, to content your people, you must go to bed'; and had been answered, 'Little man, little man, the word 'must' is not used to princes."

Neither could Richmond long preserve the life of another and very different seeker after riverside rest, that fiery particle Edmund Kean. He died and was buried there and is remembered in bas-relief on the wall of the Parish Church. The serenity of Richmond came too late to ease the pains and passions of his squandered life which ended, after all its blazing victories, in early middle age. Few actors have so singed a city with the flame of genius as did this astonishing barnstormer, once shrewdly discovered in Hardy's Dorchester; on being transferred to London he immediately conquered Drury Lane, became the talk of the town, and was master of his craft but not of his passions: he 'flamed amazement,' was sustained and destroyed by brandy, and had, most strangely, become at one time a householder in the Isle of Bute by the placid waters of Loch Fad. No stranger journey of theatrical life has been made than that of Kean from Wessex to the conquest of the capital, later to a refuge near Rothesay, then back to Richmond.

The famous terrace gardens on the hill above the river were purchased from the Duke of Buccleuch, and readers of Sir Walter Scott need no reminder of the use he made of the Richmond setting to enhance the drama of *The Heart of Midlothian*. It is appropriate that the London Scottish should play their football here and that its present M.P. should be called Sir George Harvey Watt, educated at both Edinburgh and Glasgow. Since Richmond has had so many Scottish connections, it might be thought that James Braid should have been the professional genius of its golf courses. Instead, a great and gentle spirit of the West Country, that of John Henry Taylor, five times Golf's Open Champion and for many years professional at the Royal Mid-Surrey Club, brought honour to the borough. He has gone back now to his Devonshire, but I always have him in my mind's eye, a sturdy figure, firm on the ground, steadfast against any head-wind, and as genuine as a Devonshire farm tea. He never looked like a Londoner and had the west in his eyes. Though the world's greatest master of the iron-shot to the green, he remained as modest as any 'rabbit' ought to be and probably is not. London golfers were lucky to have him for counsellor and Richmond was lucky to have him for so long its colonist.

'At Kew,' Mr. Christopher Sykes has wisely written, 'we find the cottagey side of the Hanoverians and Victorians.' The palace here becomes pleasantly parochial. Mr. Sykes speaks of

Queen Charlotte's ' rustic hovel ' and reminds us that the Dutch
House, bought for royal rustication by Frederick, Prince of
Wales, in 1730, had been built in 1631 by Sir Hugh Portman, a
trader with the Dutch and fond of their style. I like Portman's
country villa more than does Mr. Sykes, who finds Dutch
architecture ' not exportable ' and better left in Holland. Perhaps,
but gardens, after all, are permitted their exotic blooms. Kew
Gardens are a paradise of un-English beauties, an importers'
exhibition ground, a mass of alien glories.

Go there at the close of our winter period, say on a windy
day of dying March, and you will find the lawns lit with
magnolias and the keen air drenched with their sweetness, a
sweetness which, thus filtered through an easterly English breeze,
loses its sickliness, but is none the less suggestive of alien glades.
This tree came from America and was specially cultivated by
one Magnol of Montpellier; hence its name. It is a delicious
antidote to a shiversome English spring, not an expression of it.
Gardeners are cosmopolitans: what they see and love, they
annex and introduce. So why not a little alien architecture to go
with the exotic immigrants of the shrubbery and flower-beds?
I have already said a word even for Kew's preposterous
pagoda and shall reserve my right to be a friend of the Dutch
House.

Kew Gardens, entry to which must surely be the world's best
pennyworth (the charge has not risen) offer the Londoner 288
acres of lawn, hot-house, bank-side copse, bluebell woods, and
flower-bed. The size of a fair-sized farm, these acres have done
farmer's work, being for use as well as for beauty. Among the
world's crops originated or improved for service by experiment
and research at Kew are the West Indian bread-fruit, India's
quinine, and Malaya's rubber. Lord Capel had made at Kew a
display of exotic afforestation in the seventeenth century and
Princess Augusta, mother of George III, carried on the tradition
in the eighteenth. The results have rewarded much more than

the eye and lungs of the Londoner; they have provided general enrichment.

The transformation of Kew from a wilderness, much of it barren, involved, we read, 'princely expense.' Princes have often spent their money worse. Their money? Let us admit that it was, in the long run, the people's wealth that went into the creation of a demi-Eden, since princes do not spin money with their own fingers: they have officers to collect it. But, if kings, queens, and princes had not spent royally on their architectural projects and landscape-gardening, our democracy would now be far the poorer in its possession of amenities. Without Hampton Court or Greenwich or Kew Gardens, the fringe of London would have been a dismal legacy. Kew itself might have been seized by Victorian development and covered with rows of mean streets. It became a State institution in 1841 and during the following century was made continually more attractive to the seeker for beauty, more instructive to the amateur gardener, and more useful to the professional cultivator of trees and fruits.

Walking in early spring among the crocuses and daffodils, beside majestic pines and cedars of all types and climates, sniffing the magnolia-fragrant air, I could only be grateful that the Hanoverians had made this their ' cottagey ' resort. It is one of the limitations of democracy, where all may question what is done and what is spent, that the short view is most easily taken. The palace builders and the woodland planters may have had their own splendours and self-indulgences chiefly in view, but they did look forward, if only for their heirs. They planted for their own posterity, no doubt, but they did it in the clear understanding that to-morrow was worth a generous gesture, an investment on the grand scale. Modern democracy will spend recklessly on its immediate and material needs, but should anything more than a playground for immediate use be suggested, there will inevitably be cries of ' waste.' The first democracy of civilised man set the example of building for glory and almost for eternity; but ancient Athens had its slaves to do the work and, even so, the demagogues of the Left were soon vilifying Pericles for turning his noble visions into costly marble.

Nowadays a plan to make another Kew in the East End would scarcely stand a chance. The critics, after voting hundreds of millions for illusory plantations in the tropics, would denounce as fantastic and spendthirft any proposals for creating another demi-Eden in Essex. We should be grateful to those monarchs who deflected so much of their regal incomes into works of art and stately, broad-acred parks and gardens. The people have not only got their own back: they have had the benefit of the taste and discernment which employed builders and gardeners of genius.

And not kings and princes only. Chiswick House, a superb Palladian mansion with nearly 200 acres of seigneurial grounds, was the creation of the third Earl of Burlington and Cork and later the residence of the Dukes of Devonshire. Here is a glory of the Whig milords which is now yours and mine: the house was neglected and is being repaired and the grounds are in a rather wild state. But like Ken Wood in the north-west, the lawns and avenues remain for the leisured stroller and the nurse-maid with her charge. Among the senatorial statuary so dear to the Georgian grandees and historians, who made the House of Commons ring with Virgilian quotations and classical tirades instead of with the flat, conversational argle-bargle of to-day, we may admiringly meander with a faint sense of being in Italy as well as Middlesex; we have the freedom of the world of Burke and Fox: we feel eloquence bubbling within. What an outcry if Mr. Attlee were to construct and plant on such a scale as that of Kew or Chiswick, even though he ordered it all for common usage! Well, we can thank the Whig Pantheon that somebody was once thus profligate and covered the banks of London's great river with the demesnes that it deserved.

Whether we go to Kew for the lilac-time that Alfred Noyes recommended or for the daffodils that raise their lamps at the end of the dark months, we are the beneficiaries of Hanoverian 'waste.' 'Tax not the royal saint with vain expense,' said Wordsworth of King's College Chapel in Cambridge. The Hanoverians were not notably saints: let us tax not the royal sinners with any vain expenditure at Kew or the Whig grandess with having been wastrels at Chiswick. Their disbursements— word dear to honorary treasurers when they draw up the annual accounts—have been turned to our amenities.

And at Greenwich, if we skip across London, and take the river at its saltier, marine, commercial end, we are again profited by royal magnificence. Once more old palace becomes new pleasaunce. Indeed it began as Placentia or Pleasaunce, the riverside residence of Humphrey Duke of Gloucester and later a favourite mansion of the Tudors. A few miles from the older Eltham, it served the kingly need for refuge from a capital that was insanitary and often plague-stricken. Elizabeth's life was spanned by the Thames and its domestic palaces, for she was born at Greenwich and she died at Richmond. All that phase of Greenwich's glory has been swept away, while a fragment of Eltham lingers on. But it was not a case of destruction merely: the rebuilding could not have been happier.

Greenwich is not wholly public now: but the Museum in the Queen's House is for all to see and the old Naval Hospital is partly open. Moreover it is a splendid spectacle whether viewed from the brow of the park to the south or seen from the river: there is, too, a riverside path running downstream to the east which is public. It is a thousand pities that the old water-front inns, so long famous for their white-bait parties and other festivities, have been destroyed by the enemy or turned to other uses. They were the resort alike of the eminent statesmen and the young man about town and they have not been replaced. What Greenwich now disastrously lacks is places of refreshment and the Government should see to it, if they take the tourist industry at all seriously, that something is done to provide catering of quality for those who come down by river or by land—preferably by river—to enjoy the sight of what our seventeenth-century building could achieve in moods of plenary inspiration.

Here again ancient extravagance is something which pays its dividend to us and earns our gratitude now. Charles II, who was never in funds but had an eye for beauty in stone as in flesh, determined to build anew and palatially on the site of the old royal Pleasaunce. The rulers of the Commonwealth had no respect for regal birth-places and so the original Greenwich Palace had fallen into decay. It was a bauble of the housing-world: so, like the offending mace, let it go. But the architectural gallantry of Charles could not be carried far in his own life-time and on his precarious budget; so others had to complete his grand conception.

Queen Mary II, after the naval victory of La Hogue, saw the fine new foundations on the bank of the Thames close to the naval base at Deptford which Pepys used to visit—not always for the most virtuous purposes; she generously decided that another palace was less needed by the nation than a naval hospital. That was an unselfish decision and it was backed by a brave artistic resolve. The new hospital was not to be scamped work, cheaply run up for common mariners. It was to be as palatial as the original design: only the use was to be altered. William III sensibly supported his sensible queen: so Wren and Vanbrugh were commissioned to finish what Webb had begun. And nobly did they do it.

But there was already in the setting one pre-eminent jewel which had to be fitted into the new pendant of buildings appointed to adorn the neck of land beneath the fine brow of Greenwich Park. This was the Queen's House designed by Inigo Jones for Anne of Denmark, queen and widow of James I, and finished in

1638. I find this one of the loveliest things in London: what beauty of site as well as of structure it must have had before Greenwich was urbanised! As a country mansion between hill and harbourage it must have gratified a queen whose own country has been particularly rich in countryside palaces of happy placing and design.

Very properly the view from the Queen's House across the river was not to be interrupted and this command has shaped the lawns and the layout for the four main structures between the Queen's House and the water. These have been named after four monarchs, King Charles and Queen Anne, King William and Queen Mary. The general public have only partially inherited the results of Caroline and Orange policy; the Navy, as was intended, has been the chief beneficiary. The Queen's House became the Royal Hospital School for the sons of sailors and marines, but recently the school was removed to Suffolk and their superb building is now the National Maritime Museum and therefore open to the public.

The Hospital became the Royal Naval College in 1873 and is now a species of Naval University. It had been shrewdly realised that naval officers, chosen younger than most other Service men, often almost in boyhood, for their career, were too highly specialised in training and too much detached from the ordinary problems and interests of the day. Furthermore, the Lower Deck was being populated by better educated men who expected fully educated officers. What was needed, therefore, was more contact with general knowledge, political and economic issues, and the liberal arts. So young officers who have undergone their first stage of intense professional training are given at Greenwich nearly a year of general education, which they receive not only from a resident staff but from visiting speakers who initiate discussions on all kinds of topics. There is considerable freedom, ' leave ' is not stinted, and the proximity to Central London makes it possible to follow up interests of all kinds. Few students, even including those of Magdalen College, Oxford, and King's College, Cambridge, are housed amid greater beauty, and there can be no doubt that both the original alteration of purpose made by William and Mary and the second change from Hospital to Academy have been excellent improvements. With his original design for royal living Charles II founded better than he knew.

The Painted Hall in King William's Building is open to the public in the afternoon. It was once a dining hall and has become so again. It is used, at rare intervals, for State occasions and rightly. It deserves the compliment. For it has the sumptuous quality of its period, a heartless period which cared nothing about the poverty and hunger round about, but a period which backed its own judgment and had no scruple about expense when handsomeness was the determined end. Our eyes are now the gainers, as in the case of so many sumptuous foundations, by what the people of England did in fact pay for. Sir James Thornhill, with his agile assistants, worked for twenty years in the beginning of the eighteenth century to cover ceiling and walls with the paintings; these are formal, deferential, and, to a modern radical, perhaps rather absurd salutes to royal pomp and royal personage. By all this ingenious ladder-work kings and queens and their offspring were given Olympian backgrounds. The classic conventions are the base on which the House of Hanover sits or struts triumphant. The whole thing has a peacock quality. (Was it George III who spoke of the Upper House of Parliament as his 'Lords and Peacocks'?) The children are especially interesting. There, a sweet little innocent looking as though he would not 'swat' a fly, is he who was to be 'Butcher' Cumberland; this is not a hall in which a Jacobite could dine at ease.

But it is foolish to measure achievements of this kind by historical calculations based on subsequent events. One must take the Painted Hall for what it was, the contribution of the throne to a series of buildings devoted to the Navy, not to royal use. What did the legless or fevered seaman make of it? Perhaps he did not much notice this rich pictorial commingling of the age of Pope with the age of Virgil. The average man can live contentedly amid strange and even glorious spectacles without considering their strangeness or their glory. But we, coming in to see this rare curio to-day, have ample scope for pondering on this piece of our Georgian legacy. Also we can be grateful for some recent, expert, and courageous fire-watching, which prevented the German airmen from turning the Painted Hall into a burned out shell, grateful, too, for a certain amount of luck. Greenwich was an obvious and convenient target, but the Hospital suffered far less than did many a humbler area round about.

The original Chapel was burned down in 1779. No fire-watching in those bombless days! What a period that was for conflagrations. London, between 1660 and 1860, lost even more by its carelessness than we had to let go under pressure of unparalleled incendiary and explosive attacks. What 'Athenian Stuart' and subsequent restorers recreated in Greenwich on the Chapel's site has the eighteenth century's frequent blend of richness with common sense. The churches of that time invite no wonder. We are not awed by them. Religion had ceased to be a challenge and a mystery and had became an implement of tranquil living: herein, you feel, sermons would be preached with a view to maintaining order with dignity. Christianity had become an official religion and was given its due of elegance, sharing with Crown and Parliament the duty of preserving a world in which rank and precedence were to be decently maintained.

What has all this, you may ask, to do with the Jesus of the Gospels? The answer must be little enough. The Church was never more secular than during the Age of Reason; the miracle of faith was not in its complacent mind. Men did not question heaven because the affairs of earth seemed rational and secure. But, lacking humility—and what humility is in the grandeur of St. Peter's at Rome?—they yet had taste. Accepting what was, they gave it of their best as they conceived the best to be. Their notions of the stately were not corrupted by vulgarity. Deficient in feeling, they had the virtue of that vice and were never weakly sentimental. In this kind of ecclesiastical architecture there is little to inspire, yet much to appreciate.

I experience the same emotions in Stuart's Chapel at Greenwich Hospital as I do in trim St. Ann's Church on Kew Green. The former is later and richer in style. But both are sedate. The heavens—so the builders assure us—are far above and earth is well fixed below them. The transience of the social order and the perishability of the great globe itself, a thought which had occurred to Prospero-Shakespeare quite as much as to the atom-splitters, were not in those contented minds of the Anglican bishops and their master builders. The whole gracious serenity of the Greenwich which began with the Queen's House proclaims the dignity, the sanity, and the confidence of man. The mystics and romantics have had other visions and built nobly according to their richer imaginations. It takes all sorts to make an architectural world and intolerance in the arts is a wasteful folly. We all have preferences according to our fancy, and I have my own deep affection for the curious success with which the centuries that followed the Reformation and the Renaissance married the logic of the first with the balanced beauty of the second. On the banks of London's river the examples of this union are as persuasive as they are elegant.

Afterword

W HEN DOES London's winter end? For some it is when
the gates of Lord's Cricket Ground and of the Oval are
opened and cricketers, huddled in sweaters, blow on their fingers
for warmth, like Shakespeare's Dick the Shepherd in icicle-time,
and wonder whether the oncoming cloud will empty snow on
their heads. In April, 1950, a team from the West Indies arrived
to meet an April considerably colder than Christmas, with an
icy hurricane hurling waves over the seaside promenades and
whistling round the corners of London streets with rheumatism
and influenza as its Easter offering. But we have all, at one time
or another, felt like casting clouts before May was in, so fixedly
has summer's first anticyclone settled on our perspiring heads.
We can only say that London's winter ends by accident and at
almost any time between the middle of March and the middle
of May.

London's Easter means huge, serpentine queues for the railway
stations and the Zoo and Madame Tussaud's, for football matches
and picture-houses. Of Tussaud's I have written. The Zoo I
dislike, having all William Blake's hatred of cages, and resenting
the general idea that wild animals are, when safely imprisoned,
a Great Joke, at which the millions are right to go and giggle.
I suppose that some animals have an exhibitionist side to their
nature and enjoy the attention of a gaping crowd. But most of
them obviously loathe it and I think it is damnable practice to
put a beast in a cage with little or no cover and leave it exposed

to an endless succession of staring human eyes. To the open spaces of Whipsnade there can be very little objection, but to creatures whose very life is movement the confinement of any ordinary zoo—and much worse still of a travelling circus or menagerie—must be torture.

And is irremediable boredom less than a torture? Boredom in its extreme is grimly exemplified by one of the larger beasts pacing up and down its cell. You may say that it gets regular meals and need not worry to find them, that its cage, in a well-run zoo, is large, and that it has a chance to hide somewhere. (This excuse does not apply to most menageries.) But these things are no antidote to tedium. The sloth may be true to the character we have given him by nomination and so he may enjoy the cribbed and cabined life of a Zoo, but I refuse to believe that idleness and free victuals are the spice of life to most of the incarcerated beasts and birds.

At this point of an old, old argument we shall be told about children and education and bringing home to them the wonders of nature. Of course I know that all the motives of the cagers are exemplary and that their methods are as humane as may be. But dourly I insist that the proper fate of Giant Pandas is life in the Panda country and not a slow death in a European Zoo. It is true that certain of the Zoo's animals now acquire as much fame and favour as if they employed publicity agents of their own, but they plainly do not appreciate the status of a film-star and often show the fact by keeping themselves to themselves when the holiday myriads are jostling for a peep.

As I have begun to natter, after promising not to be a natterer, I shall get it all over at once and have a word about the contemporary Fair, whose year begins, in London as elsewhere, at Easter. As a Hampstead citizen who usually spends Easter at home, I always wander round the shows that are massed on two portions of the heath. They make a horrible mess and din, but they have the right of years behind them. They are traditional and generally popular. One must be very intolerant to wish them forbidden or 'planned' out of existence by the austere busybodies of reform.

To an old observer the whole thing becomes more monotonous as it becomes more wealthy. There are bigger and better (and probably safer) swings and roundabouts. The showmen are now obviously well-capitalised. Many of them arrive with sumptuous motor-caravans and I am glad that they have come up in the world. Their huge apparatus of dodgem cars, ghost trains, walls of death, giant racers and so on have obviously thousands of pounds of investment behind them. The charges for having your entrails thrown into your mouth on a switchback railway are high, but thousands think the turbulent game worth the silver. (Coppers get you almost nowhere in a modern fair-ground.) The turbulence of the Fair is now all in the convulsive frenzy of the machines. The people who attend are far more orderly and sober than they used to be and the magistrates have only a few trifling charges to deal with on the day after. Also there is much less buying of paper caps and of the long paper implements which you jocosely blew into the face of a chance acquaintance or of any adjacent victim. ' 'Ere you are, sir. 'Arry Lauder Scotch Cap, one penny. 'Ave a tickler. Tickle 'em up, sir, tickle 'em up.' The cry is heard no more. Even at sixpence you do not become an Easter Monday Highlander, nor do you assault the other sex with the flimsy brush once known as a ' tickler.'

All that has diminished, or even vanished, with the lessened sense of a proletarian Cockney carnival. The proletarian of to-day is much more eager to seem middle class and to behave as such. Apart from the occasional antics of a few loutish youths and tittering girls, the Fun Fair is scarcely a gay encounter and not at all the minor riot that it used to be. Family parties walk sedately round and spend their shillings on the circulating midget motor-cars which have supplanted the out-of-date horses,

ostriches, and queer beasts of all kinds on which the jovial used
to have their holiday ride. There are still a few of the old model
roundabouts and a pleasant sight they are among the stream-
lined, chromium-plated speed-cars of the new and mechanised
fun. They were products of a genuine folk-art, practised largely
I believe in King's Lynn, where the carving and painting of
stylised beasts and birds for the roundabouts was for long an
important and attractive industry. The surviving specimens of
the old style will not, I fancy, be replaced. Youth of to-day
must have its machinery and to gallivant on a wooden horse is
to be far behind the times.

The absence of mass-drunkenness is certainly a gain, and the
general abandonment of the alcoholic revel, which ended with
' forty shillings or a week ' is not to be lamented. But what the
older connoisseurs of the Fair ground miss is the absence of any
individualism. In my boyhood the central revels had a rich
fringe of solo performers. There were buskers, there were men
who sold nougat in mass by Dutch auction, carving off chunks
from a central deposit as big as an iceberg with a knife as menacing
as a sword and crying their wares with a magnificent flow of
eloquence and raillery. The pieces were gradually lowered in
price until a purchaser was found and the purchaser was usually
not found until the crowd had been called every name that would
not lead to arrest for blasphemy and indecency. Since the
rationing of sweets nougat by the hundredweight—' Fine French
Nugget, all pure confectory '—could hardly be the staple. But
this business of selling by exhibitionism—how that sword flashed
above the sticky iceberg!—and by inventive rhetoric might have
been applied to other objects. But it is not in the mood of to-day.

Then there was the man who invited anybody (he even took
a chance with sailors) to rope him up so that he could not
possibly escape and then did somehow extricate himself. Passing
round the hat for such feats of expertise lingers on in a small
degree at theatre and cinema queues, but I do not see it at the

Fair. High and assured wages for more orthodox occupations must have deflected the old-time specialists who were ready to put a cap on the ground and collect the coppers later. The stone-smasher who somehow cleft large pebbles with a blow of his ungloved hand is no longer to be seen nor is the sword-swallower or the man who chewed up glass and even somehow disposed of razor-blades in his mouth. There used to be a happy mummer who recited the juicier passages of Shakespeare to an audience somewhat ribald; facetious interruptions seemed rather to please him than deter. No doubt the long slide in money-values has had some effect on the individualists. They could once be content with pence, but coppers buy almost nothing now and the Fair-goer, when he spends his silver, wants more than the vagrant mountebank has to offer: he has his eye on the scenic railway, immense in power, new and glittering in paint. The coconut shy, which used to be one of the Fair's main industries, has become a pitiful waste of cash and is poorly attended for ample reason. The nuts are so few, dispersed, and tightly wedged and the price of a single throw is as high as that of six aforetime, when the nuts were massed in plenty and easily dislodged by a direct hit.

There are no barrel-organ men and that means no dancing in the streets. The would-be-middle-class factory girl of to-day is used to her pally-de-danse and is not going to kick up her heels in sheer high spirits when the hurdy-gurdy starts. When the pubs were open all day and gin was twopence a nip, there was an artificial stimulus to the public display of a Cockney's can-can. The general sobriety and restraint have killed this farewell to winter as practised by the girls who flocked up from the East End or from the closer industrial regions of North London with ostrich-feather hats, long purple coats and skirts, and high yellow boots.

This is not to say that show business decays on the heaths and commons round London, of which Hampstead's Fair is only one, but probably the best known. The new machine-conscious public likes the machine-method. Only the smallest children will consent to the comparatively slow motion of the simple, antique, equestrian roundabout. The others prefer, and enjoy, the roaring racers, as they have every right to do. It is a pleasant surprise that the complicated contraptions take the strain, after somewhat hasty erection on any odd piece of ground, without more accident. The speeds and gradients of the swirling, dipping cars and swings run high and steep and this furious bucketing of the human frame is no joy of mine. Why stay on land in order to court sea-sickness in the air? But each to his own. 'Appy 'Ampstead has not ceased to earn its epithet.

Easter at home is diversified in stormy weather by the services of television, whose range now runs to the south of Northern England and will soon spread farther still. There is much hesitation in the sporting world about coming to terms with this method of enjoying an outdoor spectacle in one's fireside comfort and almost for nothing. That is natural, but I think the fears are groundless. Every new invention disturbs the purveyors of the old entertainment, but it frequently turns out that the novelty does something to enhance the antiquity. There is a much larger theatre-going public in Britain than there was before the films came in to menace it. The invention of broadcasting did not chain people to the domestic sofa. Instead, both vehicles of entertainment have created idols whom a large section of the public became almost hysterically eager to see in the flesh and to hear at close quarters.

It may not be healthy for the higher art of the theatre that your playhouses can be packed to the brim by presenting the stars of the screen and of radio. This new theatre public may be comparatively uninterested in the quality of the play and in the theatrical values of its presentation. But they may be learning to like that of which they were previously unaware and, in any case, they are, for the moment, a tremendous financial asset to theatre business. Furthermore, the presence of ' a name ' won outside the theatre may greatly assist managements to venture upon stage productions of the highest calibre which would otherwise be despaired of as uncommercial. For example, a really first-rate production of Ibsen's profound and poignant tragi-comedy *The Wild Duck* was made possible and, I believe, even profitable by the presence in the cast of film names.

I mention this, not because I want to see the theatre clinging to the coat-tails of the ' movie-star,' but because it does counter the suggestion that televising a sporting event to-day will empty the arena to-morrow. Those who have seen a great performance on their television set may be the first to queue and to pay for a subsequent glimpse of the Athlete in Person. In the Ethiopian scorchings of a July day I have sat coolly at home to watch the prime lawn-tennis combatants of the world running themselves into a bath of perspiration and a sinking of the knees in five sets of desperately contended singles. The spectators at Wimbledon were also grilled, gasping, and even fainting. But they were there ' to capacity ' and will be next year.

Television may offer some danger to horse-racing, which is expensive and often rather tiring to watch on the spot: race-going, especially in winter, can mean considerable exposure to the wind, the rain, and the mud. The arm-chair ' viewers ' get far the best of the bargain on such a day as was Easter Monday of 1950, when Kempton Park was swept by violet squalls of bitterly cold rain. Important races, revealing the early prowess and potential powers of some entrants for the great ' classical ' events of later spring and summer, were being run in deplorable conditions. But the viewer, giving the fire a kick, could settle down to watch the horses on parade and not only to see the race better than he might on the chilly, sodden spot but also to have it ' read ' for him by those knowing and long-sighted experts who can single out one horse from another in the tightly-packed bunch moving at speed on the far side of a rain-dark course. That is a feat I can never achieve for myself. If the viewer is moved to make a bet he has only to reach for the telephone; there is no splashing across to the bookmakers or to the tote and queueing afterwards in the happy event of ' any to come.'

Yet, in spite of all this, I do not believe that more television will be the ruin of the race-course or of any other sporting spectacle. The rule of our time is that publicity always pays; the more you show a thing or a person or an animal, the more curiosity you arouse, provided the article or creature is really of the kind that people want to see; and curiosity is the best possible springboard for box-office receipts. This, admittedly, is a purely commercial argument, but those most eager to deny facilities to television are only thinking of figures and may fairly be answered in their own kind.

Few of us get through a London winter without a few bed-ridden or home-bound days. I do not see how the most convinced hater of mechanical progress can honestly deny that broadcasting and television have been great consolers of convalescence and mitigants of the inertia and depression that follow influenza. In this we are really better off than our fathers, who were so much more snugly set in many other ways; it is a small compensation, no doubt, for high prices and scarce or absent ' help.' But it is, in its way, a very real one. In times of ' accidie,' to use the old word for that demon of sloth which besets us towards the winter's long-drawn, cruelly lingering, fever-fretted close, it becomes difficult for the patient to read even the lightest and the worst. Pressing a knob to see and hear all and sundry, high art or low jinks, is an easy way out; and at such times easy ways are very easily excused.

London's winter ends in flower. The random daffodils in the

parks yield to the stately procession of the tulips, less charming
in their regimentation, but so rich in their deep and various hues.
An even greater pleasure in these times has been the flowering
of paint on the houses. It was an additional affliction of the war
years and of those immediately after that London was not only
smashed in so many places but everywhere sullied and left with
a dusty, rubbish-heap look. Drab doors, lintels, and window-
frames can soon turn a handsome terrace into a seeming slum.
Dingy, flaking, scabrous stucco is a spectacle of utmost depression,
while creamy, fresh-painted stucco gives a city a lift like few
things else. If there be enchantment to the eye in the nocturne
of a town lit-up, then there is no less relief and delight in that
day-time lighting-up which the painter brings.

One noticed it especially at Brighton, that triumph of the stucco
square and of the gleaming crescent. After mouldering into dull
ochre under inevitable war-time neglect, it seemed to rise again
goddess-like from the sea, an Aphrodite serene but sparkling,
when the painters could get the ladders up once more. So,
when that grand Georgian parade, in the stucco alignment of
Regent's Park's brigade of terraces, once more could be put into
ceremonial kit, there was a similar sense of resurgence. It was
as though spring had infected the architecture as it quickens the
lawns in front. And, now that house-painting, though costly,
can be managed, the end of winter is the beginning of a new town.

Londoners are individualists and, unless some landlord of a
wide domain can place discipline on the brush-up and titivation
of a street, there is apt to be some unruly outburst of taste in
colour. Here a blue door jostles a green, there a yellow a scarlet.
We are not to be drilled.

> *Unkempt about those hedges blows*
> *An English, unofficial rose,*

sighed Rupert Brooke amid the regimen of the Kaiser's Berlin.
And now, in April, the nosegay of a London terrace 'done up' is

an unofficial posy of contrasted, and perhaps conflicting, tints. There is a wild gaiety, none the less, about this anarchy of preference. The inhabitants of Central London live in numbered houses; they cannot indulge their sense of independence, like the suburbans, by writing Mon Abri or The Nook upon their gates or raiding the countryside for arboreal and landscape names. But they can declare themselves in hue and No. 47, with its trimmings a study in scarlet, cries 'Yah' to No. 49, whose owner has saffron predilections. Poor civic spirit? Perhaps, but a show of spirit none the less. So winter once more passes from us with a painter's carnival in being.

Leaving the clatter and clutter of the new-style, highly-geared Fair on what Macaulay knew as North London's 'swarthy moor,' I wander into hill-top Hampstead and a light breaks from steely clouds on the Georgian villas, just as it descends on the gleaming horses in a Munnings' canvas. This old, tiny suburb of the summit, suburb of Mrs. Siddons and of Romney, of George du Maurier and of John Galsworthy, had lost lustre for a while like the rest of London, but now the sadness of aspect was dispelled. The painters had been doing their work, so much an hour to them, a keen, sharp smell to the nostrils of passers-by, and a heart-breaking bill of costs for somebody. But the jumble of houses, squeezed and piled among twisty passages and lanes between the Tube and the Pond, a quarter-mile of village *de luxe*, had been touched by sudden magic. The hill-top had been refreshed. (What a word that ought to be and what a poor, weak thing it has become! Does the sight of 'Refreshments' outside a door stir up rejoicing in a Briton's heart? Refreshments are baked beans on toast and a cup of the acrid tea that is vaguely, but I fear, accurately known as 'stomach-stain.') Well, if refreshed has now no touch of Primavera in its faded syllables, let us say re-born.

So much can colour do, when there is light in the sky, the transient, radiant, sun-shaft among April storms, to give to the urban panorama a whole range of flickering beauty and so raise it to a higher power. I began with a salute to much-maligned November, whose sunsets are a London glory, and shall end with gratitude to much-praised Eastertide. Then, with winter waning, the citizen collaborates with the illumined sky, turns colourist, and resolves that an Englishman's home and garden are not only his castle but his canvas.

INDEX